AGENT
PATERSON

D1582016

For Win

AGENT PATERSON SOE

**FROM OPERATION ANTHROPOID
TO FRANCE: THE MEMOIRS OF
E.H. VAN MAURIK**

Lieutenant Colonel Ernest Henry
van Maurik OBE

Preface by John van Maurik

FRONTLINE
BOOKS

AGENT PATERSON SOE
From Operation Anthropoid to France: The Memoirs of E.H. van Maurik

First published in 2018 by Frontline Books,
an imprint of Pen & Sword Books Ltd,
47 Church Street, Barnsley, S. Yorkshire, S70 2AS.

Copyright © Lieutenant Colonel Ernest Henry van Maurik OBE, 2018. Preface and postscript copyright © John van Maurik, 2018.

The right of Lieutenant Colonel Ernest Henry van Maurik OBE to be identified as the author of the relevant section of the work has been asserted by him in accordance with the Copyright, Designs and Patents Act 1988.

ISBN: 978-1-52673-416-7

All rights reserved. No part of this publication may be reproduced, stored in or introduced into a retrieval system, or transmitted, in any form, or by any means (electronic, mechanical, photocopying, recording or otherwise) without the prior written permission of the publisher. Any person who does any unauthorized act in relation to this publication may be liable to criminal prosecution and civil claims for damages.

A CIP catalogue record for this book is available from the British Library.

Printed and bound by TJ International Ltd, Padstow, Cornwall
Typeset in 10.5/13 point Palatino

Pen & Sword Books Limited incorporates the imprints of Atlas, Archaeology, Aviation, Discovery, Family History, Fiction, History, Maritime, Military, Military Classics, Politics, Select, Transport, True Crime, Air World, Frontline Publishing, Leo Cooper, Remember When, Seaforth Publishing, The Praetorian Press, Wharncliffe Local History, Wharncliffe Transport, Wharncliffe True Crime and White Owl.

For more information on our books, please email: info@frontline-books.com, write to us at the above address, or visit:
www.frontline-books.com,

Contents

Foreword

I would like to borrow the words that Winston Churchill dedicated to the RAF pilots for their actions during the Battle of Britain: 'Never in the field of human conflict was so much owed by so many to so few.' This expresses for us – the men and women of the French Resistance and, therefore, the whole French population – how much we owe to the SOE and its brave agents.

I have had the privilege of meeting, amongst others, Ernest van Maurik, Agent 'Paterson', in 1989. In the following book, you will be able to trace his journey, and his difficulties, from Izernore, where he was dropped by parachute, to his exfiltration to Switzerland.

During this time, he was under the care of Romans, Chief of the Maquis of the Ain. He stayed for two weeks in the Ain, visiting several Maquis camps. He was able to witness and report upon the good organisation of the camps, and the willpower and enthusiasm of the Maquisards.

But he could see that the Resistance fighters needed more weapons and he promised Romans that he would explain this to Maurice Buckmaster at SOE's headquarters. As a result, as soon as Van reached Bern, and was able to contact London, he arranged for numerous deliveries of weapons that were parachuted into the Ain.

I can assure you that forty years later, when the Resistance Museum was created in 1983, it would have been possible to arm a whole battalion with the hidden weaponry that had been parachuted, hidden, kept as relics in attics and cellars, and then donated to the museum.

Pierre Mercier,
President of the Association of the Friends of the Resistance Museum,
Nantua, France,
September 2017.

Introduction

The place was Charlottenlund, a very pleasant suburb of Copenhagen, and the time was late August in 1967, also known as 'the summer of love'.

I was sitting round the dining table with my father and mother, Ernest van Maurik and Winifred van Maurik, best known to their friends as Van and Win, and decided it was time to ask a key question that had been troubling me for some time. I was then a rather bolshie, but at the same time unconfident teenager, studying Sociology at Leeds University. Having finished my first year and seeing the prospects of employment in the not-too-distant future, I wondered what people actually did at work and although I had done some research as to the content of various professions, I badly wanted to know the details of what people did on a day-to-day basis. I was now starting to think about the future and what I might be able to do with my degree, when I finally got it. In addition, my confidence and motivation had not been helped by a caustic definition of Sociology that I had recently come across: 'Sociology, the study of those who do not need to be studied, by those who do!'

I did know that Van was a diplomat and had been since before I was born, having been posted to Egypt, Russia, Germany, Argentina and now Denmark. But I had no real understanding of what that entailed. All I knew was the fact that he went to work, came back, had different international postings and that we all managed to have some very interesting holidays as a result of his profession.

The time had come to confront the issue.

I put down my lager. 'Dad,' I said, 'I've been wondering for a while what people actually do at work. For a start, could you tell me what you do?'

Van sighed, took a sip of his beer and looked me in the eye. 'Unfortunately, I cannot do so.'

'Why not?'

'The reason ,' he continued, 'is that I work in the rather more "hush hush" side of the diplomatic service and therefore cannot describe to you, or anybody else, what I actually get up to.'

I was not sure whether to be excited or disappointed. Here was my father, apparently owning up to the allegations that 'diplomats are just fancy spies', that my fellow students had made when I had told them Van was in the diplomatic service. This added an element of glamour – but it did nothing to answer the burning question as to what people did at work.

Win stepped in. 'But you can tell John how you got into that branch of the service, what it was you did in the war.'

Van smiled, took another sip of his drink and then continued. 'Yes, I guess I can do that. During the Second World War I found myself increasingly involved in an organisation called SOE, the Special Operations Executive, and this led me into eventually being parachuted into Occupied France to help the French Resistance, where I operated under the name of Agent Paterson'. I gasped. This had never been mentioned in any detail before. Van continued: 'Most people know that I did that and it was a very exciting experience; what is not so well known is something that I was involved with before that.

'Earlier in the war I was involved in training other agents up in Scotland in commando tactics including blowing up trains and assassination techniques. Although I did not realise it at the time, I trained a group of Czech soldiers who later went on to assassinate the important Nazi leader Reinhard Heydrich in what was known as Operation *Anthropoid*.' I must have looked amazed as he continued swiftly and emphatically. 'But you must not tell anybody about that. There may still be some Nazis around who might feel strongly about that. We don't want to push our luck!' This, after all, was only twenty-two years after the end of the Second World War.

I looked over my shoulder and fell silent. Enough had been said and I still did not know what people did at work.

Win stepped in again. 'One of these days, Van, you should write your memoirs. You have hardly begun to describe all the things you got up to.'

This Van did many years later, in 1993. The ex-soldier, Member of MI6 who had a Dutch name owing to the fact that he had a Dutch father who had come over to the UK to marry an Englishwoman and start the London branch of the family cigar business, sat down to write the memoirs of a long, involved and exciting life, initially for the benefit of his family and close friends. His mother had insisted somewhat zenophobically that he should not learn Dutch despite his name and ancestry and this fact, paradoxically, saved his life in later years. But in his 'diplomatic' career the origin and context of his name was never questioned and he remained unquestionably British.

Not much more was spoken of his exploits in the war for several years after that initial conversation, until after a most sad event in his life in 1984 when Win, who had been such a tower of strength for him in his travels, work and 'diplomatic' social life, died prematurely. Shortly after this tragedy, however, he suddenly found himself back amongst the veterans of the French Resistance and involved in relationships that would blossom, flourish and have, as will be revealed, positive and emotional consequences up to the present day.

John van Maurik,
Hartfield, East Sussex,
September 2017.

CHAPTER 1

A Tough-Love Education

Clad in a camouflaged jump-suit, a padded helmet on my head, a foam rubber spine pad pushed down my trousers and a parachute strapped to my back, I sat perched on the rim of the hole in the belly of the old two-engine Whitley bomber as it trundled over Tatton Park close to RAF Ringway.[1]

How the devil did I get into this unenviable position, I asked myself; but I knew the answer. From my earliest connection with the Army I had learnt two important lessons, or at least until this moment I thought I had – a good soldier makes himself comfortable under all circumstances and a soldier on principle never volunteers for anything. Why, when at camp, volunteers for potato peeling were called for, I used to be among the first to take to my heels. One soon got to know the sergeant with his 'I want three volunteers, you, you and you'. Potatoes, indeed! Yet here was I up in an aircraft for only the second time in my life: the first had been an 'introductory' twenty minutes flight yesterday, and now they expected me to jump out of the beastly thing. Yes, the answer was simple, all my own damned fault. Easy to be noble and brave in the distant Highlands of Scotland and to say you would accompany your students down to Manchester and set an example to them, but for God's sake, what was I doing up here?

The RAF despatcher at my side shouted something to me and pointed at the red light suspended on the other side of the hole, but the roar of the engines drowned his words. They say some silly bastards

---

[1] RAF Ringway was the home of Central Landing School from 21 June 1940, later becoming No.1 Parachute Training School, until it moved to RAF Upper Heyford on 28 March 1946.

actually enjoy this; they must be out of their minds. Jump I know I must, but assuming I survive they might as well realise that this is the very last bloody time I'll ever … The mesmeric red light suddenly switched to green, the despatcher yelled 'Go' in my ear and I jerked myself into the centre of the hole. I did not quite go out at the ramrod-straight position the instructors would have us do and when the slipstream hit me in the face I could neither see nor think properly for a second or two. Then quickly everything came into focus and I realised I was suspended in a sea of blessed silence and below me the lake and the tranquil English countryside stretched out far and wide in the July sunshine.

A wave of euphoria swept over me. I'd done it! All my fears and worries of a few moments ago had been carried away in the aircraft now circuiting before dropping its next customer. As I looked around me I thought I could never remember the countryside, indeed the whole darn world, looking quite so marvellous. I'd have been happy to stay up here the whole morning, no urgency to go down and join the little gaggle of instructors and students way below on the ground. Funny, I had no sensation of vertigo such as normally made me afraid of falling or throwing myself off high buildings, but then, I smiled to myself, there was nothing to fall off up here.

I realised, of course, that there was no way of arresting what appeared to be my gentle glide down towards earth, no brakes to be applied, yet why worry? But shortly I noticed that the further I descended the faster the ground came up to meet me and the thought forced itself into my mind that the impact with these modern wartime parachutes was the equivalent of jumping off a ten-foot wall.

'Keep your feet together, bend your knees,' shouted an instructor from quite close below me.

When I land I must try at the moment of impact to pull myself up on my parachute lines to soften the blow and then be prepared to execute the forward roll I practised on the soft and accommodating sand dunes of the Argyllshire coast. Before I could do any of this the forward swing on my harness combined with the motion of the parachute itself thumped and bowled me over and then started to drag me along the ground. Somehow, I managed to regain my feet and run round the parachute to spill the air from the canopy.

Thank God that's over. I beamed and waved back as the Chief Instructor shouted his routine congratulations but then, when a nearby colleague reminded me that another jump was scheduled in two or three hours' time that afternoon, a cloud seemed to obscure the sun and rob the scene of its colour and I knew in my heart that I would be no less scared the second time round.

It was a chance meeting with Fatty Stephenson in late 1936 that set in motion a chain of events which, combined with the advent of war three years later, was to alter the course of my life.

We had neither seen each other nor kept in touch since leaving prep school six years previously, this despite having at that time been the closest of friends. As a new boy one term after my own arrival, Peter had been short of stature but ample in girth – hence his nickname – and had earned my instant gratitude by rescuing me from the teasing attentions of a boy bigger than either of us by offering to knock the offender's head off. This led to a mutual defence pact between the two of us which, if nothing more, kept at bay the more cowardly of the school bullies.

As I came to know him I learnt that Peter was one of a large family fathered by a Sussex rector, a disciplinarian and a particularly ardent guardian of his children's morals. Meticulous observance of the sabbath went without saying, but in addition he denied them many of the small pleasures granted to other young people. Among these, a total ban on all cinema-going was an especial irritant to young Peter. In modern times, this was the equivalent of proclaiming the rectory a television-free zone and forbidding access to anyone else's TV as well. This claustrophobic regime merely intensified Peter's desire to taste the forbidden fruit of the outside world and the tedium of the long Sunday school walk was forgotten while Peter drank in my lurid account of a Dr Fu Man Chu film, or we both laughed merrily as I described the antics of Harold Lloyd to which my more liberal upbringing had given me access.

St. Andrew's near East Grinstead, a small boarding school whose numbers seldom exceeded forty, had been founded by a kindly and learned clergyman and this no doubt played a part in persuading the rector of Waldron to entrust first one and later another of his sons to this institution. The Reverend Reginald Bull had, however, handed over the headmastership the very term I arrived to his son Kenneth, but he remained in the background and was still responsible for our religious instruction. The new headmaster – Captain Kenneth he liked to be styled – had volunteered during the First World War to join the Army and fight the Germans; indeed, it was rumoured that he had fudged the date of his birth to get to France still earlier. He had undoubtedly been a gallant officer and had the Military Cross to prove it. Now, less than seven years after the signing of the armistice an aura of glamour still

3

surrounded him, at least in the eyes of us boys. My parents began to hint that academic standards had slipped under his guidance – my brother had been a pupil there before me – but the macho image required of the boys had not. All the year round, morning cold baths were inescapable and if the water in the enamel jugs standing in their metal washbasins ranged under the wide-flung dormitory windows occasionally iced over in winter, we dare not complain since we knew that things had been much worse in the trenches.

The school was housed in a rambling nineteenth century mansion, aping on the exterior some of the features of a fortified manor house. It had once belonged to Alfred Beit, the South African diamond millionaire, a fact which intrigued my mother since her father, also German by origin, had worked in Port Elizabeth, where she herself was born, and had like Beit been associated with Cecil Rhodes, if not as intimately as he. The grounds were spacious; in front large terraced lawns led away up steps to a full-sized cricket ground. Flanking the lawns, and parallel to the road outside, ran an immense rhododendron hedge which continued along the boundary of the cricket ground to the house. It accommodated within itself a hidden 'secret' passageway running back from the cricket ground to the house, thus affording an escape route for the few brave enough to absent themselves from compulsory attendance at school matches. At the back of the house there were further gardens and a path leading down through trees to parkland, in the centre of which was what once must have been a modern swimming pool with its own changing-rooms.

During summer term, mercifully only then, Captain Kenneth would lead first the Junior and then the Senior School down through the trees and into the park for its weekly swim. The nearer one approached, the more apprehensive many of us became. Few could swim and only the more adventurous managed to learn, but on one point our headmaster was most insistent, namely that every boy must duck his head under the water, on the pretext that one risked sunstroke with a wet body and a dry head. Even at my tender age, as I shivered in the often-sunless slimy waters of the shallow end among the temporally dispossessed frogs and water-beetles, I felt this to be a somewhat spurious contention.

However, although Captain Kenneth demanded a spartan life-style for his pupils – at a later stage the school grapevine suggested that he himself was rather too fond of his whisky out of school hours – he was fair and provided you were seen to be trying your hardest and provided you paid periodical homage before the photograph of the Old Boy who

4

had won himself a VC, you could earn words of praise and a pat on the head.

My first term, before the arrival of Peter Stephenson and the companionship he offered, I was a sitting target for bullies in that I was the only new boy. Away from home for the first time, I was homesick without any other burden being placed on me. My mother had always insisted that my brother and I be brought up as little English boys and, as middle-class English boys went to boarding school at the age of eight, I must naturally do so as well. My father, who was discouraged from talking any Dutch in front of the children, a fact which in later life I came to regret, may have felt differently but in our family mother had the last word. But now the simple fact of having a foreign-sounding name became a nightmare to me.

'So, what's your name?'

I stammer it out

'That's a funny name. So, you're a little foreigner.'

'No, I'm not.'

'So, tell me your name again or I'll pull your hair.' I repeat my name, knowing it can only bring further retribution. 'There you are, you see, you are a little Dutchie and we don't want any here, do we?'

At long last my first term dragged to its close and the autumn term with its crop of new boys took at least some of the pressure off me, and it was much longer before the bouts of homesickness entirely ceased.

Mr Heywood joined the staff of St. Andrew's a term or two before I became a pupil. It was rumoured that he had been taken on by the Reverend Bull solely on the strength of his being the son of a bishop. True or not, Reginald Bull got his money's worth out of the deal, in that the bishop graced the little chapel built alongside the main house on a number of occasions and regularly confirmed the older boys once a year. It was certainly true that the bishop's son was no intellectual but he made up for this with a cheerful outgoing personality and an unforced sympathy with the boys, not least of all the smaller and more down-trodden. This could perhaps have been because, as a small boy himself not so many years previously, he also might have been teased, not because of his name but because of the size of his nose. Trunk was his nickname, we gathered, but we never called him this. His nose was not the only large part of him; he was solidly built, six feet and over, and we marvelled at the size of his shoes. He was a good cricketer and although he was careful to temper his pace when bowling at boys, the genuine speed he engendered when other members of the staff ventured on to the pitch contributed to his popularity. He was a well-liked man and I was destined to get more than my fair share of his company.

Mr Wright, our music teacher, was not one of those who ever appeared on the cricket field or indeed ever took part in any form of sport. If he had, there would have been plenty hoping to witness his discomfiture. He was not liked and, in turn, he clearly found small boys, individually and in mass, distasteful and irritating. He was of slim build and his lean face was surmounted by an ample head of hair, which already showed signs of turning a distinguished shade of silvery grey. Unlike Beethoven, whose portrait hung in my mother's bedroom at home, he did not have the wild, dishevelled hair-style I had come to associate with musical genius; on the contrary, he groomed his hair carefully and trained a voluminous lock to fold from his forehead to the back of his head. On his narrow-pointed nose, he wore a pince-nez, a form of spectacles even at that time obsolescent, which had a peculiar propensity to reflect the light and glint back at you with an unnerving effect.

Our headmaster Captain Kenneth seemed to hold that we were lucky to have so gifted a musician as Mr Wright on the staff. We were in no position to judge or even care about his ability but we held strong views on the question of our luck or lack of it in having him. I remember my parents coming to an end-of-term concert at which Denis Wright performed one of his own compositions on the piano. My mother thought perhaps he 'had something' and might eventually 'go far'. The sooner the better, I said to myself. My father found the composition strong on noise but weak on melody. My mother turned out to be right as so often was the case in our family. Indeed, from the early thirties onwards Wright made a name for himself in the world of brass bands and during the first years of the war was in charge of the BBC's popular brass band concerts. He not only composed and orchestrated for them but, according to the reference books, surprisingly enough he founded and taught the National Youth Brass Band. One could have supposed he had already had his fill of the young at St. Andrew's!

Mid-morning break at St. Andrew's was a bit of a misnomer. After those boys whose parents had paid for extra milk had gulped it down, half the school went to Mr Wright's singing class while the other half was taken by Mr Heywood for Physical Training. The following day the roles were reversed. For those who could sing, and they included my friend Peter – one presumes he had had plenty of practice at it from an early age in his father's church – Mr Wright's classes were not too painful an experience, although no one was exempt from the risk of becoming the target of one of his temperamental outbursts. I who could not sing tried, not always successfully, to avoid trouble by miming. When caught out at this, Mr Wright would make me sing a solo passage to the amusement of the rest of the class and his own evident distress. Unlike Peter I had the added disadvantage of having private piano lessons with him.

A year or more before going to boarding school my mother, who was genuinely musical, decided I should learn to play the piano and sent me to a Mrs Bottle who was a neighbour of ours in Edenbridge in Kent. She was a very pleasant and kind lady who had devised a system of teaching the rudiments of music by representing the staff as five telegraph lines and the notes by robins perched on these lines. The robins hopped up and down and one's fingers very roughly followed suit. She also helped one to compose little tunes which one then took back to Mother as one's own compositions. I quite enjoyed my weekly visits and did not demur when my mother, pleased with my apparent progress, fixed up for me to continue my instruction at St. Andrew's.

The music room, where lessons took place, was reached from the main school passageway by a very short flight of stairs which performed a right-angled turn half way up. It contained an upright piano, a music-stool and a chair; there were no windows and illumination came from a skylight. It is difficult to imagine what use was envisaged for such a small and unusual room in the original design of the house but it now provided a perfect eyrie for Mr Wright and his glinting pince-nez.

I soon discovered that we no longer dealt in telegraph lines and robins but with crochets, semiquavers and other unintelligible symbols. I was not long also in realising that the discords I often produced had an electrifying effect on my teacher seated on the chair behind my stool, and that little further provocation on my part was required to bring forth a torrent of verbal abuse. My knees trembled as I climbed the stairs for my lessons but I suffered this weekly torture for a term or two until matters came to a head.

I had, as usual, practised a piece to play at my lesson but, somehow, I had also acquired the habit of dropping my head towards my hands each time I made a mistake. I perched my music on the piano and started. A few notes and the first mistake came and I bobbed my head and restarted.

'Don't duck your head,' hissed Mr Wright over my shoulder.

I tried again but my fingers felt numb and I found I was physically incapable of preventing my head from bobbing when the inevitable mistakes occurred.

'Don't duck your head, boy, don't duck your head,' shouted Mr Wright.

From then on it seemed to me to be a confusion between my head bobbing and Mr Wright shouting. Finally, the future guru of the brass band movement could stand it no longer. He rose to his feet and, ruffling his now less than immaculate hair with one hand and pointing desperately at the door with the other, he yelled at me:

'Get out of here. Just get out of here.'

I was off down the stairs so fast that I was fortunately just round the bend before my music, slung after me by my teacher, hit the wall at the turn of the stairs and slithered down the last lap after me.

I vowed I would never climb those stairs again and I never did; probably Denis Wright was concurrently vowing he would never again allow me up them. The following week I did not appear for my lesson and no one ever enquired why. Mr Wright did however stop me in the passage a day or two later with what might have been intended as an ingratiating smile.

'Oh, van Maurik, I've been thinking about your attendance at my singing class. As it seems you have little to contribute, I wonder if it would be an idea if you did PT instead?'

It was thus that I became perhaps the only boy in the school's history to do PT every single day of the working week.

I reckoned I had gained both ways; I was shot of Mr Wright and now had the pleasure of seeing more of Mr Heywood. The latter was slightly puzzled when I turned up for my first additional class but, when given a watered-down version of the reason for my unexpected presence, he welcomed me with his usual good nature.

The fairly elementary arms-and-knees bend type of exercises we indulged in might perhaps have become somewhat monotonous on a daily basis had it not been for a new idea introduced by Mr Heywood. He had heard or read of the resilience of even young boys' stomachs and was keen to experiment. Perhaps on the basis of my doing more PT than other boys and thus having well-developed muscles, he got me to lie flat on my back and stretch my arms over my head until they touched the floor. Then I had to lift my feet an inch or two off the ground and he tried putting some of his considerable weight on my abdomen by placing his foot on it. My feet of their own accord shot higher into the air but the weight was not unbearable. Within a few days he was placing his full weight on my stomach, the only slightly uncomfortable feature being the imprint of his size 11 golf shoe on my skin. The technique thus established, he decided to introduce the exercise to the Upper School. After he and I had given a demonstration most of the older boys volunteered to take part. In the end, we had a dozen boys lying on their backs side by side with Mr Heywood able to start at one end and walk across the bridge of stomachs and reach the far end without his feet touching the floor. The successful participants became keen to demonstrate their unusual achievement before the parents at the forthcoming Sports Day but wiser counsels prevailed, thus safeguarding the susceptibilities of nervous mothers.

Not long before my career at St. Andrew's drew to a close we returned from holidays to find that Mr Wright had left the school for other fields. Unlike most of the other boys I did not celebrate but feigned indifference over the news since it scarcely affected me one way or the other, or so I thought. He was replaced by a Mr Leighton, tall, bespectacled and inclined to be earnest. By instinct rather than by design I avoided close contact with him and it was not until around half-term – celebrated, if we were lucky, by an extra half-holiday spent at school – that we had any substantial conversation.

'I've slowly become conscious of the fact that you never seem to attend either of my singing classes. Is that indeed so?'

'Yes sir,' I replied.

'But why is that?'

'Because I do PT every day, sir.'

'And why do you do that?'

'Because I can't sing, sir.'

'And who told you that?'

'Mr Wright, sir.'

'Hm, I see. Well let's give you a try.'

He led me off to the grand piano at the end of the large dining-hall where singing classes took place. He played a scale and made me sing the notes.

'Well, yes, a bit breathy, but more or less in tune. I'd be most grateful if you would attend Upper School singing, starting tomorrow. We'll be glad to have you. I'll have a word with Mr Heywood.'

I had been taken by surprise and, realising I was trapped, I decided I had better make the best of it. So came the end-of-term concert when the Upper School sang sea shanties. My parents were surprised but gratified to see me singing lustily at the back of the group. What they did not know, and I suspect Mr Leighton had not tumbled to either, was the fact that I wasn't really singing – just miming.

By the time I left St. Andrew's at Easter 1930 I had spent exactly five years of my life there. The miseries of being a very small boy with a very odd name had, of course, long since passed but with the hindsight of later life I would never subject anyone so small to the rigours of some of the features of life there, a glaring example being the forcing of seven- and eight-year-olds from a warm bed straight into an icy cold bath, be it summer or winter. But there was nothing deliberately Dickensian or sadistic about it and it was commendable that corporal punishment, then common in many schools, did not exist at St. Andrew's. The Reverend Bull had founded the school on the precept that boys should be clean in mind and body and even if these two objectives were not always achieved the fault lay more with the boy than with the school. Pleasurable amusement was indeed built into the school routine. A small, but important, instance of this was the luxury of an extra hour in bed on a Sunday morning; no talking was allowed, but who wanted to talk when one could revel undisturbed in a Percy F. Westerman adventure or the latest volume of the William stories.

Half-an-hour's obligatory rest was ordained after lunch every day to assist the digestion. In summer rugs would be spread out under the lime trees at the edge of the lawns and Matron, the headmaster's wife and the masters, would read aloud to the various age groups. Choice of books was left to the readers and it was Matron who hit the jackpot by appearing one afternoon with a quite newly published slim volume entitled 'Winnie the Pooh'. A year or so later she again achieved a first with the eagerly awaited sequel. Other splendid characters such as Dr Doolittle added to the enjoyment of that magical moment in the day.

One of the highlights of the year was the observance of St Andrew's Day. There was no flag-waving or parading, just an unusual but civilised entertainment known as 'Pickwick and Chestnuts'. Before the show commenced the boys were provided with sheets of paper to make themselves miniature paper hats. At a given signal we all trooped into the library where a log fire blazed in the large old-fashioned fireplace surrounded by its brass fencing. Two or three boys were appointed chestnut roasters and sat on the padded top of the fireguard. When the remaining boys were seated on the carpet and members of the staff on chairs at the back, the star of the show appeared to general applause.

10

The old headmaster would not have dreamt of foregoing this chance of displaying his quite extraordinary skill at bringing the Pickwick Papers to life. He settled his thick-lensed spectacles more comfortably on his nose, his white beard softened as the main lights dimmed and then the cockney vowels of Sam Weller and the high-pitched tones of Mrs Bardell began to flow round the room to the genuine enjoyment of his listeners. I doubt very much whether Charles Dickens himself could have done better.

Every so often a short interval was taken so that the roasting hot chestnuts could be passed round from paper hat to paper hat. When Reginald Bull at last closed his volume, and announced that the reading was over, the boys pleaded for more and when, after a discreet pause Captain Kenneth added his voice to the others, Mr Bull senior discovered he had just one more extract prepared. The encore concluded, he sent us to our beds with his blessing.

Whilst many of the unhappier events of my prep school life had to be dredged up from somewhere deep within me, the happy memory of Peter – or Fatty as he would have been to me then – sitting at my side on the carpet drinking in Reginald Bull's brilliant one-man show, and then juggling hot chestnuts from hand to hand until they were cool enough to eat, has remained close to the surface.

CHAPTER 2

Down to Business

Ihad arranged to meet Peter in a London pub after finishing work for the day. We chose the Charing Cross area as it was convenient for me to catch the Circle Line from my office in Eastcheap and afterwards to commute home to Tunbridge Wells where my parents were now living. It was equally suitable for Peter who worked in London Transport headquarters and shared a town flat with a sister. Our first accidental meeting had only lasted long enough for me to observe that Peter had grown into a tall, well-proportioned young man, dark and good-looking and for him, for his part, to make it clear that he no longer answered to his schoolboy nickname. As I now battled with the rush-hour crowds in the Underground, I speculated as to how much of his rectory upbringing might have remained with him and whether its emphasis on alcoholic abstinence any longer held sway. I need not have worried, for Peter ordered beers with total assurance and consumed his first pint with what seemed to me almost professional competence. We exchanged news about our families but hardly touched on our five years of public school life, which we deemed to be only of interest to oneself or someone who had been at the same school. One thing we did have in common; neither of us had been to university due to lack of parental funds and this had thrown us both into the hard, daily, slog earlier than otherwise might have been the case.

At length Peter raised a topic which I realised later must have been at the back of his mind ever since we renewed contact.

'By the way, have you ever thought of joining the T.A.? You know it's really great fun and breaks the ghastly monotony of business life. You mix with a lot of good chaps and what's more you can double your annual holiday by claiming an extra two weeks for summer camp.

If you were to join the Artists Rifles I'd see you got into 'B' Company and we'd be together. Why not come along any Tuesday or Thursday evening, have a drink and see what it's all about? No obligation, of course, to join.'

It was not just the influence of the beer that persuaded me to agree to go along and have a look. Ever since the age of fifteen I had spent summer holidays in Germany staying with relatives on my father's side, ending up with a seven-month stint on leaving school in 1935. This gave me probably as good a working knowledge of German as I might have acquired at university but, in addition, it gave me a frightening insight into the growing militaristic threat of Hitlerism. My German relatives, I knew, were appalled by the creed and the deeds of the National Socialists but my uncle, several times removed, was a senior doctor-administrator in the Hanover Pensions Office and, realising that one word of dissent would lose him his job and perhaps endanger his wife and daughter, he kept quiet. Easy to criticise in retrospect but the danger was real. His younger brother, a major on the German General Staff, did, in the early days of the war, throw caution to the winds and was privy to the first conspiracy against Hitler. If a paralysing stroke had not removed him from office a few weeks earlier, the firing squad which liquidated General von Fritsch and other colleagues would have done so. However, without any such foreknowledge of the future, I had already heard and seen enough during my time in Germany to convince me that Britain and France must take defensive precautions against the ever-increasing might of Hitler's armies.

Whilst my joining the Territorial Army would scarcely have much effect on the balance of power in Europe, I took Peter's point that my newly entered business world of five-and-a-half days' work a week for fifty weeks in the year, might be cheered up by the comradery of like-minded young people and, not least of all, by the two extra weeks away from the office which summer camp could offer. It was not that I disliked my job in the tea trade but, after seven months on the loose in Germany followed by a pleasant and easy-going half-year in Switzerland at the École Supérieure de Commerce at Neuchâtel to polish up my French and learn some elementary business skills, the restrictive regime of working in London with its additional two hours daily commuting came as rather a shock.

Of course, it had always been taken for granted, when my brother and I were small boys, that one or both of us would join the family cigar firm which had been handed down from father to son since 1794. It was

13

my father who, as a young man, brought the main branch of the business over from Amsterdam and it became a treat for me in pre-school days to be taken to London by my mother and left at the factory in Bath Street off City Road, while she went shopping in the West End. I was placed in charge of Miss Brown, my father's secretary, seated in the comfortable leather chair in front of his desk while she went off to alert him. On the wall behind his desk I could see the portrait of the founder of the firm, my father's exact namesake, since eldest sons stretching six or seven generations back had all been christened with the single forename of Justus. My father liked to point out that he was named after the biblical character who just failed to become one of the twelve apostles and, had he not just missed out, the name of Justus would have been as familiar today as Peter or Paul. Alongside the founder hung framed certificates recording gold medals awarded at long-forgotten exhibitions in the Low Countries. Had I been old enough to think about such matters, it would have seemed logical for my brother, the present Justus in line, to inherit the business but I was too busy anticipating the coming tour round the factory with a mixture of fascination and trepidation, knowing that I would be the focus of attention for the work-people on the floors above.

My father bustled in in his long brown dust-coat which he wore in a forlorn attempt to prevent the reek of tobacco permeating his suit. He smoked a newly and roughly made-up cigar to test a particular blend of tobacco. The factory was housed in a narrow but tall building, one of a row in a short city street and must, even then, have been one of the few remaining where cigars were entirely hand-made. He led me up to the first floor where bench-loads of well-covered East End women were at work. As we entered chatter ceased, heads turned and eyes ogled the boss's little boy. My father, who was on the best of terms with all of them, had no doubt put the word about in advance and was more gratified at this attention than was his young offspring. But my embarrassment all but disappeared as we moved from one group to another. The first were strippers, that is to say they were removing the central stalk from good grade tobacco without damaging the leaf itself. The lightning-quick twist of the wrists as they did it held me enthralled.

'Would you like to have a try, luv?' they asked whilst their revolving wrists scarcely stopped.

'No, thank you,' I replied and shuffled my feet.

We moved on to the cigar makers who were taking the stripped leaves and wrapping them around small sliced tobacco known as filler.

The embryo cigars were then fitted into wooden moulds. Even I could see that the process was more complicated and more difficult than they made it seem. The completed moulds were now moved into the drying-room which was hot and aromatic when one was allowed in for a moment. Being a handy man himself, my father's pet department was almost certainly the workshop on an upper floor. A large proportion of cigars were still sold in individual cedarwood boxes and these were all made on the premises. The guiding genius here was a tall, slim and shy man by the name of Huntley. We at home were often the beneficiaries of his skill since, after he and my father had put their heads together, the latter would arrive home with any variety of tailor-made box; a box to hold cutlery, a box to keep toys in, a cabinet to hold gramophone records. The more demands made on Huntley to demonstrate his ability, the better, it seems, was he pleased.

But this friendly family business, which augmented its domestic sales with exports to South Africa and Australia, was doomed, had one but known it. It was the Great Depression a few years later which first hit it, since cigars were near the top of most gentlemen's dispensable luxuries. My father just had not the capital and possibly lacked the hard business acumen to survive and the business fell neatly into the hands of his main tobacco supplier. My father's expertise – he was said to be one of the best judges of tobacco leaf in the business – was still required but only at the price of a small annual salary. In the long run, there would, in any case, have been insufficient capital to compete with the large mechanised manufacturers, as indeed eventually proved to be the case for the purchaser himself.

The decrease in income made it a struggle for my parents to keep me at school. My mother came to the rescue by running a chicken farm in the orchard of our house and sending the eggs by rail to a London market in reusable wooden crates, especially made for the purpose by Huntley. Unwanted cockerels were sold to the local butcher and on one occasion, when the gardener was absent, my mother persuaded my father to undertake the neck-wringing. After several false starts he laid the two inert birds on the grass. A few minutes later when my mother came back to fetch them she found them running around squawking their heads off and clearly complaining of nothing more than a sore throat. Delivery to the butcher was delayed until the gardener was next available.

At the same time, the family took in foreign paying guests who wished to improve their English. Many of these 'PGs' were relatives of ours, or friends of theirs recommended to us. During the holidays, it was my task to talk to them and sometimes to escort them to London by train or to take them by the excellent local bus service to other places of interest. This experience taught me how to talk to foreigners so that they both understood and reacted, by the simple expedient of speaking slowly and clearly and avoiding slang and too many idiomatic turns of phrase. This may seem an all too obvious precaution but it has always astonished me how many otherwise intelligent Englishmen follow a diametrically opposed course when faced with persons with an imperfect knowledge of their language.

Fortunately, for the family exchequer, I was now reaching a stage at Lancing College where one had to begin thinking about a future career. Studying Modern Languages, and enjoying them, it was natural I should lean towards a profession that would take me abroad and allow me to make use of them. To be a diplomat required private means but the Consular Service, so I was informed, paid a living salary. Despite the absence in those days of any form of government grants, my parents said that if I were accepted as a Consular candidate, somehow or other they would find the money to send me to university; and Lancing offered me an exhibition which would have paid at least something towards my expenses. My application forms were duly filled up and, enclosing a recommendation from the Consul-General father of a school friend of mine, despatched for consideration. The reply, when it came, was in the negative. It explained very politely that the Service occasionally made exceptions for someone with one foreign-born grandfather but then went on, probably unintentionally, to paraphrase Lady Bracknell's observation to Mr Worthing: To have one foreign-born grandfather may be regarded as a misfortune, to have two looks like carelessness.

I next obtained an interview with the Anglo-Iranian Oil Company but this came to nothing, not on account of my grandfathers but because, they claimed, of the large number of applicants after very few vacancies. Other large firms when approached replied in similar terms.

It was when I had just left school that Cousin Paul came forward with a proposition. He was one of our numerous Swiss relatives, related to my father through their respective grandfathers, and had been long resident in England and a close family friend over the years. He ran a small tea export firm in the City known as The Blen-Chi Tea Company. Its basic function was to buy tea at the London tea auctions on behalf of its foreign customers and ship it out to them. To keep the customers coming, the largest proportion of whom were in his native Switzerland,

Paul Hatz had to travel extensively. He suggested that if I joined him to learn the trade, he would be pleased for me eventually to take some of this load off him. His offer was gratefully accepted, not least as it obviated the need for university education and I went off to Germany and then, at his suggestion, on to commercial school in Switzerland to prepare for the job.

As I stepped out of my train at Cannon Street Station on the first day of gainful employment in the City of London, I was dressed in my new business suit, I carried the regulation umbrella but I wore a trilby on my head. I had drawn a line at a bowler since, although still the preferred wear for city workers, I had found that there was something about me and a bowler which reduced my girlfriends and later my wife to helpless laughter. I hated the things anyway. I said goodbye to my father with whom I had travelled up together to work and trod the seven-minute walk down Cannon Street, through the pedestrian subway and on to the end of Eastcheap, a route which I was able to reduce to a three-minute gallop when on countless future occasions I looked like missing an evening or a Saturday lunchtime train.

No. 71, which towards the end of my time was knocked down to make way for just a small corner of the massive new Plantation House, was at the point where Eastcheap suddenly used to narrow into Great Tower Street. It was a corner building and the entrance, instead of looking across the street, looked back up the pavement towards Cannon Street. From the outside, it resembled many another smoke-begrimed London stone building, but climbing the two or three steps up from the street one seemed to be going back into Victorian times. Indeed, subsequent acquaintance with the office accommodation and at least one or two of its occupants suggested 'Dickensian' as a rather more fitting epithet. Certainly, there was a lift to the upper floors but this, like everything else, was antique. The porter-caretaker, a red-faced lumbering fellow surly to all save those in authority, indicated with a jerk of the head that the firm I wanted was two floors up.

Coming out of the lift I was faced with a door whose frosted-glass panel bore the inscription: 'The Blen-Chi Tea Company'. Behind this door was what, in a larger set-up, might have been termed the General Office. Here, apart from the boss's office, which led off a door in the opposite wall, it was the only office. The room was not particularly large; it had a sizeable table-cum-desk in the centre, a much smaller typist's desk in a corner, filing cabinets and card-indices occupied one wall and along the length of the opposing wall stretched a long window with a somewhat taller than waist-high counter running underneath it. The main feature of the remaining wall was an antiquated fireplace complete with coal scuttle, shovel, poker and other implements to keep the fire going in cold weather. The presiding presence over this office was one Thomas Hesse, who in appearance and habits, if not in other respects, was the most Dickensian of them all.

Mr Hesse, as he was always known, sat at the far side of the big desk with his back to the door leading into Paul Hatz's office. To save the jacket of his suit from further wear and tear, he wore a very old light brown tweed jacket, whose leather cuffs and elbow patches no longer succeeded in holding back the frayed material from sticking out round the edges. (I came to see how adept he was at whipping off this jacket if unexpected visitors knocked at the door and appearing in his more respectable shirt-sleeves, if he had not had time to go the whole hog and substitute his better jacket). He had a roundish, clean-shaven face, large spectacles and the beginning of a bald pate. His ginger hair sprouted out at the sides matching the similar phenomenon at his elbows and cuffs. Placed behind his right ear was his bulky penholder with its schoolboy nib. This remained permanently there until he actually needed to write, or unless he required it either to stir his tea or to pick his teeth after the biscuit he took with his afternoon cup.

Opposite Mr Hesse sat Wallace, an amiable young man with protruding eyes behind spectacles. The typist desk was, for the time being, unoccupied.

When Mr Hesse pushed me through to Paul Hatz, the latter was on the telephone to a Swiss client and I sat and tried to follow his voluble Swiss-German without too much success. The Cousin Paul I so far knew was an intellectual who enjoyed discussing the German philosophers with my mother and who spoke as fluent French as he did his own Swiss-German. He also liked to hold forth on the merits of the poets who wrote in Romansch, Switzerland's little known fourth language. I was to find out that in business he was a live-wire with considerable power of persuasion over his customers, but whatever happened he always managed to remain the born gentleman.

He extolled the virtues of Thomas Hesse to me, but I said I should try to ignore his less admirable habits, advice which Paul himself must have found difficult to follow, being the most fastidious person I ever met. Hesse was an intelligent man who had taught himself to write, if not to speak, remarkable French. He could teach me about many facets of the business and I would be wise to heed him. Paul then said he would take me through to meet the members of our sister firm, Theodor & Rawlins.

Theodor & Rawlins had made quite a pile of money in the good old days when they operated out of Shanghai but now the only survivor of that period was old Mr Seymour – and he really was old! He shuffled around with his white beard and somewhat vacant look but it was clear from the deference paid to him by his small staff, which included Mr Arthur his unimpressive son, that he must still hold the purse-strings. As far as I could gather Theodor & Rawlins had put needed finance into Paul's business and they now kept our books and indeed issued the very lightweight salary envelopes to Hesse, Wallace and myself. Worst of all, often to Paul's frustration, they exercised a veto over deals which appeared to contain an element of risk. I never really discovered what independent business they undertook themselves but it seemed to me that they mostly sat around waiting for our side to make the money. Their only genuinely friendly and cheerful staff member was Berry, a true cockney, who was in and out of our office with the latest gossip and who, among other jobs, organised the tea-tasting. Paul usually took the broker's word for the quality of a tea but at times teas were tasted before being offered to customers. Old Mr Seymour, presumably for old times' sake as much as for any opinion he would offer, often shuffled down the passage to Berry's sample room for this ceremony and after smacking his lips over a tea would shoot his contribution into the large spitoon provided. If only Paul took part, I would be invited to join in as part of my training.

Hesse, I was glad to find, in no way resented my arrival in his domain; indeed, he did not hesitate to admit that it made a nice change to have someone who could follow his homilies on the idiosyncrasies of French grammar and his occasional references to similarities or dissimilarities with the Spanish. As no one else knew Spanish he could not be contradicted, and correspondence with our only Spanish agent, who knew not a word of English, had to be left to him. Paul, often brave when faced with a big gamble, was basically a very nervous man and he suffered agonies over the few orders we received from Spain in case a mix-up due to linguistic difficulties should occur. Hesse, however, remained unperturbed and no such misfortune ever occurred.

Polio in his youth had left Paul with a permanent tremble in his right hand and this seemed to emphasise his nervousness. He would lean over you when, for example, you were preparing samples for despatch overseas and with his hand-held cigarette dancing a quick jig in front of your nose and his urgent enquiry whether you were sure you hadn't put the right reference number on the wrong sample, it was difficult not to become affected yourself. In a way, I sympathised as I could imagine what a blow-up would take place with our sister firm if a costly mistake were made.

My first office task in the morning soon became established. With no multi-lingual shorthand secretary available, Paul came in most mornings with a batch of letters handwritten the previous evening. Hesse took those in French and I took the rather fewer number in German and any French overflow. Soon I was able to compose routine letters in German myself to forwarding agents in Hamburg, Gdynia and elsewhere while Hesse was hammering away in French. Meanwhile Wallace, apart from his usual office-boy tasks, was fetching from the brokers samples of teas coming up the following week at auction, thereafter getting them labelled up in their little tin boxes for posting to customers. When two or three days before the auction telegrams hopefully arrived ordering so many chests of this and so many of that, Paul went into action with the brokers, briefing them to bid for the required lots.

It was felt that I should learn the job of fetching the tea samples from the various brokers so that I could stand in for Wallace if required. The only difficulties involved in this were that the brokers expected you to help yourself to the samples you wanted and to know which tin box out of row upon row was the appropriate one for that particular sale and, more frustrating, the method of wrapping up the samples once selected. To have had paper sachets in which to place your sample would have been too simple but not, of course, traditional; no, you had to take a plain sheet of paper measuring no more than 6 by 8 inches and wrap a good dollop of loose tea up in it. After considerable practice it became easier, thus sparing you the indignity of arriving back in your own office only to find that your sample packets had unfolded into one communal heap of tea. It was lucky that I did get practice with the kind help of Wallace because that poor boy slowly seemed to sink into a world of his own until a terminal brain tumour was diagnosed.

This, for quite a time, left Hesse and me, with some unofficial help from the ever-obliging Berry, to cope with everything. My respect for Hesse increased in proportion to the amount of work piled on him. He developed a boyish good humour and sense of fun even though the pressure of work did seem to aggravate another of his less than admirable habits. When composing one of his letters in French and trying hurriedly to work out the grammatical implications of a particular sentence, he would gaze at the ceiling and then, just when you were least expecting it, very loudly suck his teeth. Until then I had only read in books of men indulging in this distracting habit but, like most things, one slowly became accustomed to it.

Another of my duties was to help to look after agents and customers of ours who visited London. Sometimes I would go to their hotels and escort them to the office, but if they had been here before they might find their own way. On one such occasion the door of our office opened unannounced and a foreign-looking gentleman stepped in. The effect on Hesse was electric; he leapt to his feet, turned tail and fled through the door of the boss's office, leaving me to deal with the visitor. It turned out to be Monsieur Ritier, our long-standing agent in Marseille. As Paul Hatz was temporally out of the building I naturally did my best to entertain him. As we talked I noticed that Berry frequently put his head round the door or made some excuse for coming in. It was not too long before Paul arrived back and took charge of the visiting agent.

Berry again put his head round the door.

'Has the boss returned?' he asked.

'Yes. Are you trying to see him?'

'Naw, it's not that but you see old 'Essie's taken refuge in my sample room and wants to know if he can come back.'

'Why, what's the matter with him?'

'Well, he's terrified of being left with that Ritier bloke. He knows 'Essie writes some of the letters to him so, if he gets the chance, he says things to him in French and expects him to answer. That doesn't 'arf put the wind up 'Essie so he keeps out of the way until the coast is clear.'

I was subsequently called into Paul's office.

'Monsieur Ritier is in the throes of a tiresome lawsuit in the French courts,' he explained, 'and seems convinced that things are done much better and speedier over here in England. So, he'd like to see an English court in action. So please be ready tomorrow morning to take him to the Old Bailey and then just go into the one of the courts with him for a short while. If you get the chance, tell him roughly what's happening.'

We took a taxi next morning but I was unable to warn our agent of what he was likely to experience as I only just about knew what the Old Bailey looked like from the outside, let alone from the inside. Arriving there we entered one of the courts and sat down. Proceedings were in full swing and it was not long before Ritier wanted to know what was afoot. He was a small but insistent man and his stage whisper seemed to carry a long way. The more he wanted to know, the louder his voice became and he paid little regard to my efforts to calm him down. It was not surprising that we soon attracted the attention of the clerk of the court who followed up a series of angry glances with a formal admonition that we would be removed from the court if silence was not observed. For a time, this had the desired effect on Ritier until an unusual turn in the defence evidence overcame his sorely tried patience.

It happened to be a case that was attracting considerable coverage in the press. A gentleman had taken a light lunch at one of the top London hotels – I think it may have been the Savoy – and had ordered a sandwich but to his disgust had discovered a cockroach in it. This persuaded him to claim damages from the hotel. Counsel for the defence, trying to make the best of a difficult job, began arguing that a gentleman as wealthy as the plaintiff had no need to have chosen a sandwich. Why, the hotel's main restaurant was, as always, offering its unsurpassed food. Then with a flourish he produced the menu for that particular day and began to read it out dish by dish. It was, of course, in French. It took a little while for Ritier to recover from his initial astonishment but then he turned to me with a high-pitched stream of questions: what in the name of God was all this about, had that strange lawyer gone off his head or could it have some relevance to the matter in hand or was this perhaps what we should now call a commercial break for the court's restaurant?

Faced with this loud and unseemly behaviour, Counsel came to a halt just as he was coming to the entrées, the clerk advanced menacingly on us and requested us to leave before we were forcibly removed. I dragged the puzzled Ritier after me and was relieved to escape the court without further incident. When I delivered my charge back to Paul Hatz he was still shaking his head and mumbling something to the effect that the English judiciary appeared to be just as time-wasting and perhaps even more eccentric and irresponsible than the French.

We used to like to boast that we had customers from Finland in the north-east down through Europe to the French colonies in North Africa. Mr Vainio Einio in Helsinki – or was it Einio Vainio, I have become confused with time – corresponded rather infrequently but in good English and just as infrequently put in an order; our German agents had gone quiet because the Nazi government, short of foreign currency which was reserved for military purchases, normally only sanctioned barter deals, but Mr Kanal, our agent in Warsaw, made up for them all by the frequency and length of his letters if by little else. 'Mein Gott,' he would write in ungrammatical but understandable German, 'I have to support a wife and five children (the number of children was apt to increase with the intensity of his feelings) and now you do not take my close friend Herr Josef's word of a gentleman and you demand bank guarantees!! How can one operate without good faith on both sides?? If you would do this and at the same time reduce your excessive prices we could sell to every merchant in this city.' So forth and so forth. We used to welcome his letters as providing light relief in an otherwise generally humourless postbag, but it has to be admitted that every so often he did pull off a properly safeguarded deal.

It was a matter of some surprise when Mr Kanal, who judging by his letters was, together with his variable family, on the edge of starvation, announced his intention of visiting London to try to barter Polish textiles against tea, all naturally with our assistance. Paul was basically opposed to our wasting time over attempted barter deals but perhaps there was a measure of sheer curiosity which prompted him not to dissuade Kanel from coming. There was considerable speculation about him before his arrival but he turned out to be well-dressed and certainly far from the breadline. As I composed many of the replies to his letters I was appointed his guide and interpreter.

The first task before thinking about tea purchases was to try to help him sell some of his cloth and it was in this connection that my boss made the only slightly risqué remark I ever heard from him. 'If you made a pair of trousers from this material,' he said to me, 'one good fart and you'd be through them!' The merchants Kanal and I visited in Wood Street were clearly of the same opinion since they lost little time in sending us packing. But then, relating our lack of success to a business friend, Paul was given the address of a firm in Whitechapel. Kanal and I trooped off there and found the place to be a small and shabby warehouse. Going through the outer door we came into a short passage with a door at its end with a shuttered window let into it. In reply to our ring on the bell the shutter shot up and a lined face, partly hidden by a long black beard, surmounted by black hair with a skull cap perched on the back, peered through at us. I opened my mouth to explain our mission but Kanal got in first – in Yiddish. We were admitted to an inner office, joined by several other persons and discussions and much handling of samples continued in Yiddish. Eventually I left them to it, having received an assurance that our agent would be despatched back to us. A lot later a radiant Kanal appeared in our office. We suspected that he had sold more than he was prepared to admit but we did, at least, get some orders for tea out of it. This was our one and only visit from this agent and I fear that when the Germans invaded his country some two years later he and his children fared ill.

Whilst Kanal's success in selling his cloth was almost entirely his own, about that time I did earn the gratitude of colleagues by making a small, if unusual, sale of tea myself. Out of the salary I earned I paid my rail season ticket, and my lunch and all out-of-pocket expenses, but I still had to rely on my parents for board and lodging and clothing. This was not thought to be too unusual in those days for a lad just passed twenty, who was at the same time learning a trade. But how Thomas Hesse managed to run a house in the southern outskirts of London at Thornton Heath and care for a wife and two daughters approaching teenage on the contents of his pay package from Theodor & Rawlins I failed to understand. It was thus not surprising that it was his idea that the left-overs of tea samples collected from brokers over the years might bring in a little additional money. These left-overs were always available to be taken home for the family teapot but the vast majority were thrown into a spare tea-chest. This was now full, with an unusual mixture of almost every tea which came to the London auction market from top-class orange pekoes to the cheapest fannings. Hesse suggested we bring Berry in on the scheme as he had considerably more tea tucked away in his sample room. But who would want such a strange blend? Paul suggested we start at the top and go to the tea purchasing department of a firm whose products were household names in every grocery store in the kingdom. But who should go? The embarrassable Hesse was out of the question. Berry declared that he was not posh enough to approach a firm like that, so without lots being drawn, the choice fell on me.

Berry prepared a carefully doctored sample, using only the better teas, and then the question of the asking price arose. On the basis that one could always lower but never raise prices, a highly improbable figure was arrived at. I went off and found the firm whose offices were over a shop of their own not far from St. Paul's Cathedral. I explained what I had come for to the manageress of the shop and was told the chief tea-buyer would come down. In strutted an elderly and rather irritable-looking man, I explained the nature of the goods on offer and he sniffed at Berry's sample. Asked the price I took a deep breath and gave the outrageous figure we had half-jokingly arrived at. Either I had overstressed the high proportion of superior tea or Berry had excelled himself over the sample but, for some reason or other, this pompous little man seemed to think he was on to a bargain. 'All right,' he snapped,

'I'll take as much as you've got. Here's my card. Telephone me when I can send a van to fetch it. I'm busy, so goodbye.'

I bussed back to Eastcheap in a daze and when I broke the news to my companions they were dumbfounded. Then Hesse in a strangled voice asked, 'He really said he'd take all we'd got?' Then coming to life: 'Oh, then what are we waiting for? All hands to the pump!'

For the next few days I staggered back to the office from the brokers with as many and as large tea samples as I could manage. Meanwhile Hesse and Berry had a second tea chest and then a third rapidly filling up and spent all available moments searching the dusty cupboards for stray tins or age-old paper-wrapped samples. I even caught Hesse sweeping up a few leaves escaped on to the floor with the brush from the fireplace. After every source had been exhausted, a van arrived to collect the three chests and to hand over the resulting cheque. When the share-out came I received the equivalent of four weeks' salary while Hesse sat humming to himself, interspersed with the occasional satisfied sucking of teeth, planning what treats he could afford to give his family.

Our North African customers exclusively bought green teas from China, the most unappetising-looking of which was known as Gunpowder, with leaves rolled up into tiny cannon balls and dyed a fearsome mauve colour. I came to believe that if, and when, the time came for me to travel in the place of Paul, North Africa was the area he would most willingly release to me. I remember him coming back from there and describing to me the tea-tasting he had had to endure. As he spoke he rubbed his hands together as if trying to wash away the memory, and the distress and repulsion showed on his face.

'You know, out there everyone doesn't have their own cup to taste out of and even if they do' – here a shudder – 'they insist on handing you the cup they have just tasted from, almost as a compliment so you can give them your opinion. And you stand there wondering how many of them have contracted syphilis and how long it will be before you do.'

But circumstances were against me travelling anywhere on behalf of the Blen-Chi Tea Company. In the first place, I was still considered too young for such a task and pre-war the older you were, within reason, the more capable you were thought to be. The war, of course, changed all that, with everyone thankful to have fighter pilots hardly turned twenty years of age winning the Battle of Britain for them, and a future colleague of mine parachuting into France and organising resistance against the occupying Germans over a large stretch of south-east France at a similar age. But more cogently, I still had much to learn about tea and the tea trade and always in the background lurked the threat of war, which now increasingly neutralised efforts to sell tea in a number of once profitable markets.

Changes were indeed in the air as 71 Eastcheap eventually had to give way to the creeping growth of Plantation House and we moved to offices in Mincing Lane, the traditional centre of the tea trade. These were more modern, cleaner but definitely lacking the antique character of No. 71, to which we had become quite attached.

Then in summer 1939 my brother, a tea planter in Ceylon, came back on leave. He brought back with him a promise, provisional on my being found suitable on arrival, of a job in the Colombo headquarters of Whitall & Co, the large produce company, the owners of tea plantations including my brother's, and exporters to the London Tea Market. It was agreed within the family that, with the experience gained in London, the job in Colombo would offer me better chances of promotion and better financial prospects. The fact that Paul had recently taken in a middle-aged partner, who had little or no experience of the tea trade but who had put in money, probably helping to counter-balance the influence of Theodor & Rawlins, was held to be a further reason for branching out to Ceylon. The decision involved sacrifice on my parents' part, as leave from Ceylon was only granted once every four years, and, because of this, they were only seeing my brother for the second time since he left England nine years earlier.

I left Paul's office in July 1939 to have an extended holiday before sailing away to Ceylon with my brother. But Hitler got in first with his invasion of Poland and I was mobilised into the Army. My brother's attempts to join up were disallowed as, being a member of the Ceylon Tea Planters Rifles, he was forced to hang around until transport back to Ceylon was available. Some months after arrival there he was able to join the first draft sent to India to be commissioned there.

It was not really until the end of the war that I was fully able to piece together what fate had held in store for my friends in the Blen-Chi Tea Company. If not at the outbreak of war, certainly with the collapse of France, the firm's business ceased to exist and Paul, with no longer a reason to remain in London, retired to Wales with his wife for the duration. However, in 1948, visiting my bank in Eastcheap prior to a Foreign Office posting to Moscow, to my surprise I spotted the well-remembered name on the door of an adjoining building. Here I found Paul's partner in sole charge of a resuscitated business and happy to reminisce.

Thomas Hesse brings this chapter to a happy ending and at the same time proves the doubters as to his ability in the Spanish language at fault. Finding himself without a job, he made his language qualifications known to the War Office who sent him to our embassy in Mexico City as clerk to the military attaché. So well did he prosper – with a larger salary and language allowances thrown in – that he decided to stay on after the end of the war. I am sure he soon discovered that, with a little practice and a little courage, speaking a language is really easier than writing it, and I like to think of him regaling Mexican acquaintances with his tales of the complexities of the French language and contrasting them with the relative simplicity of their own.

CHAPTER 3

Second Lieutenant van Maurik

The fact that I was mobilised the day before war was declared stemmed from my meeting with Peter Stephenson three years earlier and my acceptance of his invitation to visit the headquarters of the Artists Rifles.

Instead of my habitual dash for the six-three at Cannon Street – leisure hours were too precious to risk having to take a later train – I had walked with unaccustomed measured pace one Tuesday evening to nearby Monument underground station, taken an Inner Circle train to Euston Square and, following Peter's instructions, walked three blocks along Euston Road and turned into Duke Street. This short side-street was dominated by a large drill-hall, the home of the Artists. I entered and found Peter waiting for me.

He suggested we begin with a conducted tour of the building. The front section on two floors consisted of offices, storerooms, armoury, the bar and mess-room, the sergeants' mess, the officers' mess and other necessities. At the back was the spacious drill-hall itself, with small groups of men practising firing drill on a Bren gun, signallers played with equipment in a corner and, at the far end, two masked figures were engaged in bayonet fencing which, I was told, was an Artists' speciality.

As we walked, Peter gave a short talk on the regiment. One of the original volunteer forces raised in the second half of the nineteenth century, it still had one or two men of artistic ability in its ranks but they were now there almost by chance than design. It was brigaded with the Honourable Artillery Company and the Inns of Court and all three had been nominated Officer Producing Units; that is to say, in the event of war they would not fight as a unit but provide officers for other regiments. The Artists, as its full title suggested, was a rifle regiment

28

and the attached staff came from the regular Rifle Brigade. The latter traditionally recruited smaller-sized men and to accommodate them they marched with a shorter but faster pace. The Artists Rifles adopted this fast pace on ceremonial occasions but, as they were mostly large fellows, the pace rate dropped on route marches and exercises to a slower and longer pace which came natural to them. This said, Peter concentrated on the comradeship, the splendid chaps you mixed with, the great fun and outdoor life of the annual camp with its two extra weeks' holiday a year, and the Army paying you on top of your firm's normal salary. But I shouldn't run away with the idea, he said, that one didn't have to be efficient, in fact super-efficient, because there was great esprit-de-corps and the Artists liked to think themselves the real stars of the brigade. As an example, no one became even a lance-corporal without at least four years' service behind him and as for the sergeants, not only was it said to be more expensive to be a member of the sergeants as opposed to the officers' mess, but to a man they would be capable of holding down a senior officer's job.

As we went around Peter introduced me to particular friends of his and others, including one or two officers, but as everyone was in his city suit it was not easy to sort people out. However there seemed to be a common reaction when they realised a new recruit could be in prospect. 'See you later in the bar,' they all said.

I was not so naive as not to realise, as young men vied with each other to buy me beer at the bar, that a modern but pleasanter form of press-ganging was taking place. I vaguely knew that the London territorial units were in competition for suitable recruits to swell their numbers but, had they but known it, I had already decided to join up even before entering their building and without any expenditure on their part on beer. When Peter and his friends judged that the softening-up process had reached an appropriate stage, I was escorted to an office – whether it was the adjutant's or someone else's I was not quite clear next morning, let alone now many years later – where I happily signed on the dotted line. We then repaired again to the bar for one or two more to seal the contract.

From then on, I visited Dukes Road once a week, arriving home in Tunbridge Wells late but mentally and bodily refreshed. It was fixed that I should join Peter in 'B' Company but first I had to take part in the next new recruits course. This was not too arduous a task as, in common with most of my fellow recruits, I had been a member of the Officer Training Corps at school; indeed, by my last year at Lancing

I had been made the officer cadet in charge of the Corps, under the supervision, naturally, of the Commanding Officer, who was one of the masters. It may appear that I was a rather militaristically-minded youth but I don't think this was really true. I had no desire to be involved in fighting battles and I was frightened of being scared if I had to do so. But I did enjoy it, and I was good at acting as an instructor, and the less bellicose arts of map-reading, fieldcraft and compass work appealed to me. Luckily so, as this stood me in good stead later on.

We learnt, of course, more about the history and traditions of the regiment, of the regimental badge portraying the heads of Mars and Minerva and the motto 'Cum Marte Minerva', denoting that the God of War must go hand in hand with the Goddess of Wisdom. Of how the Artists were raised in 1860 by a group of artists, sculptors, musicians and actors and had their first headquarters somewhat naturally at Burlington House. As a result, the Artists Rifles were accorded the right of providing each year a guard of honour at the opening of the Royal Academy's Summer Exhibition. To be a member of this guard, we were told, was an honour to which every Artist should aspire.

While I was imbibing all this, my mother informed me out of the blue that Uncle Harold Weekes, of whose existence until then I had no inkling, had been a member of the Artists many years back. He was, it seemed, descended from Henry Weekes RA, the Victorian sculptor, and his second wife, whilst I was descended through my mother from his first marriage. Harold went on to be a regular officer with the Gurkhas and, returning with the rank of lieutenant colonel, was appointed Black Rod to the House of Lords. Now, my mother said, he and his wife, but principally his wife, ran a country hotel just along the coast from Worthing, which he found both deplorable and degrading. Families being such as they are, no suggestion was made that we might get together and from the little I have since heard about Uncle Harold I suspect he would have been singularly unimpressed at meeting a distant young relative who happened to have joined his first regiment.

I do not recall the exact date of my joining the Artists but it must have been some time before December 1936, since I heard the news of the abdication of Edward VIII which took place on the tenth of that month over a radio in the bar at Dukes Road. I can remember how stunned I felt, how unbelieving that a King of England could give up his throne for the sake of an American divorcee. Kings simply did not do such things. I could see similar shocked reaction mirrored in the faces of those loyal young subjects standing around me. We were a generation that had known no royal scandal in our lifetime and the British press in its reticence had given us very little warning of what was to come. True, the American and other foreign papers had been running stories for some time but with neither our press nor the wireless making more than scant mention of them, only a few unsubstantiated rumours filtered through and we had chosen to disbelieve, indeed to ignore them. To us the monarchy had been immutable and sacrosanct and while we could not avoid perhaps some feeling of being let down, we knew it to be our duty to rally behind Edward's successor. Many today might argue that an undemocratic muzzling of the press aggravated matters but the press was in fact following an agreed code of practice, and I doubt whether a free-for-all by the media would have done anything other than compound Edward's problems.

My first ceremonial parade with the Artists reflected a happier royal occasion – the coronation of King George VI on 12 May 1937. The Artists were allocated a stretch of the route to line on the south side of the Strand, stretching eastwards from the junction with Villiers Street. This was my first experience of anything of this sort and I enjoyed it. We naturally had to take up positions long before the procession was timed to pass but the massive crowds were there even earlier. We were, of course, standing at ease during the long waiting period and able to enjoy the good humour of the crowd, the cheers for the occasional officials passing by, for the road sanders and especially for the removers of the horse-droppings deposited by the mounted police. Spaced out at three or four feet intervals, we were not there primarily to control the onlookers but, when the procession was soon to appear, we were reinforced by police behind us who looked inwards rather than outwards. Our main worry was whether we would hear the words of command and when the royal coaches approached, the roar of the crowd was augmented by a band close behind us striking up 'God save the King'. It was probably more by watching the straining figure of the officer, rather than much sound reaching us, that we were able to present arms on time.

This was the first occasion I had seen either the king or Queen Elizabeth 'live' but a second occasion presented itself two years later. I had never put myself forward as a candidate for the Royal Academy guard of honour, perhaps because it would have been difficult to absent myself from 71 Eastcheap on a working day but somehow, I forget how, I did manage to participate in the guard of honour when the king and queen opened the completely newly rebuilt Westminster Hospital in April 1939.

The Artists Rifles certainly lent a new dimension to my life in the immediate pre-war years when I was acclimatising myself to what appeared at the time to be an open-ended commitment to hard, although not uncongenial work, combined with limited leisure and low reward. This is a prospect faced by many young persons in any age but today they expect, at the very least, a living wage from the start, which in my case I had still not quite attained after three years. The practice, adopted by enterprising employees in the boom years of the sixties onwards, of changing jobs frequently to work their way up the ladder, was far from common in the thirties. I was brought up with the idea that this would be counter-productive as employers would regard anyone behaving in this manner as unreliable and unable to settle down to a good job of work. So, the idea of looking for more lucrative employment hardly arose, especially as, without some sort of private "pull", there appeared to be little chance of finding any. But thanks to board and lodging, plus modest financial infusions from my parents, I was able to enjoy my non-working hours, even though my weekends, after arriving home from London, effectively began at 15.00 hours on a Saturday afternoon, a Saturday morning off being unheard of in the City of those days.

My parents had given up their house in Edenbridge just before I left school and for nine months or so had lived rent-free in a cottage on the estate of very good friends of ours. The savings effected together with the cessation of school fees helped towards the purchase of a house in the Frant Road in Tunbridge Wells. It was from here that I commuted back and forth to work and it was my home base throughout the war.

As they prepared to move from the Edenbridge house, which had been my home for the first eighteen years of my life, an incident occurred which might have solved many a problem for my parents. On a patio open to the elements at the back of the house stood a small carved statuette which my father said was a Vishnu, but which, by the way he pronounced it, we thought was something called a Fishnu. It had been there ever since I could remember and had become part of the scenery. My father had been given it, or had bought it cheap, on a visit to the Dutch East Indies, where he had been sent by his father as a young man to expand his horizons. He always said that he believed it had some value but my mother, brought up on the German philosophers but uninterested in Hinduism, doubted this and could not see why anybody would want such a thing. The English climate was doing it no good and my mother thought it would be an embarrassment in the move. So, no objections were raised when my father proposed offering it to the British Museum. Their reply to his letter stated that they would be interested to see it. So, father wrapped it up – his parcels were always works of art – and took it off to London. The Museum judged it to be a good specimen, probably stolen from a Hindu temple and they accepted the gift with gratitude. When subsequently asked for a rough estimate of the value, they quoted a sum which would have gone a long way towards buying the new house. My mother, after slogging away at chicken farming and catering for paying guests, was decidedly not amused. My father, right for once, took me up to the British Museum and proudly showed me the Vishnu in its glass case with a card neatly inscribed 'Kindly donated by Justus van Maurik Esq'. I felt happy for him as we went off to find a Lyons where he could stand me lunch.

Even before we made the twelve-mile move from Edenbridge to Tunbridge Wells we had a few friends in and around the town. Tunbridge Wells, much more so than today, was known as a refuge for retired and often eccentric people and collecting sightings of the more unusual characters became quite a game with us twenty-year olds. One could win the jackpot outright with a confirmed sighting of either the Lady with the Horns or the Lady in the Barouche. The former was quite short, always on foot and dressed in Edwardian style, which was a trifle unusual but not unique in pre-war Tunbridge Wells. Her main distinction was the enormous, capacious and flowing hat which three-quarters covered what was either mountains of piled up hair or a grotesque wig. Where the story that her headgear was designed to cover her horns originated I do not know, but it was certainly not invented by us. A scheme was formulated for several of us to walk behind her and, accidentally bumping into her, to dislodge her hat but fortunately this was never proceeded with and the mystery remained unsolved.

The Lady in the Barouche was more flamboyant but the only mystery about the poor woman was whether she was just partly or entirely deranged. We called the vehicle she travelled in a barouche, not because we really knew what a barouche looked like, or we thought this resembled one, but because the term took our fancy. It was an open vehicle propelled by electricity and it was painted green throughout, the upholstery being of the same identical hue. It did not have a steering wheel but instead had a horizontally-placed long handle which was moved in the same plane. There were four attendants, all of them attired in smart uniforms of the same shade of green – the driver and a footman who sat beside him and two further footmen standing on a platform built at the back of the vehicle. On the rear seat between the two rows of footmen sat the lady herself, once again dressed in elaborate Edwardian costume, which naturally was entirely in green. It was said that she lived in one of the most expensive and fashionable addresses in the centre of Tunbridge Wells and had once been an actress; it could well have been true. Her extreme eccentricity, and the fact that she did not sally forth very frequently, made her highly collectable.

My prime sighting happened once when I was walking down Mount Pleasant, the wide shopping thoroughfare in the centre of town. The barouche overtook me with only a slight whine from its motor and then pulled up half-way down the hill in front of the town's best provision store, these days swallowed up by a department store. I saw the two rear footmen jump down from their perch and one went into the shop. The manager in his habitual morning-coat came out and stood on the pavement beside the barouche and, clearly knowing the form, made quite a deep bow to the lady in green. I stood and watched as from her seat she dictated a shopping list, long enough to show why it was all worth the manager's while. He then took a step back, gave another bow, a green glove gave him a regal wave, the flunkeys jumped into their standing positions at the rear and the barouche continued down the hill.

There were other less valuable sightings to be made; several caricatures of Indian Army colonels and their ladies, other persons of varying degrees of dottiness and always the chance of coming across someone so far unidentified, possibly a new arrival to join Tunbridge Wells' established eccentrics.

Our main organised entertainment took place of a Saturday night, when the Old Barn was our favourite port of call twenty minutes' drive away at Hildenborough. The thirties was the era of the roadhouse, where one could drink and dance, the Ace of Spades, close to South-West London, being one of the best known. A generation brought up on twice-weekly visits to the 'flicks', we were all avid fans of Fred Astaire and Ginger Rogers and, although we could not emulate their skills, we could at least dance cheek to cheek to the music of Cole Porter and Irving Berlin.

The Old Barn was not the brassy type of roadhouse and it suited us well; indeed, its owner would not have liked to hear it described as such at all. In the afternoons, it catered for Women's Institute busloads and others keen to experience its cream teas. It consisted of the old barn itself, a converted oasthouse and other built-on attachments. Around the outside of the circular oast was painted in giant white letters 'Oceans of Cream' and their teas justified this boast.

On a Saturday night, it was transformed. Tables lined the walls of the barn and a large area in the middle was left for dancing – no pocket-handkerchief floor, this! The eight-or ten-piece band was on a platform reached by steps, built in the rafters of the building.

The owner was a prematurely white-haired retired naval officer and he was very much in command. He did not interfere unless a group got too out of hand and then, if they did not come to heel, they knew what to expect. They would go on his black list and no further bookings of theirs would be accepted. A censure few wanted to contemplate. He by no means discouraged the consumption of alcohol – drugs as far as we were concerned had not yet been invented – but for reasons of his own he had never applied for a licence. It was therefore accepted practice that you bought your own bottles beforehand and carried them in to your table in shopping baskets (plastic bags had also not yet been invented). The liquor worked out cheaper that way, of course, but with ten or a dozen of us in our party, each boy bringing a contribution, we drank more than if we had had to fork out cash at the bar. Luckily breathalysers on the way home had also not been invented!

Evening dress was obligatory. Late teenagers came in black tie and dinner jacket but, as soon as this stage was passed, any self-respecting twenty-year old felt he had to come in white tie and tails. Dinner jackets could still be bought at the Thirty Shilling Tailors for the equivalent of £1.50 in decimal currency, but I remember that my tails, tailor-made in Tunbridge Wells, cost the vast sum of £11, for which I had to rely on my parents.

Dancing started at 19.30 in the evening to give us time to enjoy ourselves, as we were forbidden by law to continue into Sunday morning. The naval commander took good care to see that we didn't and the last waltz, followed by God Save the King, was played at 23.55 hours. There was no law however to prevent his staff serving eggs, bacon and coffee after midnight and this was a popular end to the evening, when one had money to spare. From start to finish we enjoyed ourselves. The band kept up a succession of quicksteps, foxtrots, slow waltzes and the occasional old-fashioned waltz. This I had been taught to dance by my German cousin, Christel, who spent a year with us in return for the time I had spent learning German with her family. When she returned home I found I could reduce an unsuspecting girlfriend in little more than half a waltz to a dizzy heap, having to support her back to the table. Then there was the polka which was enjoying a revival and was fun, provided you and your partner could coordinate your hops.

The valetta brought everyone on the floor where you formed up in long lines and progressed slowly along with high kicking and stamping of feet. The Paul Jones, played a couple of times an evening, helped to mix the guests up together. Conversation with your unknown partner traditionally started with 'Do you come here often?' and sometimes went not much further. Only seldom did it cause real embarrassment. I was still in the teenage black-tie stage when a Paul Jones lined me up with a highly sophisticated-looking twenty-five-year-old, who did not bother to disguise how too utterly boring it was to have to dance with such an infant. As a result, I found it impossible to avoid treading on her toes. The Paul Jones refrain rescued me but when the music stopped again I found I was once again opposite the same sophisticated lady with no avenue of escape. The ensuing foxtrot with its inevitable toe-treading became the longest dance of my life.

There was only one establishment which in any way challenged the supremacy of the Old Barn and this was the recently built Hilden Manor close to Tonbridge. It lacked the old-world charm and personality of its rival and its dance floor was very much smaller, but we occasionally patronised it because of its outstanding pianist who, with the aid of percussion accompaniment, thumped out an irresistible rhythm. Mr Pilbeam was short and dumpy and bounced about on his stool as he played. He beamed all over when complimented and would play all our requests, but his short-fused temper became known and some of the regulars liked to provoke him just for the hell of it. At that time, there was a precocious schoolgirl acting in British films by the name of Nova Pilbeam and a couple of young men would engage the pianist in conversation between numbers and slowly begin to bait him. 'Oh, come off it, Nova', they would say when they saw his colour rising, as he stomped out of the room. This was the moment for a conciliatory delegation to be formed to go in search of him and, with profuse apologies, to persuade him back to his instrument. All a waste of good dancing time was our own verdict.

When the war came the Old Barn was, I believe, requisitioned by the Army but the Hilden Manor remained open. Visiting it when on leave during the preliminary 'Phoney War' the scene was but changed in small ways. Outside all was blacked-out but inside people enjoyed themselves as much if not more than before, practically all the men were in uniform and baiting Mr Pilbeam, who welcomed pre-war clients as old friends, had gone out of fashion.

It was late September 1938 that war first appeared imminent and probably inevitable. Hitler had earlier that year annexed Austria and was now on the threshold of invading Czechoslovakia. France had given a guarantee of the latter's independence and was honour-bound to intervene. Britain was bound to support France. The Royal Navy mobilised, gas masks were issued to the civilian population, trenches were dug in London parks to act as air-raid shelters and the Artists Rifles sent an SOS to any members available to help put up air-raid defences round Dukes Road headquarters. I requested permission in view of the national emergency to absent myself from the office to help in this task. Short-staffed as we were, Paul hesitated, but Thomas Hesse spoke up bravely.

'Let the lad go,' he said, looking up from his ledger and firmly replacing his pen behind his ear. 'He's got a job to do. If this all blows over he'll be back in a couple of days and I can manage until then. If it doesn't, it won't matter one way or another whether the customers receive their tea samples.'

For the next three days thirty or forty of us unloaded trucks and filled sandbags, raising a barricade in front of the Dukes Road facade designed to protect against shrapnel, although certainly not against a direct hit. Other sandbag walls were simultaneously sprouting up in front of public buildings all over London. The completion of our task and my return to the office coincided with Chamberlain's return from his meeting with Hitler in Munich, waving a piece of paper which proved to be quite worthless and proclaiming that he had brought 'peace for our time'. The sandbags remained where they were as not everyone was as trusting as our prime minister.

From then on the Artists Rifles had no difficulty in attracting recruits but by the time our next annual camp came round in July 1939, the situation was again precarious. After obtaining large frontier areas of Czechoslovakia under the terms of the Munich Pact, Hitler was now eyeing Poland. That year our brigade – the Artists, the HAC and the Inns of Court – was encamped at Warminster in Wiltshire; at least, we were encamped until torrential rain flooded our tents and we were found accommodation in nearby Warminster barracks. Whilst some were prepared to take bets that we would be mobilised even before camp ended, no one let this spoil the usual fun. We may have route-marched a bit further and taken some aspects of training a bit more seriously but basically things were unchanged: the camp concert, the evening sorties into town to dine on giant-sized mixed grills and pints of ale (it all got sweated out the next day), the good-natured rivalry between the Artists and the HAC and attempts, usually unsuccessful, to persuade any raw recruit to report to the company office where he was wanted for a fatigue to whitewash the Last Post.

Mounting the Guard was always a great time for spit and polish. At the previous year's camp 'B' Company had been detailed one evening to provide the guard and I was one of those chosen to take part. The smartness of our turn-out was as much the concern of the whole company as it was of any one participant. After a great deal of polishing and honing of toe-caps, I was ready for inspection by my fellow company colleagues. The only item which the self-appointed inspection team considered below standard was my bayonet scabbard and that was less my fault than that of the scabbard which had always refused to respond properly to treatment.

'Well, who's got a really good one?' they enquired and soon a scabbard with a magnificent sheen on it was produced. My scabbard and bayonet were removed and replaced by the new set. When overall satisfaction had been achieved, the members of the guard were then carried bodily to the guard house so that boots remained unsullied by the dust and sometimes the mud of company lines.

When our new guard was fallen in for inspection by the battalion orderly officer of the day, I saw that he was none other than a pompous young man who had been on the same new recruits' squad as me. He had then done what to the rest of us was the almost unthinkable by getting himself an immediate commission and remaining attached to the Artists. We had little time for him. He now took an age coming down the line, examining each man as if future promotion depended on it. I had every reason to feel confident of my own turn-out and I felt I practically challenged him by my demeanour to find something wrong; and he did!

'Sergeant,' he exclaimed, turning to the orderly sergeant, 'this man has rust on the base of his bayonet. Put him on a charge.'

I was angry as I did not like letting the guard down, particularly as it didn't happen to be my bayonet. I was angry, too, as I had no real justification for being angry with this officer. He had done his duty, even though the spots of rust proved to be small indeed.

Peace did outlast our Warminster camp, but not by very much. Hitler's onslaught on Poland commenced on 1 September 1939, and we were mobilised the following day which was a Saturday.

Dressed in uniform, our personal kit stuffed into our kitbags, we reported to Dukes Road. There we submitted to a fairly thorough medical examination, we signed documents, were issued with identity discs which we slung round our necks with cord that became dirtier and greasier as the war progressed and, finally, we had to report to the paymaster. Here to our astonishment we were handed five pounds against signature, the equivalent of accepting the King's shilling, and instructed to report again two days later on the Monday morning.

Peter Stephenson and I finished signing on about the same time and he asked me what I intended to do until the day after tomorrow. When I said that I would have to return to Tunbridge Wells, he volunteered to accompany me as far as Charing Cross station where we could have a quick drink. With five pounds in our pockets we felt remarkably rich. Either in the Underground or in Charing Cross station we fell in with three of four more Artists and we all repaired to the station bar. Someone said that port and rum was the appropriate tipple and, although neither Peter nor I had ever heard of it, we readily agreed. We all, of course, had to stand a round and in between more than one City Gent insisted on pushing the boat out to the 'boys in uniform'.

We all ended up pretty drunk, but just sensible enough to realise that a train journey was not immediately advisable. First Peter said that he would accompany me to see I got home safely but as he, if anything, was drunker than I, this had its disadvantages. But when he suggested I spend the night in the flat he shared with his sister, this was agreed upon. It had the advantage, he suggested, that we could have further drinks when we got there. My memory as to how we got to the flat and how much we imbibed thereafter is blurred – by the passage of time no doubt – but I do remember being woken up by his sister around eleven o'clock on the Sunday morning and being told we should have some breakfast before the prime minister made an important announcement on the radio at noon, which was when the Allies' ultimatum to Germany expired. Getting up, except for a slight unsteadiness, presented no difficulty, since both Peter and I discovered to our surprise that we were already fully dressed even down to our Army boots.

We listened to Chamberlain's short announcement that since Germany had failed to cease hostilities against Poland, France and Britain were now at war with her.

As the prime minister stopped speaking the air-raid sirens began to wail, followed by whistle-blowing and shouting from down on the street as London's ARP went into action for the first time in earnest. We had little doubt that we were about to experience an air attack of the sort that the Luftwaffe had just let loose on Warsaw. Betty filled the bath with water, explaining that this was one of the requirements demanded of householders in instructions they had received; if water mains were disrupted we should at least have something to drink and to cook with, assuming of course we had gas or electricity. This precaution taken, we sat down to wait but the all-clear soon sounded. This was the first but not the last of the false alarms of the early war days.

The following morning Peter and I reported at Dukes Road in more or less good shape. All we were told was that we should don full battle order and would shortly march off but no one knew where to. Wartime secrecy had already descended on us. Our march through the streets of London took us to Charing Cross station, where we boarded a special train. Once under way, we followed my daily commuting route as far as Tonbridge but then branched off towards Folkestone and Dover. By this time, we were all convinced our officer producing status had gone by the board and that, as in 1914, we were bound for France to fight as a unit. But as we neared the Channel ports our train halted at Sandling Junction and we were ordered to detrain. We formed up by companies and were marched off down small lanes but still no word of our destination. As we approached the outskirts of Hythe the terrain became familiar from past camps spent in the neighbourhood.

'I'll tell you what,' declared one wag, 'we're going to war on the Hythe and Dymchurch Railway'. This was a miniature railway, a tourist attraction, which ran along the flat coastal strip between Hythe and Dungeness.

We laughed but when we came alongside the toy-town railway station we halted. We were ushered down the platform and embarked four to a carriage. Each with his rifle, side arm, water bottle, back pack, gas mask and rolled gas cape, together with webbing belt and ammunition pouches, it was a tight squeeze. The engine-driver perched behind his chest-high steam locomotive, we puffed along level with the coast.

Our destination, we discovered only on arrival, was St Mary's Bay Holiday Camp. Judging from appearances it had been unoccupied a while and the bleakness of its barrack-like huts indicated it had never been in the luxury class. The beds were wooden frames a foot or so off the ground with canvas stretched across. Once we had exchanged a couple with split canvas for others from a nearby hut, whose inhabitants had not yet trained in, we set about making ourselves as comfortable as circumstances permitted.

40

On morning parade, we were informed that the Artists Rifles had been transformed into 163 Officer Cadet Training Unit (OCTU) and that we, ourselves, were now cadet officers and that the training course to turn us into officers would be of three months duration, although those with sufficient length of service in the Artists would pass out in six weeks. Meanwhile the only other parade of the day would be for medical inoculation and men would be excused further duties in case some felt some reaction to the injection.

We stood in long lines for the jab and the first inkling that this might be somewhat more than a mere pinprick was when a man two or three in front of me passed clean out at our feet. He was indeed an exception but slowly and surely, we all discovered that we had developed swollen and painful arms and many felt ill enough to writhe and groan on their bunks. We realised later that not only had the army combined all necessary inoculations into one bumper shot but as none of us had been through the treatment before the effect was all the greater.

We paraded next day looking rather bedraggled and were then put through half-an-hour's arms drill with our heavy old Lee-Enfield rifles. This was an unpleasant experience for everyone but agonising for those worst affected, the theory being that the exercise worked the serum more quickly through the body and one thus recovered all the sooner. We did recover quickly but no one was prepared to give any credit to the arms drill.

We were kitted out afresh. Our old-fashioned Artists uniform with its button-up neck, reminiscent of the Tommy's 1914 wear, was exchanged for the new-fangled battledress. We were sorry to lose our Mars and Minerva buttons and badges but we came to appreciate the comfort and easiness of the new everyday uniform. No buttons to clean, no puttees to threaten to unravel on the march and in their place gaiters one could buckle on in a third of the time. Into the bargain it made a pleasant 'walking-out' attire for now we remained in uniform all the time, not as in the days of pre-war camp changing into civvies as soon as the day's work was done. In our exalted capacity of officer cadets, we wore a forage cap with a white band round it and the battledress top unbuttoned at the neck with a khaki shirt and tie showing through; gaiters were only worn on parade, and civilian shoes, off duty, took the place of Army boots.

Peter and I remained together as we were both in a squad aiming to pass out within the six weeks limit. The weeks passed quickly but not unpleasantly, as a fair proportion of the training was revision rather than being new to us. The Hythe and Dymchurch Railway, which ran to a regular timetable, was a blessing as it enabled us every so often to get to Hythe and thence to Folkestone, where food rationing had yet to have any effect on the restaurants.

We were now given forms on which we could express a first and second choice of regiment to which we would prefer to be posted. After passing out we would be sent home on some two weeks leave during which time the War Office would inform us of the regiment we had in fact been commissioned into. This would enable the appropriate insignia to be affixed to the officer's uniform, which we would have to acquire during that period.

This inspired Peter to put a proposition to me. He was sure to be posted to the Wiltshire Regiment. One of his brothers was adjutant at the regimental depot at Devizes and he was arranging it all with the War Office. Would I not like to come to the 'Wilts' with him? I thought hard and finally replied that as I had lived in Kent all my life and was attached to the place, I felt I would like to apply for my local regiment, the Royal West Kents. I would put the latter down as my first choice but put the Wilts. down as my second. I felt slightly mean about this as in many ways I would have liked to continue to serve alongside Peter, but I reckoned, in any case, that I was just as likely to get my second choice as I was my first.

Passing out day came; no peacetime Sandhurst affair this, just a few handshakes and a few beers. I wished Peter good luck, promised to keep in touch but thought it quite likely that we would meet up again in two weeks' time.

Home again in Tunbridge Wells I set the making of my uniform and greatcoat in motion, for which I now received a uniform allowance, bought my Sam Browne belt and my bed roll from the local saddlers and awaited notification of my commission. When it came, although not my first choice I was nevertheless delighted – the Wiltshire Regiment. My uniform arrived with regimental buttons and badges all complete and I put it on for the benefit of my parents. My mother approved and declared that Joce the tailors always did an immaculate job but she was bitter about the Germans putting young men's lives throughout Europe at risk for a second time this century. My Dutch father, the least belligerent of men, was nevertheless unashamedly proud of his son in British officer's uniform. As far as I was concerned, if I had to go to war I preferred to do so as an officer and, rightly or wrongly, I now felt qualified to do so. I celebrated by organising a foursome to go to the

Hilden Manor and getting a beaming Mr Pilbeam to play our favourite tunes.

I received notification of which day to report to the Wiltshire depot at Devizes, together with a railway warrant for the train journey. I found the imposing regimental headquarters on the outskirts of the market town and I made my way to the adjutant's office to report in. The orderly-room sergeant received me and said that the adjutant would be free in a minute or two. I noticed with some surprise that the name he quoted seemed unfamiliar.

'Is Captain Stephenson not the adjutant?'

'Oh, no sir. He was recently posted to one of the battalions. It's rumoured, sir, but that is of course top secret, that they're on their way to India.'

'But I believe that his brother Second Lieutenant Stephenson is reporting here, quite possibly today?'

The sergeant consulted a paper. 'No sir, there's two others and of course yourself. But we've no notification of a Mr Stephenson. Ah, the adjutant will see you now, sir.'

A few days later a postcard addressed to my home was forwarded on to me. It had a strange field post number on it and it simply said: 'I'm in the King's Liverpools. Where are you? Peter.'

CHAPTER 4

Defending the Coast

I spent several weeks at Devizes awaiting onward posting and it gave me a slight taste of what peace-time soldiering must have been like at a home base. True the officers, other than those on the permanent depot establishment, were a job lot. One or two were like me only marking time but there were also several older officers who did not seem to fit in anywhere, and whose future employment may have posed problems. One of these was a major called back to the colours, who was until early evening jolly and sociable, but who usually became the worse for wear after dinner. But to a man they were friendly and, with a shared batman to wake me up in the morning with a cup of tea and generally to cater for my needs, I settled in very comfortably. Meanwhile I learnt the etiquette of commissioned life; never to commit the cardinal sin of forgetting to remove your Sam Browne before entering the officers mess, never to talk shop in the mess, how to behave at dining-in night, how to be respectful to officers of field rank and above but how to talk to them without embarrassment if they engaged you in conversation. So, in a way I was not entirely wasting my time.

I was sorry, of course, that Peter had not also found his way to the Wiltshires but in wartime the luck of the draw seemed to play a larger role than it does at other times. I sent him a postcard telling him where I was, but I would indeed have been depressed if I had but known that this would be the last communication between the two of us. It was only long after the end of hostilities that I discovered through the Artists Rifles' veterans' association that, having survived the war, Peter had elected to stay on as a regular but had been killed in the Korean War in 1950. But with a salary much in advance of what I had received in Mincing Lane and with board and lodging, not to mention the services of half a batman thrown in, I was, on the contrary, feeling rather elated and beginning to wonder why I had not joined the Army a long time ago. One of my first duties at Devizes did nothing to dispel this impression.

The adjutant called me in and told me that he had to provide, as was customary, an examiner for members of Marlborough College OTC taking 'Cert A'. He added that as I was probably young enough to remember what it was all about, he was sending me. I was provided with a 15-cwt truck and driver and, with the amount of traffic on the roads considerably diminished even though petrol coupons were still not too difficult to obtain, we covered the fifteen miles to the college in good time. I was met on arrival by the uniformed master in charge of the OTC and was offered refreshment and profuse thanks for coming. It was a crisp but sunny late autumn day on the playing fields and, with my clip board at the ready, I took the boys through the prescribed tests and got each one to drill, march and counter-march the remaining candidates. All went well and only one boy lost his head and needed help to prevent his squad ploughing into a boundary fence. When all was over and the marks and results tallied up, I was again offered refreshment and thanks before trucking back to the depot.

Some of my older colleagues in the mess seemed to think I must have had a long and tiresome day. But not I. For me it had been a most enjoyable way of spending a working day. But the climax came when I next had to call in at the orderly room.

'Would you mind signing here?' said the sergeant, pushing a paper towards me.

'What is it, sergeant?'

'Oh, just your claim for expenses on your trip to Marlborough, sir.'

I looked down at the claim and a major item seemed to be transport expenses.

'But, sergeant, you provided me with a 15-cwt truck, if you remember.'

'Well, yes sir, indeed,' and he gave me a friendly smile which somehow seemed to indicate that he thought that young officers still had much to learn. 'It's customary, sir. You would oblige by signing, sir.'

So, I signed but not before I had rechecked the total at the bottom. Sixteen shillings! Why that would go a long way towards settling my month's mess account. Put another way, in my previous job it would have paid for three weeks rail commuting.

As I swung out of the office I asked myself: 'What were you doing all your young life when you might have been enjoying yourself in the Army?'

The men were all Wiltshire reservists who had been called up at the outbreak of war, but for whom postings had not yet been organised. Like me they knew that they would be moved on but meanwhile they were making the most of a soft billet.

'Are you glad to be back?' I asked a tough but articulate corporal.

'Oh yes, sir. Suits me fine.'

'Is that because you're looking forward to a scrap when the time comes?'

'Oh no, sir, it's not that. It's the grub. You see you get used to yer three good meals a day in the Army, even if we did used to complain sometimes. But when you go into civvie-street you're darn lucky if the missus cooks you one meal a day and she don't come round asking, 'Any complaints, my man?' or if she do, joking-like, you keep quiet. But 'ere, if you do yer stuff on parade and then steer clear of any fatigues, you're free for the rest of the day.'

These reservists had needed little retraining to bring them up to scratch, except that they had been brought up on the now obsolete Lewis gun and its replacement, the Bren, had only been introduced after their time. This relatively new weapon was becoming available in larger numbers and the depot now had several for training purposes, more indeed than they had instructors fully trained in their use. The junior officers biding their time at Devizes were detailed in daily orders to supervise the two or three training squads of reservists. Normally all one had to do, or really could do, was to tell the NCOs to get on with it, then stroll around giving one's shin an occasional whack with one's swagger cane and having to say every so often: 'Yes, thank you, sergeant. Carry on again will you, sergeant?' It was apt to be a somewhat languid affair, since the men remembered just as much of the well-worn subjects under instruction as did the NCOs. But when the Bren gun was the subject, the men's interest perked up - though it was more a question of the semi-ignorant leading the ignorant.

At St Mary's Bay, we had had the Bren gun drummed into us until we could almost literally handle it blindfold. So, when the Bren was brought out I felt it was up to me to play a more active role. I would get down behind the gun and strip it down to its component parts, naming them as I went: then put it together again. I was gratified to find that the NCOs as well as the men were keen to follow suit. Then came the IA, the Immediate Action to be taken in the event of a malfunction, which had to be practised again and again. On such mornings, I felt I was actually being of some use.

My only other active participation in a morning parade was entirely unplanned and maybe just marginally useful as an unintentional boost to a fellow officer's and my reputations. Physical Training in the gym was the detail for the day and a former TA officer and I had, for lack of other employment, been ordered to supervise it. The Physical Training Instructor was not in his first youth but was nevertheless a typical bouncy, self-confident PTI and very much the boss on his own ground. I had so far exchanged few words with my fellow officer who was a year or two older than me and who, living in the neighbourhood, disappeared for the day once parades were over. Talking to him I found him shy and probably introverted and he was keen to explain that his relatively short time in the Territorial Army hardly justified the rank of full lieutenant which the scarcity of pre-war volunteers had conferred on him. I liked him but felt he lacked confidence.

The usual PT exercises, performed reluctantly and half-heartedly by the men, and the often-disastrous attempts to vault the horse, being concluded, the PTI transformed the centre of the gym into a makeshift boxing-ring and called for volunteers. Several good-natured bouts were fought, the old experienced lags mixing a generous proportion of shadow boxing with a minimum of serious punches. Then the PTI turned to the two officers, taking us by surprise, and invited us to give a demonstration of our ability. We had a short deliberation during which my colleague revealed that he had never worn a boxing-glove in his life and had hoped never to have to do so. Nevertheless, we felt it incumbent on us to keep up the good name of the officer corps and, perhaps more to the point, feared that the adjutant might take a poor view of us if we didn't. So, we agreed to oblige. It never occurred to me at that stage, however, that my opponent-to-be had entirely failed to appreciate the unbelligerent style in which these 'fights' were conducted or that he would approach the matter with exaggerated seriousness.

The PTI announced a bout of two rounds of three minutes each between the two officers, and then blew his whistle for us to begin. I stepped out into the centre prepared for the usual touching of gloves, followed by some time-wasting 'sizing-up of one's opponent' with perhaps the addition of a little horse-play to amuse the troops. Instead I was surprised to find the lieutenant charging towards me and when he came in range his head went down and his long arms began flailing the air in the neighbourhood of my head and shoulders. When the blows began increasingly to find their target I tried side-stepping, but despite the lowered head, the whirligig managed to follow me round. It was then that I seemed to hear the voice of Captain Kenneth of St. Andrews, the only person who had ever tried to teach me to box, prompting me: 'Keep your own head up, boy, don't retreat but undercut him for all you're worth and force him to stop.' This tactic, during which we both took punishment, had its effect at last and my opponent stood back and raised his head for the first time. I saw his face blotched with red, as mine was probably too, and I hoped, almost prayed, that we could finish the round in relative peace. I now became aware that the spectators were on their feet and urging us back into battle. There was a wild and rather desperate look in the lieutenant's eyes and then, just when I hoped he had seen sense, his head went down and he surged in again, clearly feeling that more was expected of him. The remaining thirty seconds resulted in a nonstop slogging match and was only ended by the PTI, whistle blowing, separating us.

As I walked unsteadily and exhausted back to my corner, I seriously doubted whether I could survive very long into the second round. Sitting down on my chair I found that I had acquired two self-appointed seconds. One began flapping a rather sweaty shirt in the place of a towel in my face while the other gave advice.

'Great, sir. Just go on 'itting 'im, sir, and you'll wear 'im down. Force 'is 'ead up and 'e'll lose most of 'is advantage of reach. Just keep it up, sir.' My second obviously hoped, like all the others, that the spectacle of two officers hitting the hell out of each other would be prolonged for another entertaining three minutes.

However, I had not noticed, indeed the flapping shirt hardly allowed me to do so, that the PTI had been having a word with my opponent and had now taken the centre of the arena.

'The result of this hard-fought bout, now ended, is an honourable draw.' Then turning to the lieutenant slumped in his chair: 'Permission, sir, to dismiss the parade, if you please.'

As I entered the mess for lunch the jolly major, as yet sober, gave me a searching look.

'Hear you've bin havin' a bit of a dust-up in the gym for the benefit of the men. Take my advice, young man, you don't need to enter into that sort of thing too seriously. If you don't look out you might get yourself hurt.'

48

The routine of the morning parades was broken by my being designated Orderly Officer of the Day for the first time. For the Orderly Sergeant who reported to me after breakfast this represented nothing new, just a harp-back to his former peacetime service, but for me it somehow seemed to put a seal on my emergence as a humble second lieutenant from being possibly an over-confident cadet officer. The sergeant knew the form and, good NCO that he was, gave me the lead whenever I hesitated in my not very arduous duties. We did an inspection of barrack rooms and visited the cookhouse, where the cooks knew the standard questions and were ready with the standard answers. We toured the mess tables at midday and, 'Any complaints?' elicited nothing worse than the odd nod and grin since the men, like my corporal, seemed happy to renew acquaintance with the simple but plentiful army food.

The culmination of the day's work consisted of mounting the guard, drawn up for my inspection in front of the guard-room. The turn-out could not, I felt, quite match up to that of the Artists Rifles but I was not prepared to find fault for fault's sake at this early stage in my career. This task completed, my sergeant gave me the time-honoured invitation to take refreshment in the sergeants' mess. My greenness was exemplified by the fact that when the sergeant and several of his colleagues lifted their glasses to me exclaiming, 'Well sir, first today, sir,' I actually took their words at face value! But I was grateful to these friendly NCOs, as they respected the unwritten convention that it was up to them to help a new officer and to prevent him from making a fool of himself.

I left Devizes feeling that it had given me a good deal, allowing me to get used, as it were, to the feel of my new uniform. There had not been time for me to make firm or lasting friendships but, due to its current role of glorified transit camp, the mess had been an open society with no exclusive cliques and you were accepted for what you were.

When my posting to the 4th Battalion, the Wiltshire Regiment, came through, I hoped I might fit in without too much difficulty as it was the old TA battalion. But a shock was awaiting me. I was not necessarily expecting to be welcomed with open arms but I was taken aback when I was totally ignored, and even it seemed resented, by junior as well as senior officers on entering the mess that first evening. I was rescued from solitary isolation by the entry of a tall, upstanding man several years my senior, with fair hair and blue eyes behind regulation gas-mask spectacles, and who made a bee-line for me.

'You're an Artist, aren't you? Well, you are welcome! That makes two of us. Anyone taken any notice of you yet? No, I thought not. Well, let's have a drink and I'll fill you in.'

We went to a quiet corner where we could talk. He introduced himself. He was Roderick Maxwell, a Northern Irelander from Lurgan who, qualifying as an accountant, had settled in London several years previously. Not long afterwards he had joined the Artists, in a company other than mine, and had immediately been accepted as one of the gang.

'But it's not like that here, Van, as I discovered a week or two ago when I was posted here direct. I'm looked upon as an unwelcome interloper and I'm afraid you will be too. Part of the trouble is, you see, that until my arrival this Territorial Officers mess had remained an exclusive club for Wiltshire gentlemen. The more senior have served in the battalion over the years but most of the juniors were brought in by friends in the months or even days before the outbreak of war. They all know each other socially, most live close enough to be able to go home at night and, to a man, they are disgruntled that an outsider should be foisted on them. I have already seen enough to know that the newly-joined officers, I won't speak of the more senior, are abysmally ignorant of their trade and the fact that you and I have several years' training behind us, plus our time in the OCTU, is in their eyes as damning as the fact that we are not members of the Wiltshire coterie. You know, if we wartime officers were joining a regular and professional battalion it might be understandable, but when you discover you're being snubbed by young Wiltshire whippersnappers who are senior to you only because they walked straight into commissions two months ago …' Words failed him.

Roddy Maxwell and I kept each other company until to our delight we were very shortly joined by a further Artist, Roddy Clube. None of us had known each other previously as we had served in different companies, but we automatically became a small enclave in the Wiltshire mess for the simple fact that no one else took any notice of us.

The battalion was based on Trowbridge barracks in West Wiltshire. Although the other ranks were well below strength, they were shortly to be reinforced by a draft of conscripts from Manchester – imagine the shock to the system that caused.

The officers' mess, well furnished, comfortable and warm was not large enough to sleep anything like a full complement of officers. It was decreed that the three outsiders, Maxwell, Clube and I, should move into one of the NCO married quarters. These were relatively newly built and, it was rumoured, had never yet been occupied. Our billet was devoid of any stick of furniture and had no heating. Our moving in coincided with the commencement of the notoriously cold first winter of the war. The bedroom in which we put our camp beds was as cold as a morgue and, although we used newspaper as insulation between the canvas of our beds and our bedrolls, we spent a miserable night.

The next evening Maxwell, who by virtue of his age and his native stubbornness had become our leader, held a council of war. 'As all the other officers are sleeping in comfort either in their homes or in the warmth of the mess, it is up to us to look after ourselves. Since none of them has had the decency to enquire how we are faring and as we have no batman to organise anything on our behalf, we will not demean ourselves by complaining but will take the law into our own hands. There's a fireplace in this bedroom, although it doesn't ever seem to have been used, and at the end of the lines there is a fuel store, which I observed this afternoon is not locked. I have located three buckets and after dinner we will raid the store and provide ourselves with coal. Full vigilance will be observed as it would not do for three officers to be caught in the act.'

The resulting fire in our room on that and subsequent nights did something to raise our morale although comparatively little to raise the temperature. Maxwell continued to feel it incumbent on him to keep his two companions' spirits up and when it was announced that an officers' night compass march would take place the following night, he went into action straightaway.

'We three will leave the mess as soon as dinner is over and, without saying a word, we'll go out and have our own preliminary compass training to make certain our teamwork is up to scratch for tomorrow.'

Wrapped up in greatcoats against the cold, we went out into the fields and in clear moonlight practised our formation, the first man taking the compass bearing, the second going forward as far as light permitted, making certain he obeyed the signals from behind to keep on the line of the bearing, the third man then leapfrogging ahead and obeying the second man's signals, who was now renewing the bearing. Thereafter we continued the leapfrogging to our goal. When we were confident of this procedure Maxwell ordered that we then execute it at the double.

On the night of the exercise the adjutant (a regular captain) and the one knowledgeable lieutenant set the course and the individual teams went off at timed intervals. The snow-covered ground and the moonlight greatly aided navigation, and our trio almost literally galloped round the points of the course. We then returned to the mess and the longer the others took to arrive the more delighted Maxwell became. When we learnt that one team had become so comprehensively lost that the by now frozen directing staff had considered sending out a search party, we found it hard not to appear smug.

Slowly, the 4th Wilts. were jolted out of their peacetime ways. We were moved away from Trowbridge to Frome, another small Wiltshire town, and then on to the larger barracks at Warminster, already known to us ex-Artists. Maxwell and I took over platoons in 'A' Company and Clube went to 'B' Company and just when some sort of rapprochement between the Wiltshiremen and the ex-Artists began to materialise, a regular officer, a slightly long-in-the-tooth lieutenant, was posted to the battalion. I never really knew where he came from but whoever pushed him on to the 4th Wilts. clearly wanted to be rid of him. He was inefficient, lazy, unpleasant and verging on the dishonest and quickly earned the nickname of 'Shocker'. As an undesirable newcomer, he was wished upon Maxwell, Clube and myself and it took us quite a time to disassociate ourselves from the unpopularity he engendered.

From our point of view, the most momentous change was the arrival of a regular Wiltshire major as second-in-command. If Aubrey Coad had not specifically been posted to us to pull the battalion together, he certainly took this task upon himself. He was a taciturn man with prematurely steely grey hair and moustache and a serious, no-nonsense manner about him. After tightening up the officer training programme he turned his attention to the NCOs, all of whom had been part-time Territorial soldiers. He set up NCO training courses under his own direction and the two instructors he chose to work under him were Maxwell and van Maurik. Whilst this afforded an unexpected and welcome boost for us, Roddy Maxwell and I took care not to crow about it and we tried to take our new duties as seriously as did Major Coad.

When this rewarding task came to its end, I now had less direct contact with Major Coad but it must have been he who put my name forward when a vacancy on a course at the Hythe Small Arms School was allotted to our battalion. I was grateful for this at the time but, as events turned out, even more so six months later when it became the reason for my being sent for interview with the Special Operations Executive (SOE). It was ten years later that Aubrey Coad hit the national headlines when he distinguished himself as Major General commanding the British Forces in Korea.

I reported for my course at the Small Arms School around the beginning of May 1940. My parents lent me their car since it was easier for me to obtain petrol coupons than they, and they hoped thereby they might get a glimpse of me at weekends. I struck lucky on the first evening of the course when we were invited to drinks with the Chief Instructor and I found myself 'getting off' with his very attractive young brunette daughter. A few subsequent dates with her locally and she accepted my invitation to come home with me to Tunbridge Wells and go dancing at the Hilden Manor. Many of the others on the course had no use for weekend passes having no homes nearby to go to, but I experienced no difficulty in regularly obtaining passes covering Saturday night and Sunday.

When I arrived home with June, my parents were visibly impressed that I had found so attractive a girl so quickly and, as my mother was not slow to point out, nice that she happened to be the Chief Instructor's daughter into the bargain! When she changed into her glamorous ball gown, my father was so taken with her that he insisted on a photograph. The trouble was that father's photographs were never quick snaps, rather time-consuming portraits. But on this occasion, I encouraged the idea of a photo which I could later display to colleagues, especially as I never carried a camera myself, both because of security regulations and unavailability of film.

Father had always been a keen photographer and as a small boy I had accompanied him into his darkroom and watched excitedly as he waggled the large glass plate in the developer and the images slowly appeared. When the negative became slightly darker than eventually required, the plate would be washed down and then fixed in 'hypo', bleaching back to the right density. When slightly older I was allowed to make my own prints by exposing the frame to sunlight and then transferring the paper into the fixer.

Father was expert at developing the heavy glass plates but was inclined to be accident-prone when making the exposure. If he decided to take a family portrait he would mount his massive black box of a camera with its numerous wheels and buttons on a tripod, load his plate at the back and disappear several times underneath his black cloth to check on composition and focus. Now he was ready for the family to line up or to take their seats. Several more disappearances under the cloth necessitated persons moving a little to their left or a little up or a little down; more checks on fine focusing further prolonged matters. By this time smiles on the victims' faces became fixed and postures stiffened but finally we were told to watch the dicky bird and father pressed the shutter release. As often as not nothing at all would happen and father, in some confusion, would apologise for not activating this or not pressing that. Tension among the family would give way to genuine amusement and, if he were lucky, father would manage to operate the shutter while people were still relaxed.

June, years later, was not subjected to all this, but father's smaller, rather more modern camera was still put on its tripod and a catalogue of procedures had to be followed before the picture could be taken. The resulting photograph of June in her finery, reclining in an armchair in Frant Road, was well worth the trouble and afforded me considerable pleasure over a period of time. Indeed, I know that it still exists somewhere in my attic as I write this, but it does not seem to want to be found.

On my journeys back to Hythe, on a Sunday evening, I discovered a spot, it must have been in the neighbourhood of Tenterden, where the road ran through woods – no motorways in those days and only few cars feeling their way in the blackout – where the nightingales sang so lustily that I heard them over the hum of the engine. I would stop the car and listen to their song which I had never before heard so loud and rivetingly beautiful. But on the last week of the course I came back to a less attractive sound, that of distant, unrelenting gunfire and the rumbling roll of aerial bombardment from across the Channel. The Germans had converted the Phoney War, when nothing seemed to happen, into runaway Blitzkrieg and, overrunning Belgium and Holland, had rolled back the French and now encircled the British at Dunkirk.

Even as we were handed our leaving certificates – I hotly denied accusations that passing out in the top grade was due to my friendship with the Chief Instructor's daughter – the small boat armada was preparing to sail into the danger zone. They assisted the Royal Navy in bringing back a large proportion of the entrapped army but without, of course, their sorely needed equipment. Although much of this was happening close around us on the coast, we only learnt of the full extent of it a few days later. Meanwhile I received a message to report to my battalion at Saffron Walden in Essex, where they had moved from Wiltshire to be in a position to take an active part in the defence of Britain.

Arriving in Saffron Walden, I found that the junior officers were billeted in a partly-demolished house near the centre of the small town.

It did not appear to have suffered from enemy action but rather from the discontinuance of a job already begun. If one looked at the building front ways on, one could be excused from thinking that the right-hand end had no containing wall. Luckily this was not quite so, as some make-shift boarding had been erected to keep out the weather and to prevent officers, searching late at night for the toilets, from walking the plank off the edge of the second floor.

The mess itself was in a separate requisitioned house but after dinner at night those officers not on stand-by duty found the excellent pub close by more comfortable and welcoming. Whilst our preparations for war were seized by a new urgency, our off-duty moments, necessarily restricted to each other's company, gained in enjoyment and companionship. Indeed, moved away from our Wiltshire base, matters changed radically. We 'outsiders' found ourselves on a level-footing with the original Wiltshire officers. Our presence had slowly been accepted and, with no nearby homes to go to, cohesion was consequently accelerated. My company commander, Captain John Brown, was a friendly and nice man but, whilst it had been possible to slip home and help to supervise his farm, we did not see too much of him off-duty. Now we all had to muck in together and it seemed to me a pity that the battalion had not been distanced earlier from its home territory.

We had now been given our operational role – to be ready to round up German parachutists, who might be dropped with the aim of disrupting communications and of neutralising certain RAF airfields prior to, or concurrently with, the expected German invasion of southern England.

Few doubted that Hitler, with the French Channel ports now in his hands and airfields available to him within a few minutes flying time of our coast, would shortly invade us. The realisation of just how precarious our position must have been at that time only fully hit me when, five months later, our battalion took over the defence of a sector of the Kentish coast. Even then our line, thinly spread along the seashore, would have had no chance against a determined assault, but by then one at least hoped that some more effective defence in depth had been organised.

These were exciting times with the civilian population in the thick of it. Older men in their thousands came forward to join the Local Defence Volunteers (later the Home Guard) with improvised weapons and armbands rather than uniforms. Morale was high and much of this was due to our new 'secret weapon', the emergence of Winston Churchill in the place of the unimpressive Chamberlin. I can remember listening on the radio to his 'blood, toil, tears and sweat' speech with fellow officers and being conscious of the surge of inspiration and courage it gave. We did not know until much later that the Germans had been taken by surprise by the speed of their victory and were unprepared to launch an immediate invasion; furthermore, that Hitler held false hopes that the British would capitulate without a fight and thereby wasted precious time prevaricating, finally indeed turning his eyes eastwards.

But if the invasion did not at once materialise, rumours abounded galore. The RAF had, it was said, means of setting the sea afire and of destroying hostile landing craft before they reached the coast; this later expanded into a widely-held belief that a limited and unsuccessful invasion had actually taken place and that scorched bodies had floated ashore and littered unspecified stretches of the south coast. Reports, sometimes investigated but usually unsubstantiated, that fifth columnists were signalling out to sea to U-boats or helping to guide aircraft to their targets were rife. It was even said that Charlie Kunz, the radio pianist of German extraction, was transmitting coded messages to the enemy by varying the speed and volume of his playing.

To give our battalion added mobility, a fleet of far-from-new buses and coaches was made available to us. Each vehicle was camouflaged from top to bottom, the only window remaining unsprayed being the driver's. Now began a series of familiarisation exercises when the whole battalion embussed and made its way to what were judged to be vulnerable locations anywhere within a considerable radius of miles of our base. My platoon being the leading one of 'A' Company, it fell to my bus to lead the whole column. Given normal conditions this should not have been too demanding a map-reading task but circumstances were far from normal. From a seat behind the driver, with side windows blacked out, my arc of vision was decidedly limited. To make matters worse, there were no name places to assist one, all signposts had been eradicated and any potential clue as to one's whereabouts such as a notice on a rubbish tip ending 'by order of the .... Town Council' had the name painted out. Whilst this could well have bamboozled enemy parachutists, it was no help to our own troops navigating in an area new to them.

I was lucky to survive several trips with the help of my platoon sergeant acting as an efficient second pair of eyes as we both peered over the driver's shoulders. Then, mercifully, it was decided it was the turn of other companies to lead. The tension in our bus relaxed and we were able to join in the *Schadenfreude* when one poor officer took the whole battalion down what turned out to be a small track leading to nowhere. Most of the rest of that exercise consisted of efforts to extract the buses, not to mention the staff cars with their indignant passengers, from a dead end.

We had, of course, been officially on active service since the moment we were called up but the first sight, if not actual taste, of action we had was at the close of a twenty-four-hour exercise. Dawn found us in fields adjoining the important RAF airfield of Debden. I had formed up my platoon and we were awaiting the order to march off in search of our buses which had come to rendezvous with us, when we were surprised by a sudden burst of gunfire close-by. Looking up I saw anti-aircraft shells bursting high up in the sky and this led my eye to a whole formation of aircraft glinting in the early sunshine, making what appeared to be a direct line of flight over us. At that very moment, they started releasing their loads and the air was full of the whine of falling bombs. There was a wide ditch along the line of the hedgerow only a yard or two behind where we were standing. I swung round to shout at the men to jump for the ditch but they needed no encouragement from me. I took something resembling a swallow dive on top of them. No bomb actually landed in our field but smoke rose from the airfield. We got the order to make for our buses and we were not slow in obeying. We heard subsequently that the casualties on the airfield included several WAAF girls but that the airfield was soon again made operational.

It was not long before we were on the move again. The battalion now split up and 'A' Company took possession of a medium-sized country house in the Chesham area of Buckinghamshire. Whilst remaining flexible and mobile, we were also given the specific task of recapturing Oakington Airfield should this large new field, still in the last stages of construction, be seized by German parachute troops. This called forth further reconnaissance and a mock attack on the target. In order to be prepared to move off in any direction at the shortest notice, our company paraded on the front lawn of the house, with buses standing ready in the driveway, on three mornings out of four from half-an-hour before dawn until it became fully daylight. This was not too arduous a burden at a time of national crisis, the most uncomfortable part being sleeping fully clothed with the rolled-up gascape sticking to the nape of one's neck. It was almost a relief when around 02.00 hours, it being still mid-summer, the batmen came round with hot cups of 'char', that thick and sweet brew which I found drinkable provided I forgot to equate it with tea. But morning after morning we stood down without being called out, not even, surprisingly, for a false alarm.

Roddy Maxwell, my fellow platoon commander, kept me company in 'A' Company. This tall, blond, fiercely patriotic and efficient Ulsterman was intensely loyal to his friends and, particularly, to his fellow ex-Artists Roddy Clube and myself, but not easily forgiving to those he considered had snubbed him on joining the regiment. He could not resist a gloating laugh when he confided to me that the colonel 'had been forced' to call on him, as the only qualified accountant amongst us, to sort out the 'unholy mess' the Mess President's books had got into. Whilst I reciprocated Maxwell's friendship and had the greatest respect for him, I had in fact more in common with Roddy Clube. We were both keen on foreign languages and Roddy had probably more natural ability in acquiring them, since he spoke good French and German without having had the same opportunity to travel as I had. It was this common interest which in due course led to us spending much of the rest of the war in each other's company.

It must have been around August 1940 that the whole battalion was granted embarkation leave without, of course, being given any hint where we were bound for. I went home to Tunbridge Wells and my father, who had long held the view that a young man, in case of emergency, should know how to handle a horse, said he would pay for riding lessons for me. He himself was no horseman, though he had probably sat on a horse during his time in Java in his early twenties. As all my friends were away in the services or on other war work, I gladly accepted the offer.

Just behind our house there was at that time a small riding stable in Warwick Road. Mr Weaver, in charge, was delighted to get a customer. I took six lessons and on the last day we rode over to Broadwater Forest, a wooded and heathland area a mile or so south of Tunbridge Wells. In peacetime, I had sometimes taken the car and given the family dog a run there. I was reminded of a strange happening which befell two sisters who were part of our young society. They related to our merriment how they had been sitting on a log there, perhaps resting from exercising their dog, when a gentleman entirely naked except for his Wellington boots walked up to them and, greeting them politely, seated himself between the two of them. Wisely thinking it best not to excite or provoke him, they chatted with him until, as suddenly as he had arrived, he got up, bade them farewell and walked away into the trees. I was not to know that several years after the end of the war I was fated to meet the younger sister at an embassy party overseas. We naturally fell into a nostalgic gossip but when I started to remind her of the amusing incident in the Forest, she firmly shut me up lest, I believe, her somewhat older and rather distinguished husband should overhear and disapprove.

On this visit to the Forest no Wellington-booted nudist appeared to frighten my horse and, after trotting and cantering and gingerly jumping one or two small logs, we changed to an invigorating gallop. Coming to a fork in the track I decided to take the right-hand fork but the horse, knowing its way home, took the left-hand. I did neither, coming off on to the soft, leafy track. Arriving home to find I had sprained my ankle, I had it strapped up for me, telling my parents not to worry, as I would be sure to have time to rest it on the troopship.

Our unit, however, was not yet packing up as I had imagined, and the day after our return a sixteen-mile route march carrying full equipment, designed no doubt to tune us up again after leave, was the order of the day. I had some difficulty in squeezing my swollen ankle into my boot, afraid above all of having to endure the ignominy of being forced to fall out of line. Some five hours later, on our return to our billets, I followed the good Army tradition of inspecting the men's feet before worrying about my own comfort, but I could tell that the exercise had had a miraculous effect and henceforth my ankle was no further problem, provided I kept it supported.

The brigade exercise which was now organised, the first we had ever participated in, was generally expected by the rank and file to be the Grand Finale before our departure. In the event it turned out to be a damp squib. Our company took up positions on the orders of Captain John Brown but then matters seem to come to a halt. I no longer remember whether we were supposed to be the attacking or the defending force; I only remember that we remained a long time immobile with nothing happening around us. Our regular second-in-command Aubrey Coad, who might have got things going, had been appointed an umpire and sooner or later appeared enquiring what further orders our company had received and what action we proposed to take. The answer to the first half of the question was 'none' and the second was difficult to reply to without seeming insubordinate. When the exercise was finally brought to a close we were still in a state of some confusion and our verdict, with the arrogance of youth, was summed up in the words 'a complete cock-up'.

A few days after this disaster we learnt that our overseas posting had been cancelled and it was only natural that we should take it for granted that this was due to our poor performance. In retrospect, this seems unlikely. It became known subsequently, or at least generally accepted, that we had been destined to go to India. With the sub-continent not yet threatened, the entry of Japan into the war still over a year distant, it seems more likely that it was belatedly decided we were more needed where we were.

The month of September found us still standing guard to the north of London. The Luftwaffe's attempt to knock out the RAF and to bring Britain to its knees was reaching its climax and we listened nightly to the BBC, as did everyone else, giving the figures of German aircraft destroyed and RAF losses. On 15 September, our company was detailed to use the firing ranges near Colchester. Since Dunkirk, indeed to a great extent since the outset of hostilities, ammunition had been in such short supply that our men had fired no more than a handful of live rounds in training. Now our ration was slightly more generous and we were even permitted to fire our Bren light machine guns. Here, close to the coast, the activity in the air and the noisy dog-fights were particularly in evidence and when I was driving away from the ranges in my platoon truck a German light bomber spiralled down from the sky and crashed half a mile from our road. It did not seem, from the plume of smoke that rose from the spot, that there would be survivors but we turned off in the hope that we might nevertheless capture our first German airman. The charred remains of bodies were all that we found, together with an aircraft instructional manual which had somehow been thrown clear of the flames. I handed the latter over to the occupants of an RAF truck which shortly appeared on the scene. That evening we heard amid general jubilation the record claim of German aircraft destroyed against the relatively small loss of our fighters. Some post-war historians have considered the tally somewhat exaggerated but it was certainly high enough to force the Germans to decide that they could no longer afford the loss of so many trained crews. From then on, the RAF, during daylight, held the upper hand.

Later in the autumn of 1940, 129 Brigade, of which we formed part, moved down to the south-eastern tip of Kent to take over defensive positions in the Dover-Folkestone area. Our long convoy halted the first night at a tented camp in Mote Park outside Maidstone and as we continued next morning down towards the coast, one sensed, after several months in the leafy lanes and relative peace of the northern home counties, a heightened tension in the air. The grassy chalk down from behind which a flight of low-flying Hurricanes roared over us, the smell of the sea, the newly erected pillboxes at river crossings and road junctions, the increase in military traffic, all added to the effect.

'A' Company was allocated a stretch of beach to the west of Folkestone at Sandgate. My platoon occupied several hundred yards of the shore road which was raised above the level of the beach and, running straight along the coast, was out-of-bounds to civilians. Our billets were in terrace houses further back on the main road. Whilst it was safe to assume that the Germans could not keep preparations for a full-scale invasion secret, although the timing and thrust could not necessarily be anticipated, the danger of a limited surprise night raid was ever present.

The brigadier took an early opportunity of viewing our positions and we were warned that his inspection would take place at first light next morning. The sea mist was exceptionally thick that morning, limiting visibility to no more than ten yards, and from my platoon HQ on the landward side of the embankment I saw little more than a white blanket of mist. My worry was not caused by a fear of a German attack but lest we be taken by surprise by the arrival of the brigadier. I therefore posted one man to stand on the crown of the road and to nip back to me when he saw the lights of the staff car looming.

It began to seem that the brigadier was either making a more thorough inspection than anticipated or that he had cancelled things because of the weather, when his car followed by the colonel's crept out of the mist and stopped just short of my look-out, who sprang to attention but remained glued to the spot. I scrambled up on to the road, saluted and led the brigadier, followed by his attendant officers, to find my three sections and to explain how their Bren guns were on fixed lines so that they could rake the beach even in complete darkness or blanketing fog. I tried to answer the inevitable questions and then we returned to the cars. To my astonishment the lone private had not taken the opportunity of disappearing but was still there stiffly to attention. I was hoping against hope that the brigadier would not ask him what he thought he was doing but he walked past him talking to the colonel. Just before he reached his car he turned to me.

'What's that man there for?'

Luckily, I had had a few moments to think.

'Well, sir, the fog is so bad this morning and the visibility from the section positions almost nil that I put a look-out to sea on the road itself where he could get a slightly better view.'

'Oh, ha, yes, I see,' and he got into his car. There were one or two ha's and hum's from the staff officers and, with the solitary private obligingly stepping aside, the cars went on their way.

A narrow squeak, I thought to myself, and then thought little more about it. But when I had to call in at battalion HQ that evening, the CO was unusually gracious to me.

'I'd like you to know that your platoon was a bright spot in an otherwise not very impressive performance. The brigadier was particularly pleased by your initiative in putting out an additional look-out on the high ground. Well done!'

My next encounter with my commanding officer was amiable but not so satisfactory.

For some reason or other, as soon as we became familiar with one sector of coastline we were moved, always in an easterly direction, to another. Shortly before Christmas 1940 we spent a while in the centre of Folkestone and my platoon was given the role of defending the seaward end of the long mole of Folkestone harbour. It was a different scene from the time I travelled to school in Switzerland in peacetime, taking the day boat to Boulogne and then by rail to Paris and Geneva. Now the rails used by the boat trains were rusting and unused and the platforms and custom sheds devoid of travellers.

When not on duty we were billeted, officers and men, in a convent building overlooking the harbour, whose occupants had presumably been moved to a safer area. Prompted by an issue of posters giving aids to aircraft recognition and to combat the boredom of inaction, I cut silhouettes of enemy and friendly aircraft out of cardboard and played games of 'spot the aircraft' with the men. Not that aircraft recognition should currently have posed any problem since we had inherited standing orders which decreed that any aircraft approaching Central Folkestone from the sea should be deemed hostile and, if within range, engaged.

It was a bright early winter morning and I was inspecting our three section positions on the mole with my platoon sergeant, Sergeant Sparks, an experienced Wiltshire territorial with whom I had an excellent working understanding. Suddenly we both pricked up our ears and then started running towards our forward-most section, whose Bren gun was mounted in anti-aircraft mode with its muzzle pointing skywards. The sound of rapidly approaching aircraft from over the sea was unmistakable but, with the sun directly behind them, they were hard to discern. Then two fighter-bombers some six hundred feet up were streaking over us and to my delight our Bren gunner was blazing away with his tracer bullets arcing up towards the aircraft. Just as suddenly the heavily camouflaged machines disappeared over the town.

'Well done that gunner! With a bit of luck, you'll get him next time.' I was somewhat out of breath from running.

There was a definite buzz of excitement; it was, after all, the first time in over a year of war that any of us had fired a gun in anger.

'We nearly had him, zur. They were Messerschmitts, weren't they?'

'Not easy to tell, but yes I think they probably were.'

My elation at the way in which my men had reacted to this short encounter was entirely deflated that afternoon when a message came through from battalion HQ to put the man who had fired on two RAF aircraft on a charge. I protested that the man concerned had merely obeyed standing orders, but I was nevertheless instructed to take the action requested. When I saw the CO that evening he seemed to be on the defensive but, whilst avoiding apportioning blame, was not prepared to cancel the charge. I could only conclude that the RAF, whilst understandably disliking being fired on, had had to be placated and that we were taking the rap for someone's omission back along the chain of command. What was certain was that within the next twenty-four hours amendments were issued to the relevant standing orders. The immediate result of this storm in a teacup was that my Bren gunner was given ten days detention and I decided to step up our aircraft identification training.

A day or two later I was able to slip away to the detention barrack, hoping to persuade the officer in charge to allow me to have a word with the detainee. Such permission, as it happened, proved unnecessary as my driver and I spotted our man weeding the neglected flower-bed in front of the barrack block as we drove up.

'Don't worry about me, zur,' said the former farm labourer. 'This job's more up my street than soldiering. Quite a holiday, if you'll excuse me saying so.'

In early January we moved again, this time to Walmer on the other side of Dover. Almost immediately after taking up our new quarters I was summoned to see the colonel, whose HQ was now in Walmer Castle itself.

'I have been ordered to send one officer for interview at the War Office in London,' he told me. 'The original instruction was sent to Division who passed it on to Brigade who have now passed it on to me, so I have no option but to obey. It specifies that it has to be someone with weapon training experience and, apart from one of my company commanders who is in any case too senior in rank, you are the only officer who has been through the Hythe Small Arms School. It appears to have something to do with training Allied troops and they seem to want an officer in a hurry as you have to report for interview in a matter of days. If you like it and feel it leads to promotion, don't be afraid to accept it. If you choose to turn it down, then you'll be welcome back here again.'

I thanked my CO for those generous words and then went off to arrange a railway warrant to London.

CHAPTER 5

Commando Training in the Highlands

L ondon had the air of an embattled city, which indeed it was, with sandbags piled high against buildings in Whitehall. Traffic consisting mainly of buses, a reduced number of taxis and the occasional staff car, which presented no hazard as I crossed over to the wing of the Horse Guards building to which I had been directed. The Life Guards and their horses had long since left for other duties and tourists, with railway stations displaying posters enquiring 'Is your journey really necessary?', had become an extinct species. The building appeared to be used as an interviewing or recruitment centre and climbing to the first floor I found it crammed with twenty or more officers reporting at the same time as I was. With this competition, my CO's assumption that I would be able to pick and choose whether or not to accept an appointment, now seemed rather far-fetched.

A minute or two before the hour at which we had been bidden, a tall, grey-haired and to my eyes decidedly elderly officer, wearing the red tabs and insignia of a full colonel and followed by an attractive civilian secretary, came up the stairs and, greeting the assembled young men now springing to attention in a friendly and unpompous fashion, disappeared into an inner room. He clearly had to be a 'dug-out', the name in most cases unfairly given to those very many retired officers who, past the age of compulsory call-up, had nevertheless eagerly volunteered their services. It should have been clear to anyone with the least experience in the more clandestine aspects of warfare that the colonel's real place of work must be in some other building and that this was only an 'accommodation address' but we were all quite inexperienced. Soon the first officer was called into the inner office but as successive officers emerged from interview they seemed unable or unwilling to give any clear idea what the colonel 'had been getting at'. I sat on waiting, suspecting that, as so often happened, my name must be near the bottom of an alphabetical list.

At last I was called forward and told to take a seat.

'Judging by your name,' said the colonel, looking up from the papers on his desk, 'you must surely be Dutch and I imagine you speak the language fluently.'

'No sir, I'm British,' I replied rather stiffly, as I had been taken aback by the question and had hoped that I had long outlived the handicap of having a 'funny' name. The interview then seemed to go from bad to worse with the colonel persisting in his questions about my foreign origin and only reluctantly accepting the fact that my knowledge of Dutch was elementary.

'Well then, do you speak any other languages?' he asked almost as an afterthought.

'French and German, sir.'

'Good French?'

'Reasonably good, sir,' and I quoted some of my qualifications.

'Do you feel you would be capable of giving weapon training instruction in French?'

'Yes, I think I could, sir, provided I was given the correct translation of the technical parts of, say, a Bren gun. I wouldn't, for example, know what a body locking pin was in French.'

'No, ah yes. No, quite.' I formed the distinct impression that the colonel didn't know what this was in English, let alone in French, but then the weapon had probably not been introduced in his day.

The interview continued along more orthodox lines, the colonel probing into my past military background and throwing in a few more personal questions.

'All right, van Maurik,' my interviewer concluded, 'go back to your unit and should we have any job to offer, we will communicate through normal channels. I should add that any appointment would bring with it immediate promotion to full lieutenant. I can't give you any more details other than to say that it would be interesting work but do you feel you might be prepared to accept?'

'I would, sir.'

My marching orders came through a week later, giving me only a few remaining days with my battalion. The two Roddies were, I think, the sorriest to see me go, although it was Roddy Maxwell above all who, perhaps against his own personal interests, urged me to grab promotion with both hands and to take what was on offer. I was to be reunited with Roddy Clube the following year but sadly I was never to see Roddy Maxwell again. Much later in the war I heard that he had been attached to another unit and lost his life, gallantly I have no doubt, fighting the Germans either in Greece or in Crete.

I was sad to say goodbye to my platoon and particularly to the excellent Sergeant Sparks, whom four-and-a-half-years later I fleetingly bumped into after we had both reached our goal on German soil. Looking back, I am happy that the 4th Wilts. had finally accepted their Artists implant and that the latter had now fully transferred their loyalty to their wartime regiment, but I feel I took the right decision in leaving, as my future service brought much satisfaction and enabled me to do what I can probably do best, making friends and dealing with other nationalities. As regards the 4th Wilts. I lost touch with their further movements but I know that post D-Day they fought in Northern Europe with great distinction and bravery, suffering heavy casualties in officers and men. Today the Wiltshire Regiment, alas, no longer exists as such, having been merged with two others,

My joining instructions enclosed a railway warrant from Dover to Fort William. One of my friends produced an atlas of Great Britain and we identified my destination at the top end of the railway line in north-west Scotland.

'At least you won't be popping back for the weekend,' said one of them. 'What do you think it's all about?'

I had no idea other than its possible connection with the training of Allied troops, who might have escaped to this country after the fall of France. But if so, why the mystery?

'Come back if you don't like it,' said another, but this hardly seemed a feasible suggestion. For better or worse I was off on a new tack.

One evening at the beginning of February 1941, I caught the night train to Glasgow and I was lucky enough to have a reserved corner seat in first class. I was soon joined by others who like me were travelling with bed-roll and suitcase. A stroll down the corridor evidenced a carriage-full of similarly laden officers. With wartime security in mind I chatted with my immediate neighbours but, like they, asked no leading questions. After a reasonable sleep - the seat was more comfortable than some of the billets I had had to doss down in - we arrived at an early hour at Glasgow Central station. Here I had to change over to the early morning Fort William train leaving from Queens Street station and it soon became clear that not only my compartment but the whole carriage-load was doing the same.

Settled down in our new train, the fact that we were all members of the same group could no longer be disguised. Eager comparing of notes took place but no one ended up much the wiser. As soon as daylight permitted I turned to gazing out of the window. Travelling in new territory whether at home or abroad had always fascinated me and I had been to Scotland just once before on a family holiday and then as a very small boy. Only two memories of that trip remained with me: a visit to Edinburgh Castle where my father, thinking to give me an enjoyable thrill, warned me to beware of the enormous bang occasioned by the firing of the midday cannon. He succeeded in scaring me to such an extent that we all had to cut short our visit in order to distance ourselves from this dreadful event; and the other was staying in a hotel on the main street of Callander and gazing out at a small boy wearing the kilt.

By the time we reached the northern tail of Loch Lomond it was light enough to take in the rugged beauty of the countryside and I was undisturbed in my contemplation in that most of my fellow-passengers were still catching up on lost sleep. To our left the slopes of Ben Vorlich climbed almost vertically upwards and out of the other window one caught glimpses of the loch through trees. Then after puffing and climbing we freewheeled into Crianlarich station. To my eyes grown accustomed to the heavily populated Kentish coast and the busy skies above, this small railway station with its cluster of houses seemed the personification of isolation. Some of us got down on the platform and after a night of stuffy, smoke-laden carriages, the air was cold but gloriously fresh and clean. To be honest, Crianlarich in peacetime is a relatively busy, and not all that prepossessing a staging post for tourists, but it was nevertheless there in wartime on the station platform that I experienced the first stirrings of my attraction towards Scotland, which has never left me.

There was much better to come. Climbing again with hill slopes on either side we reached Bridge of Orchy. (The glories of Glen Orchy, which doubles back from here to Loch Awe, I only discovered years later). We set off now across the truly deserted, watery Rannoch Moor, no road, no habitation, just our train threading its lonely way, almost as if it were pioneering it for the very first time. Yes, half-an-hour on there was Rannoch station, with its hotel reached by a small road from the east, but further on, at the only other halt at a spot named Corrour, a solitary railwayman materialised from nowhere to take delivery of a small package and stood waving as we puffed on. I don't think I went so far as to say to myself 'that's the life for me!' but the attraction grew the further we advanced.

It was only when we turned into Glen Spean that real signs of life and cultivation reappeared - Tulloch, Roybridge, Spean Bridge - and then we were on the last lap to our destination. Although I didn't, of course, then know it, I was to do this journey numerous times both ways during the next seven months and, if anything, I enjoyed it more each time.

We were met at Fort William station and transferred into Army transport. Sitting hunched up on our luggage we saw little of the scenery of the 'Road to the Isles' and after a forty-minute drive, and well short of the end of the road at Mallaig, we turned into the gates of Lochailort. Clambering out of our trucks we had our first view of the fine neo-baronial building and the Army huts partly hidden by the trees. We were shown to our quarters and later in the afternoon the CO of the establishment gave us a talk which, if nothing else, told us what we had to expect in the immediate future.

Lochailort was a commando training school. (We had all heard of the Commandos although these tough independent units had not long been in existence.) He could not tell us, as yet, why we had been selected to come here, but over a period of three weeks we would be taught the basics of guerrilla warfare, how to attack and blow up enemy targets, sabotage techniques, unarmed combat, living off the land and more as well. This would be followed by a final week which would be physically more demanding than the preceding ones. He stressed the need for strict security and when writing home, we could only quote the field post number of the school but not give any indication of its location or of what we were doing. This was normal Army security but in our case, we should not attempt to circumvent it in any way.

This emphasis on security, and indeed the completely unexpected syllabus, led me to conclude that the impression I had been left with, that I was destined to instruct Allied troops, had been nothing more than a smoke screen to cover whatever lay ahead.

Once instruction got under way, I began to enjoy myself. Both the instructors and my fellow trainees were good company and most of the work was new and exciting. The use of explosives and sabotage techniques took up quite a proportion of our time, rightly so, as a half-trained man could well be a menace to himself and to others. Unarmed combat was taught by two ex-Shanghai policemen, Sykes and Fairburn. Sykes played the leading role and although a hefty man he had the face and manner of a benevolent clergyman. But when he caught you in a hold or demonstrated how to disable if not kill a man with a chop to the neck with the edge of your hand or, recommended in extremity, to gouge your opponent's eyes out, there was nothing benevolent about him. One dodge, which I felt sometime perhaps might be useful, was how to escape from someone who had taken you prisoner and then made you walk, holding a gun to your back. You had to swing round unexpectedly encircling your captor's arm with your own so that, assuming he had time to fire, the bullet passed harmlessly behind your back, simultaneously putting the man out of action with one, if not two of Sykes' and Fairburn's fancy tricks. Practising this amongst ourselves we found that the captor invariably fired too late. The corollary to this, of course, was finding yourself in the role of captor, you must always hold your gun a foot or more away from your prisoner's back. Don't copy the way they do things in Hollywood, said Sykes scornfully.

General fieldcraft and living off the land was dispensed by Captain J.M. Scott. I was sure he must know what he was talking about as I had read his books on Artic exploration and he had written a biography of Gino Watkins who, still in his early twenties, had led highly successful Artic expeditions until he was tragically drowned in a kayak accident. Gino left Lancing a few years before I arrived but Gordon, my housemaster, always held him up as a shining example of a brave and enterprising young man and it was a red-letter day when he revisited his old school. The only specific item of information I still remember that Scott taught us, and that was subsequently of use to me, was how to dry a spare pair of socks on the march by placing them between your vest and your shirt close to your chest – but fortunately I never had to emulate what a local ghillie,[1] produced by Scott, demonstrated to us – how to skin and degut a newly shot deer.

It was into the second week of the course that one Harry Hale came up to me.

'Tell me, do you speak Spanish?'

'No, I don't. Why?'

'Well, nearly everyone I talk to seems to have a knowledge of Spanish. So much so that I, with little linguistic ability, begin to wonder whether I've got into this affair under false pretences.'

---

[1] A ghille is a fishing and hunting guide.

I had to admit that I had heard bandied around a few Spanish sounding exclamations and swearwords but perhaps being less inquisitive than Harry, I had attached no importance to them. However, in view of Harry's misgivings and my aroused interest, we agreed to ask around among our colleagues and then confer again in a couple of days.

By the end of the week we had identified a vast preponderance of Spanish speakers among the thirty or more members of the course.

'You and I would look pretty bloody silly,' pronounced Harry, 'if we found ourselves sent into some purely Spanish speaking territory to raise guerrilla bands or, worse still, to act as liaison officers or interpreters and to have to try to explain by sign language to the locals that our War Office had made a balls of it.'

As a result of our doubts, Harry and I and one other non-Spanish speaker we had identified, spoke to the CO over his evening glass of whisky at the bar and, whilst emphasising that we were in no way trying to back out, we indicated we were slightly worried that the Powers That Be might have muddled up our language qualifications.

The colonel, normally approachable and at ease among his students, immediately became cagey and said he would have to make enquiries and meanwhile not to worry.

The third week was scheduled to terminate with a carefully planned coup-de-main attack on installations in the grounds of Achnacarry House at the head of Loch Arkaig, which lay some way north of Fort William. This was in fact a Commando holding unit and opposition was perhaps to be expected. A rather older and outstanding student amongst us was cast in the role of 'Captain Blood', the leader of a guerrilla band, and he was driven over close to the target so that he had a chance to make a reconnaissance. On the given day, we were all trucked to within easier striking distance so that we could cross-country march that day and be in position to make a dawn attack next morning. We were making up dummy demolition charges and generally getting ready on the eve of the exercise when the CO called Harry and myself and four other officers into his office. He now had authority, he said, to tell us that we six were destined to be instructors at other training schools and that we would not be attending the final week of the course. On the following Monday, we would be leaving for our new destinations, where we would no doubt be given full briefing.

Our faith restored in the War Office, we set to work again. I chiefly remember the Captain Blood attack for the considerable discomfort of trying to sleep on a sloping bank covered in a couple of inches of wet snow just outside Achnacary, wrapped up in a single ground sheet with J.M. Scott offering advice on how to keep warm under such circumstances. But it was only the approach of dawn and the resumption of physical exercise that I found had any effect at all.

In anticipation of our departure from Lochailort, the other four officers were given railway warrants for destinations in the south of England but Harry Hale and I were told that our unit was not quite ready for us and that we were to wait around for a day or two until we were called forward. After a quick consultation Harry and I asked the colonel's permission to continue meanwhile attending his course.

'Well done, you two,' said he, perhaps flattered at our keenness. 'Much better than sitting around. Just carry on until we get word for you to leave.'

We turned out for the first session of the final week which was held out in the grounds. The sergeant-instructor must have been a called-up reservist, perhaps ex-cavalry or ex-Indian Army; what was certain was that he was a cockney.

'Well, gentlemen, what we're goin' on with this morning is learning 'ow to saddle a mule. Now I want you gentlemen to take my word for it that this 'ere is a pukka mule.' Saying which he unhitched reins from a firtree and led forward a reluctant donkey. 'Best we can do, I'm afraid, owin' to wartime shortages.' Pause for polite laughter. 'Now the first thing you've got to remember when saddlin' a mule...' Here he stopped as he had observed the CO advancing on him hurriedly and holding up a warning hand.

The colonel had a quick word with the sergeant, then came across to Harry and me and led us away into the house.

'I just informed your unit that you had volunteered to go on with the course but they couldn't allow that on security grounds. Instead they've fixed up for transport to come and fetch you in an hour's time, so you'd better get your kit together and be ready to move off.'

Our transport came so speedily that we never even had time to say farewell to our colleagues, since they were still being initiated into the inner secrets of mule-handling. Over a period of over thirty years future friendship with Harry we sometimes had occasion to lament over a drink that serious gap in our education, our inability to saddle a mule! Looking some way ahead we eventually learned the reason for the recruitment of these Spanish speakers, who had been given the codename of Sconces and with whom we had been trained only as a matter of convenience. At the time, serious fears had been entertained that the Germans, moving through Unoccupied France, would thrust into neutral Spain and drive down towards Gibraltar, thus endangering the Royal Navy's ability to maintain her fleet in the Mediterranean. The Sconces' job would have been to organise and support guerrilla activities along the German lines of communication. Now we know that Hitler was more interested in moving eastwards into the heart of Russia and with no advance through Spain materialising, the Sconces were subsequently found other duties, some of them in the Iberian Peninsula.

The colonel, having had his fingers burnt once, was not inclined even to give a hint of Harry's and my destination and the fact that we apparently required no railway warrants still did not prepare us for a journey of only fifteen minutes. Our 15-cwt Army truck turned left up the Road to the Isles towards Mallaig and after crossing the neck of the Ardnish peninsula began to twist and turn along the wooded and indented shore of Loch nan Uamh. The snow had disappeared and the tall wild rhododendrons looked happier in the sandy, rocky soil than the more stunted oaks and pines. Before we had even noticed it, we turned left down a half-hidden driveway at the bottom of which a large solidly-built grey granite house awaited us.

A tall, slim clean-shaven captain came out of the house and, introducing himself as John Bush, welcomed the two slightly bemused newcomers as members of the staff of Arisaig Training Area. A flush of pleasure passed over me at the realisation that we were to be based, not in the south of England, which, much as I loved it, was no novelty to me, but just down the road from Lochailort. Ever since the train had groped its way up into north-west Scotland I had experienced a growing feeling of at-oneness with this wild and exciting countryside. Had it not been for the fact that I had never in my life been so far north, I would have said that there was an element of coming home to it. Harry on the other hand, although smiling and not unhappy, could not, I knew, fully share my elation as for him, with a wife and small child just north of London, a home-county posting would have been more welcome. I for my part was fancy-free and wanted nothing better than to remain in this new-found area, taking every opportunity to explore the coast and climb the mountains inland from it.

'How much have you been told about what happens here?' asked Bush as we sat down to a morning mug of tea.

'Absolutely nothing,' said Harry and I in unison.

'Well, here goes then.' He had a shy but competent look about him and had explained to us as we carried our kit into the house that he was the area training supervisor. 'First of all, Colonel Evans, our CO, is away viewing a new house we are taking over but he's asked me to put you in the picture. This is Arisaig House and we're the headquarters and administrative centre of four or five small training schools situated between here and the end of the road at Mallaig.[2] We do sometimes run courses here at Arisaig house but most of our training will be given in our satellite schools once all of these go into action. So, what do we teach and who are our students? Well, basically our training programmes are not so very different from what you have just experienced at Lochailort. Fieldcraft, demolitions, sabotage and particular emphasis on toughening up and testing out students, some of whom will have come practically straight from civilian life. To understand the why and wherefore, all you need know is that with most Europe under Hitler's heel, Churchill has decreed that measures must be taken to stir up and support resistance to the Germans in occupied countries; for example, to sabotage factories forced to work on behalf of the German economy and to tie down troops which might otherwise be used offensively against us. This is, of course, easier said than done but in order to put the Old Man's directive into effect, a special inter-services organisation has been set up with HQ in London and we here are part of its training arm. Our job is to train prospective agents who speak the lingo and who will eventually be despatched into Occupied Europe. These chaps – they've so far all been men – are first sent to a preliminary school in the south where they get tested for suitability and those who pass muster come up to us for more serious training. We act as a second filter, so it's important for us to give an unbiased opinion on them. From here they go down to RAF Ringway near Manchester, where they learn to parachute and then go on to finishing schools, where they're given specialist instruction for their coming missions in occupied territory. Have you any questions so far?'

We both shook our heads. We were enthralled but not entirely taken aback since life had been full of surprises since we set out from London.

'As you can imagine, continued Bush, 'a very high degree of security is required here if lives and projects are not to be endangered. You may not have realised it but the whole of this territory from Corpach, just outside Fort William, right up to Mallaig is a restricted military zone

---

[2] Arisaig House was, officially named, Special Training School (STS) 21.

and no unauthorised persons are allowed in. For our part, by creating a series of small schools accommodating at the most ten or twelve students, we can keep nationalities apart and also prevent too many students, even of one nationality, from becoming acquainted with each other. So far, we've only had a trickle of students sent up here but you two have arrived just in time because we're promised a steady flow from now on. I should perhaps warn you that, in general, you'll find that too much curiosity about who is who and what goes on elsewhere is not encouraged.

'Well, having given you a quick run-through, I will leave it to the colonel to tell you this evening what he has in mind for you. Meanwhile let's take a walk around the grounds and let you get your bearings.'

He led the way through the back of the house into the garden. The original outbuildings had been supplemented with Army huts which served as additional living accommodation as well as storerooms and armoury. Walking down to the beach we were shown where demolition training took place. Short lengths of railway line were lying around waiting to be severed by explosives and various thicknesses of steel sheeting appeared to have had holes punched through them.

We stood on the shore and admired the view across the Sound of Arisaig to the misty outlines of the Ardnamurchan peninsula stretching far out into the Atlantic.

'You're looking over to the westernmost point of mainland Britain. Yes, a few miles further west than Land's End. Nothing between it and America. If you're interested in history,' continued our guide, 'we're now on the beach where Bonnie Prince Charlie first stepped on to Scottish mainland in '45. He went on to raise his standard half way between here and Fort William at Glenfinnan and, if you remember, marched his men down as far as Derby but, unaware that half of London was preparing to welcome him, his courage failed and he returned northwards, finally to be defeated by the redcoats at Culloden. He ended up here again on the run with an immense price on his head, but was finally picked up by a French man-of-war near the head of the loch. You'll find the cairn marking the spot from which he was rowed away a short way down the road. If you stand there beside it you'll realise that the overwhelming beauty of that place must, if nothing else, have broken the poor man's heart. It's funny, you know, when you think about it. Here were the French infiltrating, and then exfiltrating, a man into Britain and here are we, almost 200 years later, preparing to reverse the procedure.

'But surely there's a difference,' I pointed out. 'We are trying to help the French rid themselves of the Germans, not to overthrow their legitimate government.'

'Not perhaps so different as you think,' ventured John Bush. 'Charlie was also trying to get rid of the Germans – the Hanoverians – and who knows whether that might not have been a good thing?'

Over drinks that evening the colonel, a lively little Welshman, sketched out his plans for us.

'We recently requisitioned another house further up the road just short of Morar and we've already got a group of nine or ten French speakers booked into it for a two-week course starting in a couple of weeks' time. Normally a complement for a school would include a senior officer as commandant and a training officer working under him. Well, London hasn't yet provided us with a commandant so I'm going to appoint you two jointly as acting commandant and acting training officer. You can split the work up between you as you like but I imagine that once the course begins you will both spend much of your time training, although I fear that opening up a new place will involve you in quite a bit of admin initially.

'We'll give you all the backing we can and we'll send you two good NCOs to assist you generally as well as kitchen staff. You can of course always call on John Bush to help sort out any problems on the training side. But before you go off I want you to spend the next three or four days with John. He'll advise you on drawing up a course syllabus and he'll expect you to submit the finalised version to him after you get there and have seen the place on the ground. But most important of all, he'll give you some more experience in handling explosives and advice on the best and safest methods of teaching students in their use. We don't want either you or the students blown up! The students, by the way, are always accompanied by a conducting officer from the country section in London, in this case a French Section officer. He deals with any personal problems they may have and he will naturally keep in close touch with you. Don't forget that London will expect fairly comprehensive reports from you on each man as they're still all on trial.'

I went to bed that night in more physical comfort than I had experienced for quite some time. But it was not only that which induced a feeling of intense well-being. I was now sure I had taken the right decision in leaving my regiment. It had little to do with any disgruntlement I had felt during my early days with the Wilts., that was a thing of the past, nor was it any real wish to get away from sitting on the Kentish coast waiting for the Germans who began to look as if they might not now be coming; no, it was the realisation that by some incredible fluke of fate I had walked into a world such as I had only dreamt about.

My pre-war fantasies were often related to my experiences in Germany, which had convinced me that Hitler was dead-set on military confrontation with France primarily, and Britain if needs be. Young Nazis would assure me with chilling conviction that they would avenge themselves of the indignities heaped upon Germany at the end of the First World War by the Treaty of Versailles. The Nazis had taken the law into their own hands and remilitarised the Rhineland and they would fight to regain their lost territories in the East, if the latter were not handed back on a plate. Furthermore, was it fair that Britain should have colonies and Germany not?

When a school friend and I were invited to be the only foreigners among over a thousand young Germans on a *Kraft durch Freude* tour of the Baltic aboard the *Columbus*, Germany's largest liner, we had constant reminders of the propaganda campaign being waged. He and I finally found ourselves marching through the streets of Danzig behind placards vowing to reunite the city with the Fatherland. On another occasion in Hanover I witnessed Jewish men and women being forced to sweep and then scrub the pavement on their hands and knees to remove slogans painted there by stormtroopers who, undeterred if not actually encouraged by the police, had smashed the windows of the Jewish owned C&A store. Later at college in Switzerland, a refugee German Jewish fellow student told me stories which I might not have believed, had I not had some taste of things at first hand.

These events gave me some insight into political realities which many of my elders and betters back in Britain were slow and even unwilling to accept. They also led me to fantasise, casting myself in the role of a bi-lingual or even tri-lingual John Buchan-type hero involved in secret activities to foil Nazi war plans and save his country. I was, of course, neither bi- nor tri-lingual but being a rather old-fashioned patriotic young man, I had often wondered whether my knowledge of French and German could not be put to better use. But with Consular and Diplomatic Services closed to me I had to content myself with becoming a tea salesman. Now with the war over a year old and our backs still very much to the wall, had I still been prone to fantasise I would have started my scenario with something very close to the words with which John Bush had addressed us. I was not stupid enough to imagine my French equipped me to become an agent in occupied territory but, priding myself on being a good instructor, I felt I could make a more useful contribution here in Scotland than by continuing to edge my way up the coast of East Kent. In any case, although I so far knew comparatively little, the mere thought of being on the fringe of cloak and dagger work gave me an enormous thrill and the fact that it was all to take place in a countryside which held great attraction for me and among colleagues who welcomed you and actually seemed glad you had joined them formed the icing on the cake.

John Bush was an excellent instructor who had developed a number of his own refinements to the standard sabotage techniques. We spent happy hours exploring the various ways of derailing trains and finding the critical points of turbines and other machinery which needed only a pound or two or plastic explosive, correctly placed, to put them out of action, a result an air bombardment might well fail to achieve. We placed dummy charges attached to fog-signals on the track of trains on the Fort William-Mallaig line, receiving thumbs-up from the drivers who had grown used to being 'blown up'. We received very necessary advice on measures to be taken to prevent too enthusiastic novices from endangering themselves and others, and we had fun rehearsing the use of booby trap devices. We tested out the various timing gadgets and the effect of heat and cold on their performance. We again went over the introductory lectures on the nature and various types of explosives, their methods of detonation, the calculation of quantities necessary for a given job and the useful effect of tamping. In conclusion John considered us capable of teaching our students all they needed to know for the tasks likely to befall them. If at a later date they were briefed to attack some specialised target, then they would be given further instruction elsewhere.

We got to know the other staff members at Arisaig House and contacted the NCOs who were to be attached to the new school. Harry volunteered to deal with the administrative side and made his number with the HQ quartermaster. This suited me well as it left me free to take on more instruction and to run the demolition side myself.

John took us up to see Garramor, the school which was to be ours. The road beyond Arisaig House ran through woods with tree-high rhododendrons lining part of the route. Three miles up we debouched on to open ground with the village of Arisaig before us. Harry, a quiet, thinking type rather than a tearaway man of action, was happy to confirm the existence of St. Mary's Catholic Church which kept company with a village store and the Arisaig Hotel, where local men met for their evening dram. The area round about was a predominantly Catholic enclave and Harry liked to attend Sunday mass when his schedule permitted. We continued northwards from the village over the Hill of Keppoch and down again to the small crofting community of Back of Keppoch; then the road led through flat land which occasionally gave us glimpses of gleaming white sandy beaches.

'That's your place,' said John pointing to a stone-built, slate roofed house standing a couple of hundred yards to the landward of the road.

We turned down a track running beside rough grassland and, entering a front garden well provided with the ubiquitous rhododendrons, we pulled up at the front door. The staff detailed from Arisaig House were unloading bedding and stores from an Army truck and the sergeant in charge of demolition stores came up and smilingly assured us that he already had his stock-in-trade safely behind padlocks in an adjoining outhouse.

We followed John into our home to be. It was difficult to judge its age; it certainly wasn't very old but this did not prevent it being built to last. It was too spacious and too out of character to have belonged to a crofting farmer and at a guess it had been built by a well-to-do Glaswegian to use as a base to entertain friends up for the salmon fishing in Loch Morar. The furniture was Army issue supplemented with some soft furnishing which looked as if it had come from a local second-hand sale. John filled us in as we poked around.

'This room here is for use as a sitting-room, the mess if you like. Not large but I think you will be able to fit in and this adjoining room is destined to be the dining-room, doubling up for classroom. You'll have ample room as you can see for up to a dozen. We won't know the exact number coming up from the preliminary school until the last moment, depends on how many, if any, fall at this first hurdle.

'As you've been told,' turning to Harry, 'you've got a generous supply of wine and spirits. While it's not up to you to deliberately encourage consumption, let the students have what they ask for but check how individuals hold their liquor. This is one of the items you'll have to include in your end-of-course report. Mind you, make them sign for every drink so you can check how much they've had and also as a means of discouraging the mess staff from having a field-day.

'You can take one of the small single rooms each', said John as we went up the stairs. 'The students have bunk beds in the larger rooms. We've also requisitioned the empty farmhouse known as Camusdarrach on the other side of the road as an overflow and for use by the staff. Okay, well let's go out and have a look at the demolition area at the back of the house.'

There was no real garden at the back; the ground soon became semi-moorland with clumps of dormant heather and the odd hummock, gently sloping down to a small burn. After that there was a mile-wide swathe of flat moorland, reputed to be boggy in places, before the mountains of South Morar began. The railway made its way through the moorland, further south skirting the foothills in search of firm land before looping westwards to Arisaig station.

The sergeant accompanied us as we walked down to the burn.

'If you prepared your charges somewhere here,' suggested John, 'you could set them going over there and then retire to that hummock for shelter. Once again, don't forget to insist they walk, repeat, walk back after igniting their fuses. If they run there is plenty of heather and humps they could trip over and then perhaps panic. But just watch them to make sure they cut the right lengths of fuse, please! You're getting your railway line and other props sent over here, aren't you, sergeant? Fine. And while I think of it, chaps, I wouldn't site your night compass march here at the back. You'll find good dry land further up the road.'

While the other two returned to the house I briefly examined the lie of the land with the sergeant. In this sort of demolition training there were no dug trenches or concrete observation posts to retire into. You made use of folds in the ground just as the joes – I was beginning to pick up the jargon – might have to when working in the field. Yes, I thought to myself, providing the bods – using a newly acquired alternative to joes – do what they're told and don't think they know better, we should be all right.

Back at the front door John pointed across to the other side of the road. 'Camusdarroch is a few yards up the road but you can't see it because of those trees. Take an early opportunity of going over there and have a look around and it's also a good way to get to the beach. The Silver Sands of Morar, I can assure you, are really something. Should be gorgeous on them once the better weather comes. But let's now get back for lunch. I'm told we're sampling the haunch of venison one of the sergeants mysteriously produced a week or two ago. Don't know where he got it but still, no questions, no pack-drill.'

CHAPTER 6

Two Quick Shots and the Dynamited Salmon

It had been a hectic eight days leading up to the arrival of the students. For a start, everyone from the colonel downwards had underestimated the amount of administrative work entailed in getting Garramor on the road. Harry, who had started life as a schoolmaster, was not only good at admin but positively enjoyed and thrived on it. The cook complained he would be unable to produce a decent meal with the utensils so far supplied, always assuming, of course, that someone could get the plumbing functioning properly; the batmen pointed out that pillows were missing (the joes were not required to travel with their own bedrolls) and where were the cleaning materials? The NCOs, the driver and anyone else around were all at Harry's heels. I had a steady demand for training accessories, more maps and compasses, map cases, chinagraph pencils, protractors, detonator crimpers, a powerful torch, additional storm-proof clothing – the list grew every day.

One of the urgent tasks was to finalise the course programme and this required fitting in visiting instructors at times they were available and adjusting our in-house training accordingly. I found this difficult as it necessitated consultations with Arisaig House staff and Harry was blocking the phone half the day; the other half, as often as not, I was off on a reconnaissance in the hills. I gratefully accepted Harry's offer to coordinate these visits: the signals corporal to teach the sending and reception of Morse up to twelve words a minute; the physical training instructor for unarmed combat; the arms instructor with his bag-loads of German and other foreign weapons likely to be encountered across the Channel.

For my part, leaving demolitions aside, I had to acquaint myself with the countryside and work out training schemes. As an example, I wanted to take the students up one route into the mountains and then get them to find their way back in trackless terrain solely by studying the contours on the map. Not only did I have to find a suitably puzzling tract of land but, to avoid losing face, I also had to be sure I knew the way home myself. This and other exercises always had the subsidiary purpose of toughening up the students physically. In the event, on this particular scheme they got even more physical exertion than planned, since, left to find their way back, they decided to do it by committee and after walking forty-five minutes in the wrong direction I was forced to intervene.

On my reconnaissance trips, I made it a rule to take an NCO with me both for company and as a safety precaution. On a short walk to find a suitable place to ambush the Fort William train I took both Sergeant Smith, my demolition assistant, and Corporal Senior, who had just been sent to us. Senior, who stayed with me a long time and became a trusted helper, was short in stature, the sort of man who automatically attracted the nickname of 'Titch'. We had decided to leave the beaten track through the moorland and take a short-cut towards a likely looking location. Senior was walking between Smith and myself when suddenly he disappeared into the ground so that the top of his head was on a level with our waists. Sergeant Smith recovered from his surprise a fraction quicker than I. 'What do you think you're a doin' of down there?', he shouted down at the unfortunate corporal. We both leant down and getting Senior under the armpits, we hauled him, accompanied by squelching sounds, back on to dry ground. 'Don't you ever do that again,' scolded Smith. 'You gave the officer and me quite a turn.' We didn't give him a chance to do so, as after that we stuck to established tracks in that stretch of moorland.

When it came to marking-out a night compass course, the indefatigable Harry said he needed exercise and would do it with me. That afternoon we went out with our compasses and taking bearings on convenient objects, a gap in a stone wall or a lone tree and even at one turning point erecting our own mini-cairn, we led back to our starting point. After dinner, the next night we went out into the black night and swirling mist and put our course to the test.

Pouring a celebratory drink back in the house, Harry was pleased with our handiwork.

'Well, I reckon that's a pretty good compass course,' he boasted. 'Indeed, I'd be surprised if it doesn't continue to be used until the cows come home or, shall we say, until the Germans have been sent packing.'

I agreed with him, happy that another item on our list of jobs could now be crossed off. But what neither Harry nor I had taken into account was the fact that, come the summer, there would be no real darkness up at that latitude, thus enabling the joes to romp round the course with little or no effort on their part. But at that stage we had not yet finished with winter.

After we left Arisaig House John Bush went back to whatever work it was we had interrupted by our arrival. He found time, however, to look in every so often and on the last occasion before we were due to open shop he told us of a change of plans forced on him.

'You'll remember you were going to send your students for revolver training to a range we had fixed up in the farmer's unused cowshed down the road? Well, there's been a bust up with him and he's withdrawn his permission and asked us politely, perhaps not all that politely, to get lost and to clear out all our equipment. It's a damn nuisance as Sergeant Bates had built a first-class little place there with many ingenious snap targets popping out at you where and when you least expected it. Well, all we can now do is to send him here to fix up some sort of substitute at the back of the house. It won't be the same, of course, but he'll do his best, I know.'

I didn't tell John but I had already heard something of this from the NCOs who were naturally tuned in to the headquarters grapevine. Indeed, rumour had it that it was the outspoken colonel himself who had put his foot in it. I had had the would-be firing range pointed out to me, a long-whitewashed stone building running parallel to the road a mile back towards Arisaig. I had also seen Bates in action at Arisaig House. He was good and had been trained as an instructor by Sykes and Fairburn and therefore taught their system. For our work, these experts recommended a Colt .38 as reliable, not too clumsy in the pocket or shoulder holster and with sufficient stopping power for close work. Just as you can point instinctively at a given object, so you shot with your Colt rapidly and instinctively, forgetting any idea of deliberate aim. You fired two quick shots at each target just to make sure you had well and truly stopped your opponent. If you relaxed and followed instructions it worked remarkably well.

'Nothing gained by crying over spilt milk,' went on John, 'but don't get the idea that the locals are uncooperative. Some of them have been super, but they're inclined to be insular and by nature suspicious of outsiders. We labour under the disadvantage of not being allowed to be entirely honest with them and telling them what we are about. Many of them have sons at sea risking their lives in the Atlantic and they probably think we are fooling around here far from the centre of action and, into the bargain, for no good reason disturbing their way of life. Just remember that in any dealings you have with them. Be tactful and, whatever you do, don't appear to be trying to boss them around. We don't want any more bad publicity.'

The morning our students were due to arrive Harry and I, comparing notes, decided we now understood what a stage director felt before the curtain went up on the first night. It was not that we were afraid of forgetting our lines – Harry had been able to iron out most foreseeable snags on his side and I was reasonably confident on mine – but audience reaction was something we felt unsure about. Indeed, the make-up of the audience was a bit of an unknown factor. What would budding secret agents be like? Would some turn out to be enigmas or perhaps prima donnas and would some not be amused by being flogged around the mountains? Soldiers had to obey orders but did secret agents, some straight from civilian life, have the same code of practice?

When the ten of them climbed down from their truck at our door they did look a mixed bunch; a sergeant-major might have been tempted to refer to them as 'a shower'. One or two were clearly already serving officers; you could tell that from the fact that their uniforms looked as if they belonged to them and bore badges of recognisable regiments. Others seemed uncomfortable and out-of-place in their shining new garb, were perhaps rather old for their ranks and sported General Service insignia. One or two spoke with traces of a French accent although most spoke English as well as I did. They were virtually all British subjects although many the product of Anglo-French marriages. Many had lived longer in France than in Britain and one told me he had only recently found his way to England after being stranded by the fall of France.

They had been together as a group since joining a preliminary training school in the south and their morale was high. As we revived them with a drink after their long journey from London they were curious as to what they would be subjected to in Scotland. They already knew that subsequently they had to face parachute training. I decided that they were perfectly ordinary, nice persons who had accepted a task which only someone with their linguistic ability could perform and that they were determined to undertake it. I became convinced that they were out to learn all they could – after all their lives might depend on it – and that it was up to me to do all in my power to help them.

We started off in earnest next morning after a few introductory and welcoming words from the colonel, who then left with apologies for being too busy to stop longer. My first orientation lecture elicited the fact that my students were already proficient in elementary map-reading and I was thus able to get straight on with orientation in difficult terrain. This was fortunate, because finding your way by making use of churches, with or without steeples, railway cuttings, junctions with main roads or post-offices is not exactly relevant once you get up in the mountains. Then the signals corporal arrived carrying a suitcase full of 'buzzers', those units used for teaching the Morse code: a transmitter key screwed to a piece of board with a battery and buzzer alongside. Each man was given his own buzzer for the duration of the course so that he could practise in his spare time. This was new to me and feeling that a knowledge of the Morse code might one day prove useful, I reverted to student status for these periods.

My first lecture on explosives showed that the students were entirely ignorant on this subject – indeed as I had been only a few weeks back – and this at least enabled me to play the role of 'expert'. It was at a later stage in the course that the only slight accident occurred which was the result of one of the students 'knowing better'. We had put together an explosive charge combined with an incendiary, copying one of John Bush's 'inventions'. In practice, this would probably have been used with a timing device but, in order to demonstrate its effect, the fuse was to be ignited by one of the students. In the early stages of instruction, I would stand with the student while he did this and then walk back – not run – with him to shelter; but now he had reached the point where the student was encouraged to work on his own. The fuse alight, the student knew perfectly well that he had to join the rest of us sheltering at a safe distance behind a hummock. Yet on this occasion, instead of coming back to us, he decided he would get a better view behind a fold in the ground only half way back. To have shouted at him and forced him to get up again might have meant that he was caught in the open when the bomb went off. I hoped that all would be well but the explosion sent a drop of phosphorus sailing high into the air which then landed in the middle of the seat of the student's denim fatigues. As a proof of this a thin plume of smoke rose from the man's recumbent figure. Luckily, I had been taught to apply a copious amount of water to a phosphorus burn, so, accompanied by the sergeant, I rushed down to the now seriously worried student and the sergeant and I dumped him unceremoniously into the nearby burn. A subsequent examination revealed that the only damage sustained was to his trousers and these were easily replaced. A salutary lesson had been administered to the students and to me as well. Mercifully, in six months more training this was the only mishap under my responsibility.

The days slipped by and the farewell dinner was soon upon us. The students, I felt reasonably sure, had enjoyed their stay; the weather had improved and there was more than a hint of spring in the West Highland air. If nothing else they all looked weather-beaten, if not actually tanned, and they were going up mountains without the groans and puffing which was a feature of their first climb. The only cloud on the horizon was perhaps the thought of jumping out of an aircraft in a day or two's time. They didn't talk about it but I was pretty sure that some of them were thinking about it, now that the time had drawn near. I did not for one moment blame them but there was nothing I could do about it.

Harry and my partnership, which we ourselves considered had been successful, was broken up the moment our course ended. The reason for this was two-fold. A commandant for Garramor had been found and was to move in before the next bunch of joes were due and a new school across the bay from Mallaig on the scarcely inhabited promontory of Knoydart needed an instructor. Harry packed his kit and left for Inverie but I had a few days without any arduous duties awaiting the arrival of Major James Young.

I had of course already been to the beach past Camusdarroch but now I had time to dally and admire. The early spring, softened by the impact of the Gulf Stream, brought sparkling sunshine even if it so far lacked much warmth. From the height of the dunes, anchored down by scrags of marram grass, I looked across the sands, truly whiter than white, over the progressively darkening gradations of blue sea to a stage setting background of the islands of Rhum, Eigg and Muck. Rhum, to my right, with its serrated backbone of peaks, Eigg following on with a long high plateau and Muck like a rounded full stop at the end. On the far right in the distance I could see in this good visibility the wild outlines of the Cuillins of Skye. To frame the scene were low skerries, their bases attractively outlined with yellow lichen, some so close inshore that they were reached on foot at low tide and had provided small clams for my more gallicized students who knocked the shells

86

Born of a Dutch father who was in the cigar business and an English mother. His mother unwittingly saved her son's life by insisting that he learn French and German rather than Dutch. Had he been a Dutch speaker, Van would almost certainly have been parachuted into the arms of the Nazis who had infiltrated the circuits in Holland and this book would never have been written.

A happy childhood spent in Edenbridge. Van standing beside his elder brother, Justus, as young boys. A shared joke, but later life and careers meant that they did not see much of each other.

Bakers Street, the SOE HQ. There were demanding schedules for agents in preparation and members of FANY but there was still some time off to enjoy one another's company on the roof.

A lunch break in the sun at Bakers Street. In the middle of those present is a young FANY, Winifred Hay.

Another break on the roof but the seriousness of the underlying wartime situation is emphasised by the sandbags in the background.

A FANY officer who was to come into prominence in Van's life. Captain Winifred Hay, a Scottish girl looking very formal in her uniform. Their first meeting was stressful when they clashed about how to keep the car she was driving on a 'special duty' running. Later she came to work for Van at Bakers Street and saw him off at the aerodrome in order to say a fond farewell when he left for France.

The start of a romance. Van and Win looking happy together. The demands of the SOE were to separate them in 1944 for a considerable time, but, nevertheless, their relationship flourished.

The demands of war often made genuine friendships flourish. FANY Muriel Smith, who achieved the rank of Lieutenant, was one such friend of Van and Win. The friendship was to continue for the rest of their lives and into the next generation with Muriel becoming Gillian van Maurik's godmother.

A team of friends making the most of time off from SOE work. Roddy Clube, SOE and future diplomat, was to remain a friend for the rest of both their lives and to become John van Maurik's godfather.

Van dressed informally, but in a uniform that enabled him to train people to carry out the demands of sabotage and other clandestine activities.

The family wedding of Win and Van. From left to right are John Hay, Sybil van Maurik, Roddy Clube, Van, Win, Muriel Smith, Fanny Hay and Justus van Maurik.

The happy couple. Van's uniform has the parachute wings on his chest indicating that he qualified as a military parachutist.

Post war. The young diplomat en route to Egypt, his first overseas posting.

Van the mature diplomat taking time off to walk the hills of southern Scotland whilst on leave from his posting to Buenos Aires, Argentina.

off the rocks and with the aid of Swiss Army penknives ate them on the spot. This was a place, when off duty in summer, I would frequent, sunbathing, feasting my eyes but seldom braving the deceptively cold water.

If time permitted or if I could thumb a lift I might go a further mile up the road to the little hamlet of Morar with its railway station and hotel. Not much more than a track led off the main road climbing up to Loch Morar. Before you got there, it crossed the river over a wooden bridge; here you could lean over the wooden railings and look down into the pool formed by the waterfall which brought the water down from the loch. This was a well-known salmon leap and at virtually any time of year there were one or two salmon contemplating and gathering strength for the prodigious effort of clearing the obstacle and gaining access to their spawning ground. During the spring and autumn 'runs' the pool literally seethed with fish.

The track ran along the north bank of Loch Morar past the little Catholic church for some three miles and then became no more than a footpath. The loch, twelve miles long, had the distinction of being the deepest stretch of inland water in the United Kingdom and boasted of its own legendary monster but Morag appeared to be more class-conscious than its counterpart in Loch Ness as it would only appear before the death of a MacDonald of Clanranald. Half-way along the north bank well after the road fizzled out there was, I had heard, a house at Swordland which seemed to have some connection with our set-up but as with Traigh House and other properties I took John Bush's advice and asked no questions.

The only school other than my own and Arisaig House which I visited was Inverie. In a slack period, I was told to go over to give Harry a hand for three or four days as he had more than a full complement of students. There was an old open launch based at Mallaig on which we called for transport of students and provisions. Its ancient motor was amidships among the passengers and it often took considerable effort by its skipper, a retired fisherman, to get it started. Once under way we chugged at a steady eight knots eastwards along the coast of North Morar and then across to Inverie Bay, a total of some ten nautical miles. The school was located in the only large house on the whole of Knoydart, the remainder of the tiny settlement of Inverie comprising fishermen's cottages and one or two crofts.

Having arrived I felt I must be of some assistance to Harry. But here a snag arose. The CO from Arisaig had come over in the launch with me and next day, after his customary few words to the students and a discussion with the commandant, he decided that he would like to explore along the coastal track. He detailed me to accompany him on his walks. The hillsides rose steeply from the track and were covered in heather and gorse. In some places fire had clearly swept up the slope leaving a black swathe of carbonised bushes. The colonel may have been correct in assuming that the farmer had deliberately set fire to the area in order to encourage sheep grazing but I was taken aback when he produced a box of matches and started his own fire. Soon the flames were moving merrily up the hillside to the colonel's immense delight and a cloud of black smoke was wafting back towards Inverie.

At dinner that night nothing was said of our incendiarism but I had a quiet word with Harry who naturally feared repercussions from the small Inverie community. I promised him that if I had to accompany the colonel on a further expedition I would do what was in my power to discourage further fire-raising. Sure enough, next day the CO insisted I accompany him on what turned out to be a similar exercise but this time the colonel really had the bit between his teeth. I did my best to dissuade him but short of physically restraining my commanding officer, something a junior officer does not lightly entertain, there was little I could do. I was forced to the conclusion that the man was a pyromaniac. That evening the complaints began to come in to the commandant. He had, I think, already been tipped off by Harry but I did not envy him his task of appeasing the crofters and dealing as best he could with the CO. I was not sorry to learn that a message had been received from headquarters telling me to return on the next day's boat to prepare for more students at Garramor. Whether the CO had planned in advance to return to his base I did not know but I was relieved for the sake of Harry and his commandant to find that the colonel was also a passenger on the returning launch. I am not sure how much longer Jones stayed on at Arisaig House but on the next occasion I had contact with the CO it was a different man.

The advent of Major Jimmy Young as commandant of Garramor was, whichever way you looked at it, 'a good thing'. He was a hefty Scot with a broad smile and an ability to get his own way by the charm of his personality. He wore the uniform of the Black Watch and was never seen in daylight out of his kilt. At night, he wore his well-cut trews. I knew from the moment I met him that he would go down superbly well with the students. He fitted so well into the background and was what they perhaps unconsciously expected to find up there. He lent a little elegance to our mess, which had been lacking; he liked good food and drink, he had a store of stories but was always prepared to lend a sympathetic ear to his guests.

Jimmy and I hit it off splendidly from the word go. The fact that he had been a tea planter in Ceylon before the war, and knew that my brother and I had some knowledge of the London tea market, gave us something in common. I am not sure what his war service had been up to that point but for sure he had no previous experience of our type of work. This worked to my advantage as it was I who had to initiate him rather than the other way round, and ensured that he left the day-to-day training to me. But without doubt he earned his major's pay by the manner in which he worked on the students' morale and left his mark on them. When he arrived his forty-three years of age sat somewhat too comfortably on him and I did not get the impression that his previous occupation had involved much strenuous exercise. Nevertheless, he decided he should accompany us, for some of the way at least, on several of our more energetic sorties into the mountains. This had a very definite slimming effect on his person but it might have been even greater had he not felt that it was also his duty to demonstrate to his students of an evening how a man should hold his liquor. They loved him for it!

Unlike anyone else Jimmy had arrived in the area driving his own car, an Austin 8 saloon. How he came by sufficient petrol coupons to do so was his own business. As far as both he and I were concerned this was a big advantage since it gave us transport independent of our army driver. Even before our next students appeared Jimmy suggested we investigated the Morar Hotel for a quiet drink. He drove us up after an early dinner and we made the acquaintance of the proprietress over a first drink at the bar. These were quiet days for the hotel since fishermen from further south were no longer allowed into the military area and were probably in any case occupied with more serious pursuits. The one or two locals slowly finished their drinks and saying goodnight to 'Mary' and nodding to the two of us went their way.

'What's the matter with them?' enquired Jimmy. 'Don't they like us?'

'Och, they'll like you right enough but the bar closes at nine.'

'At nine every night?'

'At nine every night, that is, except Sundays when it doesn't open at all.'

'But that's dreadful, Mistress Macdonald. What are people like us who don't finish our work until this hour to do about it?' Jimmy had been using charm but now he began laying it on thick.

'It's the law.'

'Aye, but who's going to enforce it?'

'There's the constable on his bike from Mallaig.'

'But I'll wager he doesn't often set off on a night like this. Besides he'd need a wee drink himself after that amount of peddling.'

'So, you'll be needing a second drink?'

'A further drink would be very much appreciated.'

Mary MacDonald was a middle-aged spinster, not exactly good-looking but trim of figure and her smile was shy but nice. She looked capable and probably knew how to deal with an unruly customer but she was not impervious to Jimmy's charm.

'Well, if you'll keep quiet about it you can come into my back parlour. Then if the constable comes you're just my private guests having a wee dram. Ach, but the whole village knows long before he even gets here!'

Mary MacDonald's back parlour could hardly be described as wee, being ample enough to contain several well-worn but comfortable armchairs, an equal number of badly ringed occasional tables, a couple of bookcases and an ancient upright piano against one wall. It could well have been a residents' sitting-room in busier times.

'And what can I get you?' asked Mary MacDonald after Jimmy and I had seated ourselves.

'A large whisky and water, if you would really be so kind and a pint of McEwans for the young man. But only, of course, providing you will join us.' Miss MacDonald raised bashful objections but Jimmy was persuasive and we were glad to see that she had three glasses on her tray when she returned.

'*Slàinte mhath*,' toasted Jimmy. I had noticed, whether by design or not, Jimmy's Scottishness had noticeably increased in the few days he had been up with us and it went down well not only with the students but, one hoped, with the locals as well.

'Well, this is pleasant indeed. But tell us, my dear, what goes on in the fair village of Morar? Although we have our own military training to get on with we can't help feeling a bit cut off. How do the folk here spend their time?'

'Well, there's not much that happens here these days.' Mary had the caressingly soft tones and the clear enunciation of the West Highlander, contradicting the average Southerner's impression that all Scots spoke the broadest Glaswegian. 'Most of the young ones are off to the war and the older ones are doing what they know best, fishing the herring at Mallaig or tending their crofts and animals. Aye, the herring is king along at Mallaig but here at Morar after the Almighty – they are God-fearing folk here – the salmon is king. In peacetime, they come from far and wide to fish him or even just to watch him come up from the sea and fight his way back to the loch. Aye, the salmon is part of their lives here.'

'You can pass on to the folk, Mary, that we military here are happy, indeed honoured, to be temporarily part of this community even if we do not have a great deal of opportunity to mix. I may call you Mary, may I not? I'm Jimmy and this is Van.' I feared that Jimmy was proceeding a bit fast with the charm offensive but after a short hesitation Mary nodded her head. 'It's really so very nice to get away from the military atmosphere for a short while and tonight we were lucky that our duties finished earlier than usual. Normally it is turned nine when we finish. Would it be too much to ask to allow us occasionally to pop in here after closing hours? It would really be the only chance of a little relaxation.'

Thus, our own private drinking hole was established. Although Jimmy made sure that Mary continued to enjoy his blandishments, he had no motive other than to have a place where both we and later selected students could have an evening away from the mess, where tension generated by the realisation of dangerous work ahead could be loosened.

One of the best evenings we had in Mary's 'night club' was in the company of Peter Churchill and two or three other students. Peter, as far as one could tell, was probably one of the least in need of tension-lifting but because he was such a natural leader and life and soul of his course he was an obvious choice to come with us.

Jimmy rightly made it a rule than Mary should not serve us with whisky or any other drink which, due to wartime shortage, might deprive her local customers of their normal tipple. I remember well that on the occasion of Peter's visit deliveries had not arrived and after an initial round of drinks a discussion took place between Jimmy and Mary.

'No, Mary, we won't take another round of precious liquor but tell me, have you anything tucked away which might not appeal to your regulars?'

Mary left the room and returned shortly holding an unopened bottle of creme de menthe.

'I don't know if this is any good to you. I had it in for peacetime fishermen who would sometimes take a glass. My bar customers would never touch it.'

'Beggars can't be choosers. Open it up, Mary.' I heard him add, 'Give the bill for it to me personally.'

We often had quite a party on our visits, depending on the mood and personalities of those who accompanied us. But now we let ourselves go as never before. The piano was pushed further into the centre of the room and Peter seated himself at it. I had had no real idea of the versatility of this man but I vaguely knew that, apart from being an all-round sportsman, he had captained the Cambridge University ice hockey team and later played for England. In his early thirties, half hidden by the piano, his somehow rather old-fashioned looking glasses surmounted by his brown wavy hair belied the strong physique below. We crowded round resting our liqueur glasses rather incongruously on the top of the instrument. Peter started to play Cole Porter and Irving Berlin and it was not only the drinks we had had before leaving the mess, and now the frequent fill-ups of the sickly green liquid, which convinced me that he was good. By the time the tobacco smoke was thick on the air and several of us were sure we were seeing things through a green mist Peter switched to the music of the film of *The Wizard of Oz*. He played, *When you wish upon a Star* singing softly and wistfully and if he was not wondering what the future held for him I certainly was. I asked him to play it again but he shook his head. Since then I have never been able to hear it without visualising Peter singing it in Mary MacDonald's back parlour. When later Jimmy and I put Peter and his companions on the train bound for Ringway Airfield, I would have been pleased had I known that I would be involved with him on more than one future occasion.

We did try other places but nothing ever came up to the friendliness and intimacy of the Morar Hotel. The choice, of course, was very strictly limited and we had a sneaking feeling that the security boys, had they known, would have preferred us to keep to the confines of our school. One foray I do remember was when we had a Lieutenant 'Dusty' Millar of the Highland Light Infantry attached to us as a supernumerary instructor. I subsequently gathered that he went on to a school somewhere in the Middle East and that he had been sent to us to learn the ropes. He was a likeable chap and he got on well with Jimmy, although they could hardly have been more different. Jimmy, however much he joined in, had his dignity and his accent had much in common with 'polite Edinburgh'. Dusty was a bit of a lad, as they say, and his speech was pure Glasgow and to some of us it sometimes verged on the incomprehensible. One thing they both had in common was their partiality to a drop of whisky; I on the other hand had not yet reached the age of such discrimination and preferred to stick to beer or perhaps a gin and tonic. We were in an in-between-courses period and it was decided that we should give the West Highland Hotel in Mallaig a try.

Mallaig claimed to be the busiest fishing port on the West coast of Scotland and, although it only counted some thousand inhabitants in all, quite a few of these were slaking their thirst in the bars of the hotel. The unaccustomed presence of two Scottish officers in their bonnets and trews not only attracted attention but also a steady flow of proffered drinks which I, for one, found it difficult to keep up with. Even Jimmy found it impossible to buy a round, the only consolation being that the fishermen were undoubtedly earning much more than we were. We undeniably enjoyed our evening but as we finally regained our car we all agreed that, despite the advantage of there appearing to be no nine o'clock closing in Mallaig, the sheer volume of unreciprocated hospitality might make a further visit embarrassing. But that did not worry us for long. As Jimmy drove down the narrow, deserted road back towards Morar he led us in chorus after chorus of Scottish song; the more we drove, the more we sang and the less we realised how drunk we were. We were nearly home and past the blacked-out Morar Hotel – not for fear of air raids but because everyone had sensibly gone to bed – when we reached the right-angled bend which took you over a wee bridge and then an immediate sharp turn to the left to take you south again in your original direction towards Garramor and Arisaig. Unfortunately, neither the driver nor I sitting beside him noticed the right-hand bend and, continuing straight ahead, the little car sailed over a four-foot drop and landed on its roof in the field below. Somewhat sobered, Jimmy and I opened our doors and crawled out. Having both decided we were completely unharmed, Jimmy started examining the minor damage the car had suffered. Only then did we become aware of the tones of *Annie Laurie* coming from the back seat. Looking in we saw Dusty, apparently oblivious of the fact that he was upside down, continuing the song which had been so rudely interrupted. The next morning while Jimmy arranged for his car to be towed away to have one or two dents in its roof straightened out, he decreed that we would revert to the Morar Hotel for future nights out.

Although I did not know it, I had so far been involved with the training of Buckmaster's F Section early pioneering agents. I did not know it because the rank and file in Arisaig were kept in ignorance of what went on at London headquarters. Not only did I not know that, for political reasons, there was more than one French Section; I did not even know where the HQ was located nor what its name or military designation might be. Not that it worried me as I loved the work and an enforced return to regimental duties was the only bad dream I ever had. Many of the students impressed themselves on my memory but I lost track of most of them as their identities were hidden under field pseudonyms and network code names when I later arrived in London. Ben Cowburn, who metamorphosed into Benoit and Tinker, struck me at the time as a rather retiring north countryman but he emerged as one of the most energetic and successful agents when he got to France. Vic Gerson was one of those, if my memory serves me well, who collected what they hoped were recently laid seagulls' eggs and then supervised the cooking of an enormous omelette for our dinner. It was only the scarcity of hens' eggs that encouraged us to tackle this gaudily coloured and extremely fishy dish. Victor went on to achieve great things.

Michael Trotobas was an unforgettable visitor to our school. With his flat southern accent – had he acquired it in Brighton where he was born? – his pencil-thin moustache and somewhat foxy look, one might have felt, before one got to know him better, that he could have fitted into the popular Tommy Handley radio show with the catch-phrase: 'Wanna buy a packet of fags, gov?' He seemed to be a loner but this was maybe because he found some of his colleagues a shade too pedestrian for his liking. He had no difficulty in absorbing the instruction but he liked to adapt methods to his own way of thinking. I remember saying to Jimmy that, providing he did not blow himself up beforehand, he could cause the Germans a lot of trouble. I little thought that his first independent operation would take place within a couple of days and that the trouble would be Jimmy's.

It was a Saturday evening and as the students were supposed to be doing their homework for a night exercise, Jimmy and I slipped off for a quiet drink at the Morar. Returning back up Garramor's drive our headlights caught the still moving wheels of an upturned motorcycle at the bottom of the bank to our left. Stopping the car, we got out and investigated. Trotobas rose unsteadily to his feet and, mumbling something to the effect of just having beaten us home, failed to climb the bank. Jimmy and I taking an outstretched hand each hauled him back on to the driveway. He could have been described as 'well and truly sloshed'.

'That looks like the corporal's cycle. You shouldn't have taken it. Certainly not in your present state.' Jimmy exercised an easy discipline, believing that rigid control did not teach individuals to use their wits and keep alive. 'Now Van and I will see if we can get the bike up the bank. You just stop there for the time being.'

'Okay, but please bring the shalmon up while you're about it.'

'Salmon?' queried Jimmy, but looking down we could now distinguish a large inert silvery fish a foot or two away from the bike.

'Where did that come from?'

'From the pool. Hundresh of 'em floating around. Bloody amazing what a shmall bit of plastic'll do. Could only carry that one bastard.'

Jimmy stood quite still for an appreciable moment. I felt for him. As the model Scot, I knew he must be dying a thousand deaths at the thought of being ultimately responsible for the dynamiting of a famous salmon leap. Then he shook himself, hoping against hope that Michael Trotobas was just fabricating, just a drunken dream.

'Let's drive up and see. Into the car, both of you.'

But it was no drunken dream. Not a hundred but maybe a score of silver bellies floated on the surface.

We debated what we should do. Trotobas assumed we would haul in as many as possible and take them back to the school, thus providing delicatessen dinners for a month or more. Jimmy and my aim was to cover up the crime and to avoid taking fish back to Garramor as this might make it look as if it had been an officially sponsored exploit. The night was not totally dark and we discovered bushes on the edge of the pool furthest from the road and we hoped that these would provide an overnight hiding-place for retrieved fish. Some fish had been washed to the edges of the pool and these were relatively easy to pull out of the water. Others we raked in with a length of dead branch; we had hoped that some of the fish might just be stunned but no such luck, they were dead beyond recall. Finally, we decided we had done all we could with the light at our disposal, reckoning that any remaining fish might perhaps be carried down the small length of river to the sea. We did our best to camouflage the hoard of dead salmon under the bushes with leaves and other debris and then got into the car.

'I just can't really be doing with all this subterfuge,' said Jimmy as we headed home. 'But what else can we do? The deed is done and there'll be one hell of a bust-up if it gets known in the village. For everyone's sake better we keep quiet about it.'

But it did get known in the village early next morning as the faithful wended their way past the falls to Sunday mass. There were still apparently sufficient floating bodies to attract attention and when the pile under the bushes was discovered and more than one villager remembered having heard an explosion, the game was up. I did not see Jimmy until after lunch that day and when I did he was looking pretty chastened. Spotting him, Michael Trotobas went up and made embarrassed apologies for the trouble he had caused.

'Now don't you worry, laddie,' replied Jimmy, giving him one of his warm smiles. 'You didn't realise that up here it's fair game to net a salmon but a sin to blow it up. But let me give you a word of advice. When the time comes to attack a bigger target elsewhere, make certain you have no more than one stiffener before you set out; in your state last night you might have blown you hand off!'

After Michael had left us, Jimmy continued. 'I started off by consulting Mary and she tipped me off as to the two or three important people to make my peace with. It wasn't an easy job I can tell you; it would have been less difficult if I could have explained that the brave young man in question will shortly be risking both torture and death on all of our behalves. But that can't be. I think however that this time they're prepared not to take the matter any further and there'd better not be a next time. After all that grovelling and hard work I felt in need of a drink and also wanted to thank Mary again for her advice and support. "Och, they're a bunch of hypocrites," she told me. "They've collected up every single fish and distributed them among their friends. Everyone, I tell you, in this village will be enjoying salmon tonight. I'm not for telling you that they're hoping you'll do it again but they're not quite so sorry as they make out." I just hope this is true and Mary is not saying it to please me.'

'Which reminds me,' said I, 'what do we do with the original fish which Michael brought with him.'

'The cook asked me the same question when I got back. It goes against my principles but I told him we'd have it for dinner tonight.'

I often wished after the war that I could have returned to Morar and told them of the last chapter in the short life of their salmon saboteur. They might have been astonished to learn that not very long after leaving their area he was parachuted into what was then Unoccupied France but in October 1941 he and other F Section agents, through no fault of their own, were arrested and imprisoned by French Vichy police. Trotobas was a prime mover in organising a mass escape and he was able to work his way back through Spain to Britain. He was re-parachuted into northern France where the daring but expert sabotage raids against railway targets by 'Capitaine Michel' are still remembered and commemorated. After inflicting very considerable damage and having built up a sizeable Resistance group, the safe house he was using was betrayed to the Germans but when the Gestapo raided it he shot dead their leader before being killed himself. The street where this took place is still named rue du Capitaine Michel.

CHAPTER 7

Operation Anthropoid

There were some people who enjoyed parachuting, there were some who just claimed to do so, but there were many more who definitely didn't. Ray Wooller, the chief instructor at our secret wing to the main army parachute school at RAF Ringway, now the site of Manchester Airport, belonged to the first category. It was he, moreover, who tested out new techniques including the idea of dropping agents into water. It didn't take me long to join the mob in the third category, those who disliked the whole affair. This came as no great surprise to me and I would never have volunteered to join a bunch of our students going down to Ringway had I not felt there were good reasons to do so. In the first place, I had had pricks of conscience at sending students I had trained down to what would be an ordeal to some of the less intrepid, or perhaps less thick-skinned, without having had the experience myself. I wanted to be able to reassure them that there was nothing to worry about, nothing too frightening at all, even if I had to tell a few white lies. Then instinctively perhaps I felt that in this aggressive organisation I had strayed into, about which I still knew so little but in which I wanted to make my way, learning to parachute might be a first step on some ladder or other.

I based my case to Jimmy on the grounds that if I acquired my parachute wings it would give me more clout with our students and indirectly, perhaps, contribute to their morale. He needed little persuading and submitted the idea to Arisaig House who passed it on to the training section in London. It happened that its head, Colonel J.S. Wilson, the master-mind behind the rapid establishment of the organisation's network of training schools, was on his way to visit the Arisaig area and I met him when he came to Garramor. His was a stocky, upright figure surmounted by curly, steel-grey hair. When he questioned me about my request and looked me up and down with his bright blue eyes I got the impression of decisiveness and complete integrity, as befitted the peacetime deputy chief of the Boy Scouts Movement. He seemed impressed with what he judged to be my keen approach and gave me permission to carry out my plan.

As far as the British Army was concerned parachute troops were a recent wartime innovation but their training was lengthy and hard. Our students' whole parachute training took the inside of a week and they were finished and away before a regular soldier would have even taken to the air. They were men in a hurry with much else to learn before they went into action. The sheer concentration of the course, and the fact that parachuting was not to be a profession to them but merely an unpleasant means to an end, must have increased the tension that every beginner felt.

We were driven from our quarters to a hanger on the airfield rigged up for training purposes. Our driver was a smart and attractive FANY (First Aid Nursing Yeomanry) and it was the first time I had set eyes on or even knew of the existence of such a brand of female volunteer. With her smart tunic, tightly held in by her highly polished brown leather belt, the khaki shirt and tie, her friendly smile and her cap at ever so slightly a rakish angle, she epitomized the splendid corps of ladies with whom I was to have much future contact. We swung from harnesses, we practised forward rolls on landing, we projected ourselves through holes in the floor of mock-up aircraft fuselages, we practised going through the hole in sticks of two and three and at every stage it was impressed on us that whatever happened we must keep our feet together on approaching the ground. We were taken into the parachute packing department where WAAFs were at work and it was explained to us how the static line which followed us out of the hole was attached to the cover round the parachute and then to the apex of the parachute by a specific thickness of nylon cord. When your fall reached the end of the static line it automatically pulled the cover off and also opened the 'chute but the weight of your body and the drag on it broke the nylon line and ensured you did not still remain attached to the aircraft. 'You never get mixed up with the thickness of the nylon cord, do you?' someone asked one of the packers, but none of us really enjoyed the joke.

At lunch Wooller apologised for it not having been possible to arrange for us to do our preliminary jump from a balloon so we would have to do it from an aircraft. We nodded assent and it was only later, talking to others, that I realised the lucky escape we had had. The balloon was a barrage balloon with a small gondola with a jumping hole in its base attached to the bottom of the balloon. You went up in the gondola with the instructor and then, in cold blood, on the word go you jumped through the hole. This, they said, was much worse than an aircraft, since in the latter you knew there was a sense of urgency to jump, magnified by the noise of the engines and the slipstream, if you wanted to avoid missing the dropping zone and landing in trees or in the lake at Tatton Park. In the balloon, there could be a temptation to prevaricate and decide you were not quite ready yet!

We were taken up for a twenty-minute familiarisation flight in one of the Whitleys reserved for training.[1] At least half of us had never flown before since train and boat had been the normal peacetime means of transport for holiday-makers, and as soon as the RAF despatcher lifted the covers from the hole we lay flat on our stomachs and gazed over the edge. A thousand feet was to be the altitude for the first solo jump and eight hundred for the succeeding ones. Looking down, I knew that there was no going back and that I would have to jump the next day, but I now began to scold myself for being such a fool as to get myself into this position. But this was nothing to the way I upbraided myself when togged up in full jumping attire and parachute strapped to our backs we sat in the fuselage next morning awaiting to be called forward for our first jump. The 'plane was to do a series of circuits dropping one man each time round and I had been detailed by Ray Wooller to jump first. Maybe as a fellow instructor he felt I should lead from the front, or perhaps he wanted to spare me the suspense of waiting until last. I jumped and I landed safely.

I had picked myself up and gathered up my 'chute by the time the Whitley reappeared to drop its next passenger. This was a Major Clark who, we had learnt last night in the mess, was an officer at a research institute run by our organisation. (I do not give 'our organisation' a name since as far as most of us were concerned it did not seem to have one or if it did it was a secret.) He was working on an invention which was designed to soften the impact of a parachute landing and thus make it safe for agents of more advanced years. His idea consisted of some sort of bottle of compressed air which was released a moment

---

[1] Armstrong Whitworth A.W.38 Whitley, was a twin-engine medium bomber, introduced into the RAF in 1937.

before touch down. He had decided that he needed personal experience before being able to proceed further since the project was still on the drawing board. He was a heavily built man in his forties, certainly not a 'natural' for parachute jumping.

Major Clark left the aircraft in good order and one could judge that he would land almost in the middle of the little group of instructors and hangers-on. As he came lower one could see that not only were his legs not held together but one seemed to be held half way up in the air. Wooller held his loudhailer to his mouth and shouted at him to put his legs together. Major Clark seemed either unwilling or incapable of complying and by the time he landed beside us we were all shouting at him. A broken leg was quickly diagnosed and the unfortunate major left by ambulance. Some two years later I had to visit Clark's establishment and it occurred to me to enquire what had happened to his invention. I was told the project had been dropped as Clark had decided that the whole thing was not worth the candle.

The last jump to qualify for our wings was upon us and as far as I was concerned the sooner it was over the better. As I floated down to earth I was celebrating the fact that I would not have to go through that hole again when I realised I would be landing on a rather vicious backswing; instead of performing a forward roll I was thrown heavily on to my back. No serious damage was done but I knew I would be stiff for some days to come. The truck took some of us back to the hanger where several of our group were waiting to emplane for their last jump. As I hobbled past one of the weaker members of the group, the sort of man I had originally thought I might encourage by my example, saw me and apprehensively asked what had happened. I assured him that it was only a bump due to a backswing and nothing to worry about.

When we reassembled in the mess and Ray handed out the cloth parachute wings we had earned, I was upset to discover that the young man who had seen me hobbling had refused his jump. I spoke to the conducting officer but he assured me that I had in fact done him a favour since he had become convinced that his charge was not suited to the work ahead and this incident provided the final proof needed. I allowed one of the FANYs who had arrived with needle and thread to sew the wings on to my right upper sleeve with a cleared conscience.

I was happy to get back to Garramor. There were two or three days before the next course was due and I used these to loosen up my back again with some hiking in the hills. Clearly it would have been counter-productive to have appeared before the new lot of students in damaged shape.

The main piece of news locally was that Colonel Wilson and the brigadier in charge of Operations and Training were to visit the Arisaig area in the near future. Nearer the time we were informed that Wilson and Gubbins, for such it seemed was the brigadier's name, were to be accompanied on their tour of inspection by Dr Hugh Dalton, the Socialist politician who held the post of Minister of Economic Warfare in Churchill's coalition government.

'Where does he fit in?' I asked Jimmy.

'If I understood correctly, but no one at Arisaig House was prepared or possibly able to be very forthcoming, he is our overall boss.'

'But I thought we were in the Army.'

'So did I but the longer I stay in this outfit the harder it is to feel surprised.'

We were prepared for the bigwigs – the handy acronym of 'VIPs' had not yet been invented – to arrive at Garramor, step out of their staff car, briefly inspect our training facilities, say a few kind words, re-enter their car and disappear. Instead Jimmy and I were asked to report at Arisaig House one morning and to be ready to accompany the visitors and other available members of the training staff on a short hike into the mountains.

This somewhat unusual procedure was apparently Dalton's idea as, being a keen countryman and walker, he wanted to combine meeting people with making the most of his time away from his desk. He was a strange figure among all those uniforms and with his long legs clad in knickerbockers, his tweedy jacket and his long, rather lugubrious face topped by a deerstalker, he towered over the rest of us. It seemed to me that he was more interested in the scenery than the views of a young lieutenant. Gubbins looked very small and dapper compared with the loping figure of the minister but when he addressed one or two questions to me and his almost black eyes summed me up, I had a feeling that, unlike some other senior officers I had met, his queries were not just formalities and that answers were not disregarded as soon as he spoke to the next man in line.

'I've had a word with Colonel Wilson,' said Jimmy when we found ourselves walking together, 'and he said that we would be kept particularly busy in August and September and that we should not make any plans for weekend leave. By the way, have you noticed that the brigadier has parachute wings up? I reckon he's a pretty good officer.'

The second half of August and much of September certainly did turn out to be a busy time, and a change from training F Section joes. We were notified of the imminent arrival of twenty Czech soldiers followed by a second course of the same number. To accommodate them all we had to bring Camusdarroch into full use and I moved there myself. To help with this larger training commitment we were promised temporary assistance from local resources.

Coping with double the normal number of students did not prove very much more difficult as they were all trained members of the Czech Army in Britain, most of them were senior NCOs and they were under the discipline of a young officer. Many of them had had adventurous journeys reaching Britain. As far as one could tell none of them knew exactly what they were being trained for, nor did any of us, but as far as they were concerned if it led to the opportunity of having a bash at the Germans, so very much the better. They enjoyed getting away from regimental life, they fired at targets as if they really believed they were Germans, they approached demolition training with the greatest gusto and all in all they had a darn good time. Nevertheless, they maintained faultless discipline and never overstepped the mark.

The second course of twenty came and went and they had been a replica of the first. It had been fun and rewarding teaching the Czechs but towards the end of the second course I began to feel I was in danger of slipping back into an orthodox officer myself with a sergeant-major saluting me every morning and asking permission to proceed. I desperately wanted to stay with the cloak and daggers and I found I was beginning to miss the individuality of the F Section boys and the way one could get on a wavelength with them. But I need not have worried, as just before the last lot of Czechs went on their way I was notified that I had been posted to London HQ. My suspicion that my volunteering to parachute might have had some bearing on this unexpected transfer subsequently proved to be true.

Both groups of Czechs had been accompanied by the same Czech country section officer. With the Czechs, the conducting officer had to be a first-class interpreter as many of them only had a superficial knowledge of English, and Frank Keary was more fluent in their language than anyone else at HQ. I had had time to get to know Frank and he was a gentle, kindly soul who had been a teacher of English in Prague before the war. He had contracted TB out there and, although he had been cured of it for the time being, he looked dreadfully frail and wheezed audibly at the slightest exertion. He told me that he did not expect to live long but was glad to be of a little use meanwhile. There was of course no question of him going on exercises into the mountains but he was indispensable at lectures and static instruction. When I told him that I had been posted to London he immediately said that I would need to find my own accommodation and, if I was stuck on arrival, I should get in touch with him and he could get me a room in his inexpensive hotel off Lancaster Gate.

It was under a year later that I read on the front pages of the newspapers of the assassination of Heydrich and was let into the secret that it was two of the men I had helped to train who had done the deed. SS-Obergruppenführer Reinhard Heydrich, who was No.2 to Himmler in the SS, had become Reichs Protector of Bohemia and Moravia based in Prague, and far from 'protecting' the population he had set himself the task of 'germanisation' of Czechoslovakia and was engaged in mass arrests and executions. The Czech government-in-exile under the leadership of Eduard Beneš decided that he should be eliminated and SOE, as I had now discovered our organisation was called, was prepared to provide the means – training, equipment and air transport – to make it possible. The operation was planned by the Czech Intelligence chief in London, Moravec, and the young Czech officer I had shared my quarters with in Camusdarroch had been one of his assistants. Jozef Gabčík and Jan Kubiš had carried out the attack on Heydrich's car and several other of my ex-students had acted as back-up. The German reaction was predictable. Himmler and several hundred Gestapo men descended on Prague but the terror and indiscriminate shooting of innocents they unleashed did nothing to reveal the whereabouts of the parachutists until one man claimed the reward and gave away their hiding place in the crypt of the Orthodox Cathedral of St. Cyril and St. Methodius. The men held out against an overwhelming force of Gestapo and SS, an attempt by the fire brigade to flood them out failed but eventually the survivors used their remaining ammunition on themselves rather than being taken alive. Among the atrocities to follow were the shooting of every man, woman and child in the small villages of Lidice and Ležáky, which the Germans thought had had some connection with the assassination, and the confiscation of all Orthodox Church property in Czech lands and the despatch of many priests and laymen to forced labour in Germany, with all that that implied. Professor M.R.D. Foot, who spent time in Prague assessing the operation, records the view that the German over-reaction was a propaganda gift to the Allies and that the loss of Himmler's most able deputy was a set-back for the German security services. That this was achieved with considerable loss of life cannot be denied, but there is, of course, no telling how many lives Heydrich would have continued to exact had he been allowed to survive.

But none of this had yet taken place as I said goodbye to Jimmy and other friends around Arisaig and started the lengthy train journey to London

CHAPTER 8

SOE, Baker Street and Buckmaster

The words INTER-SERVICES RESEARCH BUREAU headed the pass issued to me by the security officer I had to report to. In his accompanying talk, he explained that this was a convenient 'cover' for our offices in Baker Street since they were used by officers of all three arms of the Service, plus a number of civilians. Naturally if anyone should be indiscreet enough to enquire the nature of our research, 'mum' was the word. The enemy would love to discover what we were up to and the longer they remained in ignorance the better. We must do everything we could to avoid drawing attention to ourselves and whilst there was no ban on using neighbouring pubs and eating houses, our work must never be discussed outside the office. In the pursuit of anonymity, I would discover that no names were used in internal office minuting and this applied to the telephone as well if one spoke from one section to another. Instead, every section was designated by a symbol – I was to work in the Air Liaison Section and this was known as AL – and everyone in a section was given their own section symbol. I was to be AL/B1. If you left to go to another section you relinquished the old symbol and adopted one relating to your new section. I would pick up the symbols of the various sections I would have dealings with as I went along; it was really quite easy when you got used to it. It had the advantage that if any piece of paper went astray no names would be disclosed.

'I'm still wearing the shoulder flashes of the Wiltshire Regiment and the Wyvern badge of 43rd Division. Should I now take these down? Does one put up any ISRB designation?'

The officer looked pained.

'Good heavens, no. You don't bandy ISRB about unless you have to. Tell your parents and other friends that you're working in the War Office. Generalise, avoid details and locations. Keep your Wiltshire and Divisional signs as they are, they may help to confuse the unduly inquisitive. Now, I see you will be working with Colonel Barry and Major Dodds-Parker and they will be able to put you straight on most things but if you should have problems over your cover or anything else you are always free to pop in to see us. I'll tell you how to get to your section. It's in a rather smart block of flats just off the top of Baker Street but in a week or two you'll all be moving to Norgeby House across the street from here. Perhaps not quite so smart but much more convenient. Virtually all the European operational sections will then be in the same building and the administrative sections together here in No. 64. I'll give Dodds-Parker a ring to say you're on your way.'

This is perhaps a good moment to explain that Special Operations Executive, the official title of the organisation, was still unknown to the rank and file of those working in Baker Street and was only used in Top Secret communications with outside ministries and departments in the know. It was not until nine months later when I became a staff officer to General Gubbins, as he had then become, that I learnt of its existence. But for convenience and clarity I will henceforth use the abbreviation SOE rather than 'we' and 'us'.

Major Douglas Dodds-Parker was a very tall Grenadier Guards officer and his immaculate turn-out and sleek appearance made me feel like someone arrived down from the backwoods, which in one sense I was. He sat me down and in the friendliest manner talked to me for the next hour. It was an excellent briefing but it was all so new to me that there were moments, quite a few of them, when I found it difficult to keep pace with him, especially when he got on to the frequent divergence in priorities over availability of aircraft between the RAF, the SIS – could that really stand for Secret Intelligence Service? – and SOE and even more so when he advanced from our present phase of operations into considering future spheres of probability. As I got to know Douglas better I realised that while most people's horizon was at that time bounded by the current and difficult job of fostering resistance in Europe he was contemplating eventualities two or more years ahead; and that in wartime was a long space of time. While this sometimes tended to bemuse plodders like myself, it did not imply that Douglas was a dreamer at the expense of being an organiser. Derek

Dodson, a young Royal Scots Fusilier, had set up the Air Liaison Section more or less as a one-man-band, so I understood, and now Barry and Dodds-Parker were developing it into a complex structure upon whose efficiency the work of country sections increasingly depended. As I was to discover, it worked well.

AL was the travel agency to which country sections had to apply for air transport of their agents to destinations in Occupied Europe, and subsequently of arms and equipment to the networks those agents had established. There were two modes of transport, by parachute or by clandestine landing of single-engine Lysander aircraft. The latter, which was the trickiest and the most difficult to organise, had for operational reasons to be confined to the northern half of France, and was normally reserved for those unfit to parachute. It had the great advantage that agents could be brought home as well as taken out. There were also sea landings by fishing boat and occasionally by submarine but these were not dealt with by our section.

Up until the end of summer 1941 comparatively few air operations of either kind had taken place but, with men finishing their training and with country sections recruiting hard, a big upsurge in numbers needing to be transported had to be provided for. AL was being expanded to take the strain but, as Dodds-Parker explained to me, the one limiting factor might be the RAF's strong objections to diverting aircraft from bombing sorties to special duties.

'It's hard to get it over to Bomber Command,' he said with true proselytizing fervour and looking me in the eye, 'that, if they will give us the means to get our men into occupied territories, our chaps will carry out many of the jobs by sabotage and the RAF will then be able to reserve more of their aircraft for bombing Germany. We'll just have to prove it to them by results. You've joined us at an exciting time and I can assure you, you won't be stuck for work. Well, we're grateful to Jack Wilson for having recommended you to us and I think you also met the brigadier up in Scotland. He takes a great interest in this Section and you'll find he's a frequent visitor. By the way, I'm glad to see your promotion has come through and you've put up your Captain's pips; the rank will help you in your dealings both inside and outside this organisation. Now I'll take you to your office which you share with Philip Rea who has also just joined us.'

Captain The Hon. Philip Rea was a compact, neat, but unassuming figure, and his dark hair matched well the black buttons of the Kings Royal Rifle Corps. He was fifteen years my senior in age and in experience but such was the genuine friendliness he exuded this counted for nothing. We learnt the ropes together in AL Section but then he was transferred to another job, yet whenever we bumped into each other in SOE or in post-war days I experienced the same warmth of friendship.

From our office window, we looked down on an internal paved courtyard with a small fountain in its centre. On our first Sunday in residence both Philip and I were in the office as the moon period, when air operations were possible, had just begun. Several parachute operations had been scheduled for the night before and Philip and I had been given the job of receiving the call on the 'safe' telephone from our liaison officer at the airfield, giving the results of the debriefing of the pilots on their return. We then had to telephone the results to the country sections concerned. More often than not, as we discovered later, the country sections on tenterhooks beat the gun and telephoned us, often blocking our lines and holding things up. Waiting for our call we looked out of the window and saw below Gubbins, having taken possession of someone's female bicycle, peddling like mad round and round the fountain. Then he carefully replaced the bike where he'd found it and went on up to his office.

'An unusual but brilliant officer, so I'm told,' remarked Philip. 'I reckon we'd better telephone him first of all.' Our call from the airfield came through and we noted down the summaries of the various debriefings: 'Dropping point clearly identified and agents should have dropped on target'; 'Thick mist over target area and forced to return to base without dropping'. Between the two of us we telephoned all the sections on our list and then sat back in our chairs, satisfied that we had completed our task.

Philip's telephone rang.

'Yes, this is AL Section.' He glanced down at his list. 'And who might that be?' Philip paused as he listened, his face clouding over. 'No, sir. Yes, sir, I do apologise, sir.' Then he proceeded to give the whole list of results.

'A word of advice, Van,' said Philip as he replaced the receiver. 'If anyone tells you he is CD, don't ask him who that might be.'

'And who is it?'

'He says it stands for Chief Director and he happens to be the boss of the whole shooting match!'

Lieutenant Colonel Dick Barry, unlike Douglas Dodds-Parker, was a regular Army officer, Sandhurst and Staff College, Camberley. He had gingery coloured hair, a somewhat earnest expression and when he spoke it was in the well-considered terms of a highly intelligent organiser. When he was not speaking but thinking, which was quite often the case, he smoked an all-metal pipe, which claimed to be more hygienic than the old-fashioned briar, and which he was able to strip down to its component parts for cleaning purposes. He seemed to me to be a prime example of the best type of Army staff officer and the Army apparently came to the same conclusion, since he retired twenty years later with the rank of Major General.

For detailed instruction in the work of the Section I sat for a while at the feet of Derek Dodson. He came into the office early every morning and, until things started happening, he lounged back in his chair, stretched his tartan trewed legs far in front of him and lost himself in his copy of *The Times*. As he read, he twirled his set of keys, attached to a long chain, round his index finger and then untwirled them again. When he spoke, it was in what some considered an exaggerated drawl. A languid individual, one might have thought first thing in the morning, but once he put down his newspaper that impression disappeared. He left the Section not so long afterwards, won the MC with the Partisans in Greece, and, after the war, he exchanged the life of regular soldier for that of regular diplomat and served as ambassador in several posts.

The first essential for a successful parachute operation, Dodson stressed, was the availability of a dropping ground not only suitable for those landing on it but above all acceptable to the RAF. They demanded that it had to be as easy as possible to find in the black-out of occupied territory and the proximity of a river or other expanse of water was highly desirable if not completely essential. Even then it might be turned down as uncomfortably close to known enemy air defences or for other technical reasons. It also, of course, had to be within range, bearing in mind the length of darkness at any given season of the year. In the case of pioneering agents dropping 'blind' without the benefit of reception committees, the dropping points normally had to be picked off a map but, when these agents became established, one of their first tasks was to send back via their wireless link one or more grounds for approval. They had been trained how to indicate exact locations in France by superimposing a grid system over the widely used Michelin maps. It was AL Section's job to transfer these on to RAF navigational maps and to submit the coordinates to the special liaison department in the Air Ministry. If they were satisfied in all respects the ground was 'agreed' and the operator in the Field so informed. If the ground was not accepted, then AL had a frustrated country section on its hands who liked to point out that its agents too were risking their lives sending messages backwards and forwards to no avail. But in the end, they realised that the RAF were unlikely to budge and it was to no-one's advantage to lose one of the very few and precious aircraft allocated to our work.

Then there was the AL briefing of the agent shortly before his operation was due to take place. For this one got out one's 'commercial traveller's' suitcase and went off to the country section's hide-out. No agents were allowed to know the location of headquarters offices and each section therefore had outside 'safe' premises where the agents came for briefing. In the case of F Section, it was an apartment in Orchard Court, just off Baker Street in Portman Square. The purpose of the meeting was to tell the agent the details of his operational jump and to answer any queries he might have. First one produced maps of his dropping point and discussed it with him, giving him the flight time to get there. Then one opened one's suitcase and took out the exhibits one by one. First the camouflaged jumpsuit which was more elaborate than the overalls he had worn at Ringway. This was the best pocket for his automatic. Was it a Colt .32 he wanted? Okay, that would be ready for him. This pocket on the side of his right leg was for his collapsible spade. As he had not seen one before he found out how it worked. Essential to bury or otherwise dispose of one's parachute and other tell-tale equipment before moving away from the dropping ground. These little blue pills were Benzedrine. If he felt completely done in and had to keep going, swallow one to keep awake for an hour or two longer. This final exhibit was the L tablet. L for Lethal. Just bite through the rubber coating and it's instantaneous. No compulsion to carry one.

It was in the company of both Barry and Dodds-Parker that I attended my first despatch of agents. No.138 Squadron, the Special Duty squadron which catered for both SIS and SOE agents, was still based on the racecourse at Newmarket. Douglas drove us down in one of the office cars, FANY drivers still being a rarity. Baker Street had somehow or other obtained a fleet of American Hudson cars which were both modern and spacious by British standards. They had right-hand steering and must, presumably, have been imported into Britain shortly before hostilities started. Driven subsequently by sometimes diminutive FANYs with heads scarcely topping the steering wheel, they became a recognisable feature of the traffic-free roads of North West London.

Before setting out we had waited to see the list of those operations to be attempted that night. No point in going down should there be a total weather clamp-down, which sometimes occurred. There was one F Section operation scheduled, but I could not tell whether it was one of the men I had trained, as identities were disguised under the code-names given to the air operations. Country section code-names were issued on a generic basis: F Section kept to the names of professions, thus FARMER, STATIONER, MARKSMAN. The same code-name was retained for the resistance network which it was hoped the agent would create.

We drove to Audley End House outside Saffron Walden, which was, at that time, the operational holding school where agents expecting to leave during the current moon period could wait in comfort. It was a somewhat eerie feeling stepping into the magnificent Jacobean Great Hall and finding the family pictures boarded over and the furniture removed. But once one had climbed the dual staircase up to the first floor of the south wing the unoccupied atmosphere disappeared. It was here in the motley wartime furnishings that the FANYs produced excellent meals, catered for the comfort of their temporary guests and generally helped to maintain their morale. Not all departing agents could, for security reasons, be allowed to pass through Audley End but the Commandant, who had just concluded a long business talk with my two companions, explained to me that the strictest rules were enforced against any exchange of real identities or exact destinations. A party of Norwegians might meet a man going to France, or a Belgian meet a Dane, but that was as far as inter-consciousness extended. Indeed, more than one agent had told him that he found it an encouragement to know that other nationalities were in on the fight.

The F Section agent, I learnt, was being escorted direct from Orchard Court to the airfield but Barry, Dodds-Parker and I joined in the early dinner served to those four or five due to leave from Audley End. The meal was indeed good, but I hardly had the heart to tuck in too much with a couple of my neighbours understandably a little off their food. The meal over, we said our farewells and drove the twenty miles in the blackout to Newmarket.

Squadron Leader Benham, our liaison officer with 138 Squadron, was virtually unique in being an RAF officer who positively enjoyed the thought of parachuting. Together with Ray Wooler he had test-jumped experimental equipment at Ringway, but sadly was aboard an aircraft which failed to return after parachuting one of our agents over

Belgium a few months later. When we arrived at the make-shift airfield on Newmarket racecourse he was busy fussing around the agents preparing to leave that evening. I found the F Section agent with his conducting officer and, as it was indeed an ex-student of mine and he seemed pleased to see another friendly face, I remained with him.

His conducting officer was in the process of going through every pocket of his, to check once again that no incriminating document or article, no bus ticket or sixpenny piece had escaped detection. They then went through his wallet to ensure that his (forged) French identity card and other necessary papers were safely tucked away. He was carrying a money belt round his waist and that too was looked at again.

Benham came in with the despatcher who would be travelling with him and together they helped him into his jumpsuit, put his spine-pad in place, handed over his firearm and Benzedrine tablets – he decided against an L tablet – and then fixed his parachute over the top of everything else. Finally, he was given his silk inner gloves and leather outer gauntlets, which he was advised to start wearing in the aircraft, and his rubber helmet to be used for the jump. 'Now you've got one package containing suitcase and personal belongings on its own parachute. That's already aboard your aircraft and your despatcher will push it out immediately after you have jumped. So, you should find it a short way in front of you on the same line you yourself were travelling. Okay? Fine.'

All was set, and Benham was clearly keen to get his various charges into their respective aircraft in good time. There was an emotional moment of farewell between the conducting officer and the agent, I shook the outstretched hand and Benham ushered the despatcher and agent out to the car, which would take them to their aircraft.

On the way back to London my companions became engrossed in plans to cope with an expansion of air operations and problems relating to the expected move of 138 Squadron to a new base. I was left to my own thoughts and I found the image of the lonely figure, weighed down by his equipment, walking away from us to unknown adventures and dangers, hard to forget. The other two had seen it all before on a number of occasions but it was my first time and, besides, it was someone I knew and liked. This was indeed the sharp end of the Section's work and I was glad I had had a glimpse of it early on.

'By the way,' said Dick Barry, turning to me during a pause in their conversation, 'have you found somewhere convenient to live or are you just bedded down temporarily?'

I explained that I had taken up Frank Keary's suggestion and moved into his hotel, and that for the immediate future it was a good stop-gap until I'd had time to look around. He grunted his approval and at the time I had no reason to suppose there was any ulterior move behind his enquiry.

I had telephoned Frank on the day of my arrival and he was clearly delighted that I had taken up his offer. We took a taxi to accommodate my luggage and arrived at the early Victorian narrow-fronted, five-storey building, with its peacetime white painted facade a little the worse for the ravages of wartime London. It was the sort of hotel patronised by elderly couples, widows and widowers of only moderate income, and those of them who had not wished or been unable to move out of London and had stopped on, still occupying their accustomed seats in the lounge and in the dining-room. It was certainly a change from the lively and at times devil-may-care atmosphere of Jimmy Young's mess at Garramor but I was happy to start life in London in Frank's pleasant if unexciting company. What was more, the place was far from expensive and would not exceed my living allowance. This was partly due to the fact that Frank had a room on the fifth floor and I was offered one next to his. There was no lift and when, after a slow and halting ascent, we reached the top landing and Frank turned to me and laughed, nothing more than a protracted wheeze came out.

'It's a long way up,' he gasped, 'but I find the room adequate. It's good enough to sleep in and there's not much time for anything else anyhow. When you're ready, give me a knock and we'll go down to dinner.'

Our entry into the dining-room caused a slight flutter. Frank had told me that he was the only resident in uniform and here was he bringing in another rather younger officer. His small corner table was already laid for two and it was a moment or two before eyes returned to soup plates.

'The food, all things considered, is really not bad here,' said Frank, 'and you'll like Rosie, the waitress. She seems to think that I need feeding up' – a wheezy laugh – 'so I always seem to get more than my fair share. Mind you, I don't think some of the old dears here even eat their full entitlements. Which reminds me, you did hand over your ration card to them? Good!'

Rosie brought us our soup and Frank introduced us. She was a good old-fashioned sort, beyond the age of even considering joining up or doing anything other than what she was accustomed to.

'It's very nice for you to have some company. Captain Keary, and you can be sure I'll do my best to look after both you two gentlemen.' There was no hint here of looking for financial reward; if there was any motive other than goodness of heart it was a desire to do her little bit towards the war effort – by feeding up Captains Keary and van Maurik! Frank beamed at her and I could see that, in a funny way, they both hit it off well together. But I fear Rosie must have had moments of disappointment since, although Frank enjoyed his food and finished the second helpings smuggled to him, his gaunt face never blossomed out but his already bushy eyebrows did seem to grow bushier.

When I moved into a communal flat a few of weeks later I was sorry to leave Frank but I knew that he would continue to be well looked after by Rosie.

My coming south enabled me to take a train down to Tunbridge Wells in the non-moon period to visit my parents. My mother, with her usual energy and efficiency, was kept busy driving all over Kent giving pep-talks to Women's Institutes on behalf of the Ministry of Information, as well as being part of the local Civil Defence mobile squad. At a later stage, she became head of the Tunbridge Wells Women's Voluntary Services. My father still went up to the City to run the cigar factory and it seemed that the war had not cut down cigar smoking, perhaps even the contrary. My mother told me that he was beginning to suffer attacks of angina but would not take medical advice. When I was still a boy my mother had become a Christian Scientist and my father had followed suit but, whereas my mother had since become disillusioned, my father still read Mary Baker Eddy's *Science and Health* daily and refused medicaments. 'He derives comfort from it,' she told me, 'and I think it's better to leave it as it is, rather than have a row which would upset him but probably not change his views. What would help him is if you could ever find a moment to visit the factory, say, at lunchtime. He thinks this would be good for the morale of the workforce. I'm sure it would do even more for his own morale if he could show you off to the old cigar-makers, many of whom remember you from the old days.'

I did indeed find an opportunity to take the Underground to Old Street and to revisit the factory in Bath Street. We climbed the stairs to find old van Damm, London-born despite his name, still in charge of cigar-making where I shook the hand of various East End ladies, greyer and even plumper than I recollected them. 'Shame that Doris ain't no longer wiv us,' one of them told me. 'She remembered you comin' round wiv yer Dad when you was only a little kid. Fair 'air you 'ad, almost white. She was killed in one of them bad raids before Christmas, Doris was.'

We poked our noses into the aromatic drying room discovering Huntley miraculously still active in his cigar-box making department and, back on the ground floor again, I spoke to the rather austere Mr Mitchell who had sat in the same chair doing the accounts ever since I could remember. Then father and I walked down the road to the ABC restaurant where he stood me lunch. He had had to give up, he told me, his age-old custom of bringing up home-made sandwiches in his Dutch tin *boterham trommel* and eating them at his desk while he worked. The ingredients just weren't available any longer on one's ration card. We finished our lunch and I had to get back. He thanked me for coming and I knew that he had enjoyed our short time together as much as I had.

One of the nice things about working in AL Section was that one felt at the hub of things; virtually all the country sections had to come to us if they wanted to get their operators into the Field. That meant that one got to know the country section heads and those of their staff dealing with the despatch of agents. In the smaller sections, one got to know them all. In the early days they cultivated you, went out of their way to be friendly and pleasant, hoping against hope that in some way you might be able to promote their operations and ensure they were given priority. There was, of course, no question of this as priority stars were allocated only by Gubbins and his staff and, bearing this in mind and the weather conditions, it was up to the squadron on the night to decide which operations had the best chance of success. It did not take the country section officers long to grasp this fact but friendly relations continued with one exception. The following year the Dutch Section was taken over by a certain Lieutenant Colonel Blizzard and he made a practice of coming into our offices and trying to bully us into putting on his operations at the expense of others. When he received the written debrief on the result of one of his operations he would could come in waving it at us and pointing out that the pilot had reported strong and well-laid out reception lights facilitating an easy drop. 'Tell the RAF,' he would say in unpleasant tones, 'to forget all about the other bloody people who can't organise themselves and to concentrate on those who can.' It was long after my time in the Section that it was discovered the Germans had penetrated the Dutch circuits and were laying out the excellent reception lights themselves and hauling in the agents as they dropped! I tried not to feel any Schadenfreude over Blizzard's plight but it was at that point that I became grateful to my mother for discouraging me from learning Dutch, since otherwise I might have been recruited as an agent for the Dutch Section at my first interview at Horse Guards Parade.

All sections inevitably had their early set-backs and misfortunes but nothing on that scale. The first time I took the sample suitcase and went to brief agents on their forthcoming operation was when I visited the first two SOE Danish agents to be parachuted back into their homeland. The section head was Lieutenant Commander Ralph Hollingworth RNVR, who had run a small business in Copenhagen before the war and who, as a co-opted member of the British Embassy, had been given safe passage out of the country when the Germans invaded. He was a small and cheerful man whom we all liked and he now introduced me to his two agents, Carl Bruhn, just qualified as a doctor and tipped off as a star performer, and Mogens Hammer, a very large and heavily-built man, his wireless operator. We examined on the map their dropping point south-west of Copenhagen and I explained the operational procedure which would be followed and then displayed my wares. I had an attentive audience as this was a first time for Hollingworth as well as for the agents. In the event these men were not parachuted until 28 December 1941, by which time, as will appear later, I was on my way to Malta. I did not hear until sometime later that, by what was described as a chance in a million, Bruhn's static line became detached from its anchorage in the aircraft and he fell to his death with his parachute still unopened. Hammer luckily landed safely and survived the war.

Major Maurice Buckmaster was the head of F Section and his team was numerically the strongest both in headquarters officers and in recruited agents. I, like everyone else, got to know Maurice but I also had dealings with a number of other members of his staff: with the rather humourless Thomas Cadett, the pre-war *Times* correspondent in Paris; with the more amiable Nic Boddington, ex-Reuters; and, later on with Georges Bégué and Gerry Morel after they returned from serving in the Field. And every so often we received a visit from Vera Atkins, charming and unrufflable, with some query or some piece of information to assist us, perhaps better to understand agents' messages copied to us.

Here I should explain that AL Section automatically received copies of all agents' messages dealing with air operational matters. This not only enabled us, in cases where speed was essential, to anticipate the arrival of the ATF – the request form for air transport from country sections – and to get on with checking up the dropping ground, but also to double-check the information passed on to us, a process which occasionally brought mistakes to light.

As well as F Section, de Gaulle's Free French special services were also despatching agents to France. De Gaulle naturally considered that only his men should operate in France but the Foreign Office and the Chiefs of Staff thought otherwise. The root of the trouble was that the only British objective was to defeat the Germans whereas de Gaulle had a dual aim: militarily to defeat the Germans and politically to ensure that he took over power in a liberated France. This latter aim came to dictate his policy in Resistance matters. He planned a centralised command of Resistance within France under his control, which the British feared might be penetrated by the Germans and neutralised when the invasion came. SOE wished to create a series of independent networks reporting back only to London, reminiscent of the Communist cell system on a large scale. In its support of any émigré government working into its own country, SOE was instructed to keep the two trump cards in its hands: communications and means of transport. In the case of the Free French every facility was afforded them and they built up their organisation in France as they wished, but SOE remained aware of what was happening and were not prepared to fall in with de Gaulle's contention that only the French should run Resistance in France and that SOE should desist.

Since the Free French had to come to SOE for their air transport, this meant that AL Section had to handle their operations as well as all others. A separate country section known as R/F had been set up to liaise with the Free French and we dealt with them. They were housed in 1, Dorset Square, which had previously been the headquarters of Bertram Mills Circus and one has to admit that, early on, there were moments when one was tempted to refer to them as clowns; for example, when they passed on from the French, presumably without checking themselves, the coordinates of a dropping point which indicated it to be somewhere out in the Bay of Biscay! The first head of R/F was Eric Piquet-Wicks, whom Douglas Dodds-Parker rightly described in his book *Setting Europe Ablaze* as a gay and helpful colleague but calling him 'a little unpredictable' was perhaps an understatement. He had an assistant, an older officer with First World War medals up, who was also inclined to be 'unpredictable', but I was glad to find that the junior in the Section was Terry O'Bryan Tear, whom I had trained in Scotland and knew to be efficient. He had been a keen student but, looking much younger than his twenty-two years of age, he had not been recommended, it seemed, to be sent to the Field as an F Section agent. His only failure at Garramor had been his complete inability to climb a rope and, luckily, I had been able to hide the fact that I too suffered from the same disability. Terry survived a changeover in staff and remained a valuable member of a new-look section.

The Belgian Section known as T was at this time under the command of Claude Knight. He used to come down and discuss his operations with us and, unfortunately, he had a stammer of the type with which music hall comedians habitually brought down the house. A genuinely nice man, one dreaded the moment when one could no longer keep a straight face. If one could see one's colleagues grinning behind his back the strain was almost unbearable. I escorted one of his agents code-named MOUSSE from the Despatch Station at Audley End to the airfield on the night of his parachuting. Beforehand the FANYs served the usual farewell dinner and MOUSSE was chatty and apparently unconcerned and he confided to me that one of the things he would miss most would be Vera Lynn's radio programmes. I discovered there was one to be broadcast that evening and the FANYs let him hear it before we left. I was touched by his ability to enjoy such a thing at a moment like that and I hoped that the stark reality of life under the Nazis would not come as too much of a shock to him. I sometimes wondered what had become of him and was delighted years later to read in Dodds-Parker's book that he had eventually turned up in North Africa, having escaped from occupied territory after his subversive activities in Belgium had caught up with him.

Dealing with the Polish Section in SOE was always something of an adventure, which was almost entirely due to the personality of H.B. Perkins, its head. Perks, as he was universally known, had been a British business man in Poland before the war and, on the arrival of the British Military Mission shortly before the German invasion of that country and the commencement of the Second World War, Perks was co-opted as a civilian member of that Mission. Its second-in-command was the then Lieutenant Colonel Gubbins. Back safely in Britain, Perks set out to get himself an Army commission. He was a heftily built man, as strong physically as he was mentally; he called a spade a spade and had no time for bureaucracy. He told later how he had been posted to a cavalry regiment and had to go through further training before qualifying for his commission. In his ignorance, he took it for granted that the instruction would centre round the use of armoured vehicles but on his way by train to the Cavalry Training School at Weedon he noticed that others had riding-boots sticking out of their kit. He was asked whether he didn't agree that there was still a role for the horse in modern warfare. 'You wouldn't ask a bloody silly question like that,' he replied, 'if you'd been in Poland when the Germans invaded.' But to his astonishment he found that he was faced with tough riding instruction and whereas virtually all the other cadets had been brought up on a horse he had never sat on one in his thirty-odd years of life. But Perks was not easily beaten: he fell off at the simplest jumps, he was so sore he could hardly walk but he had just one advantage over the others, he had no ingrained bad habits to correct. He passed out top of the class and went to join Gubbins in SO2, SOE's predecessor. Perks fought hard on behalf of his Poles but until Halifaxes replaced the old Whitley aircraft, the distance factor inhibited air operations as did the months of long daylight.

His relations with his Polish counter-parts were excellent and it was said he could drink most of them under the table if need be. I attended one or two SOE staff parties at which both Perks and Gubbins were present. Perks produced his party trick which needed the presence of half-a-dozen fresh eggs. These were, of course, a very rare commodity, but Perks, who could swear like a trooper, could also wield a soft-spoken gentle persuasion to get what he wanted. Six wine glasses filled with water were lined up on a table and then a flat piece of board was placed over the glasses. He then perched the six eggs, in egg cups if I remember correctly, on the board, one egg above each glass. Announcing that not infrequently the trick misfired, he hauled out two of the more attractive FANY officers and placed them six or eight feet from the edge of the table, instructing them to catch any eggs which might, if things went wrong again, fly in their direction. He'd promised to return them unbroken. Distracting people's attention with more patter, he raised his massive fist and gave the board a smart but well directed tap. This sent the board flying towards the girls but the six eggs plopped unbroken into the wine glasses. Gubbins was now encouraged to perform his mess party trick. He called for a full glass of beer, placed it on the floor and took off his uniform jacket. With no effort at all he performed a hand-stand and doing an arm bend he somehow got his teeth round the rim of the glass and, tilting it slowly upwards, he poured the liquid down his throat – or perhaps one should say up his throat since he was still upside-down.

M.R.D. Foot records that Perks was once seen to bend a poker double with his bare hands. This was, I think, true, as was a tale about him during his post-war service with the Foreign Office. He was on the committee of a senior staff luncheon club in the basement of one of the so-called outhouses. In their deliberations, they discussed the removal of what appeared to be a partition wall consisting of some sort of beaverboard in order to make more space for tables. The administration officer of the building, a true bureaucrat and therefore a target for Perks, became more pompous than usual and declared the matter would have to be examined in detail. At the next meeting, this officer informed the committee that he had looked into things and the matter was not as simple as it might seem. The committee might be surprised to learn that the innocent looking boarding was hard up against a solid wall, one of the supports of the whole building, and could under no circumstances be touched. Perks rose from the table and went up to the boarding. 'Very interesting,' said he, 'so this is solid right through?' 'Yes, sir!' But Perks too had looked into matters and raising his fist he punched it straight through the boarding, revealing a gaping nothingness behind.

There were other good people to deal with in the Polish Section, if not quite so unique as Perks himself. George Klauber was a favourite of ours with his soft-spoken, friendly efficiency as was Vera Long, Perk's secretary, who hid behind her charming blue-eyed look of innocence a remarkable ability to keep Perks pointed in the right direction. Apparently a pair of opposites, they remained together as a team for a very long time.

The second mode of air transport to France was the clandestine landing operation carried out by 161 Squadron, the sister Special Duty squadron to 138 Squadron. These pick-ups, when I first arrived in AL Section, were infrequent, roughly one a month, and were usually handled by Douglas and Derek Dodson who already had experience of them. By the time I left the Section some year later their number had arisen to around ten a month and the Lysanders, limited at a pinch to three passengers, had been supplemented by twin-engine Hudsons which took up to ten. *We Landed by Moonlight*, the invaluable and indeed only researched complete account of these operations, gives the astonishing minimum total of 443 men and women ferried into wartime France and 635 exfiltrated. Hugh Verity, its author and pick-up flight commander from December 1942 onwards, earned a double DSO and a DFC leading his intrepid team and I leave his book to tell its tale. There is no doubt in my mind that the exploits of this select group of pilots, some of whom lost their lives on the job, made an indelible impression on the French countryside over which they operated. On a trip through

'Resistance Country' made forty years later Hugh Verity, Vera Atkins and I discovered that the code-word of 'Orion', given to a large meadow on which both Hugh and Bob Hodges, later to become Air Chief Marshal Sir Lewis Hodges KCB, CBE, DSO, DFC, had landed Hudsons, had now become the official name of the main square – Place D'Orion – in the nearby little town of Bletterans. Furthermore, monuments had been put up on the edge of other fields once used by the pilots of 161 Squadron. Elsewhere a shop-keeper engaged us in conversation and, bringing the topic round to wartime Resistance, told us of the great book written by one of the gallant RAF pilots who risked their lives to help the French. When I could get a word in edgeways I introduced my companion to him as the author of that book, rendering him speechless for more than a moment or two! It was nice to know, however, that local memories were both long and warm.

I did get the chance to escort one or two parties of agents down to Tangmere Airfield, which was the forward base from which pick-up flights took place. For security reasons when operations were scheduled, the pilots and the passengers kept away from the main airfield buildings and used a small cottage just near the main gates of the RAF station. Instead of returning to London after seeing the agents off, conducting officers and their FANY drivers had to wait five hours or more until the aircraft returned. One could perhaps doze off a while but the tension mounted as the estimated time of return came near. In this small and closely-knit group, where the pilots not flying that night were nevertheless personally involved with the success or otherwise of their colleague out over enemy territory, the excitement and joy when a returning lone aircraft was signalled was spontaneous and heart-warming. If all had gone well, then a fitting welcome to the incoming pilot and passengers took place before the convoy of Baker Street cars set off for London.

One occasion that stuck in my mind was after I had left AL Section and was already on Colin Gubbins' staff. I was asked to take a newly joined senior officer down to Tangmere so that he could see how things worked. I do not remember the identity of the Lysander pilot who flew that night but I well recollect the long wait in the room used as ops room and mess. Wing-Commander Pickard was then the CO of 161 Squadron and he organised a poker school; I was not a poker player but luckily my visitor was and four or five of them were soon apparently engrossed in their game, although I knew that part of their minds were focused elsewhere. I remember the sudden break-up of the poker school when the news came through that the Lysander was overhead and the excitement as the pilot and his incoming passengers arrived back at the cottage. I found I could not take my eyes off the Frenchmen's shoes with the mud of France still sticking to them and the First World War rumour, that Russian reinforcements had been identified in Britain through the snow on their boots, came to mind. But this time our passengers, if they themselves hardly believed it, were really in England and the mud was genuine.

Pickard, the CO, large, fair-haired and good-looking, was a nationally known figure as he had 'starred' in a very popular and stirring Ministry of Information film *Target for Tonight* in which he played the skipper of bomber F for Freddie. He had already had a distinguished career and now he was to fly a number of successful pick-up operations before moving on to take command of a squadron of Mosquito fighter-bombers. He led the low-level pinpoint bombing raid on Amiens prison in February 1944. This had been requested by French Resistance and had the object of releasing prisoners shortly to be executed. The outer walls of the prison were breached, the guard posts attacked and the internal main gates shattered. In the confusion 258 prisoners, of whom some eighty were members of Resistance groups, made good their escape but fifty-six who failed to do so were shot by guards. Pickard's aircraft was shot down and he too sadly met his death.

As regards Hugh Verity, he continued with his pick-up operations over the space of fifteen moon periods up until the end of 1943. He was then given a well-earned rest and came to work in AL Section, bringing with him unique experience and great charm of manner. I was not in Baker Street at the time but colleagues and friends had the benefit of his company.

But going back to the run-up to Christmas 1941, I had now been in the Section for three months and changes were happening all around me. Philip Rea had moved over to No. 64 and, pleasantly enough after his gaffe at not recognising the Chief Director on the telephone, was soon to become personal staff officer to the new CD, Charles Hambro. Colonel Wilson, mainly responsible for my move to London and who always gave me a friendly smile when we met in the lift, had handed over Training and was now in charge of the Norwegian Section. So far, the Norwegians had made little or no call on the services of AL but this was to change in the new year. Our Section itself was expanding all the time and new packing facilities near Tempsford Airfield, to which the Special Duty squadrons had transferred, were set up for the increasing number of arms containers being sent to the Field. These were cylindrical, indeed bomb-shaped, and were designed to fit into the aircraft's bomb bays and were released by the bomb-aimer over the target in the same way as bombs themselves. Smaller objects such as W/T sets, personal luggage and the like were still sent as packages through the hole, if for no other reason that their wrappings were much easier to dispose of. In general, new faces were appearing every day in Norgeby House, although the influx of FANY officers into AL Section was still a month or two distant.

I had so far remained in Frank Keary's hotel and, provided I got back in time, I found his gentle character a pleasant relaxation after the bustle and sometimes the panics of Section work. His work, being less operational, allowed him to take things at a more even pace and to turn up regularly every evening in the dining room. But as far as I was concerned, the more involved I was the more irregular my working pattern became. If I was not off to the airfield, I could well have to stay into the evening as a result of messages received from the Field proposing new dropping operations. I would then miss the time for dinner in the hotel and instead two or three of us, when we shut up shop, would go over to the Marks and Spencer's canteen. No. 64, Baker Street, our building across the road, had been the head office of M & S pre-war and they still had premises at the back which could be reached from a side street. There they had a canteen which kept open late at night and we were invited to use it at night-time. I was never quite certain what kept their employees busy at that hour but there was always a handful there and we were grateful for being able to get a snack which, being M & S, was as good or better than anything else around. The fact, however, that I was missing a number of dinners I was paying for did begin to strike me as a waste of money, which I could have put to better use.

I had little hesitation in accepting Dick Barry's invitation to come into a flat that he shared with several other SOE officers, and which had several advantages. It was much closer to the office than my hotel and in easy walking distance; it worked out quite a bit cheaper, provided we kept the numbers up, (hence the colonel's interest in getting me in) and dinner times were more flexible. I took the first opportunity of inspecting it.

The flat was situated on Park Road which branched off the top of Baker Street and ran parallel to Regents Park and Regents Court. It consisted of a terrace of Victorian or perhaps Edwardian three-storey houses containing custom-built apartments, and No. 22 occupied the whole of a second floor. It belonged, so one was given to understand, to a gentleman who took fright at the sound of the first bomb – or perhaps even the first air-raid siren – and retired to the depths of the country for the duration of the war. He had left behind sufficient furniture for the place to be habitable and, as accommodation in Central London was not exactly sought after during the war, the weekly rent was agreeably low. The sitting-room, at the front of the house, was spacious and boasted a splendid grand piano which had probably been too difficult to move and so had to remain. The windows looked across the road to the Georgian terraces which flanked the Park, to which a narrow passageway gave access. The central hall was used as a dining area from which bedrooms and kitchen led off. The latter was the domain of the middle-aged Swiss housekeeper and cook who had been hired by previous SOE inhabitants of the flat. I would have been interested to have found out more about her background and which parts of Switzerland she knew best but, as I was to discover, she had a permanent air of disapproval about her and was not the sort of person one lightly chatted up. She did however cook reasonably well with the limited ingredients at her disposal and she had accepted the fact that we could not always keep to peacetime timetables. Nevertheless, I was to come to miss Rosie's cheerful and obliging face at mealtimes but one can't have everything.

I finished the week at my hotel, said goodbye to Rosie and other kind people – Frank I knew I would continue to see – and then moved in to 22 Regents Court.

I now come to the final country section with which I then had dealings - that which concerned itself with the Soviet Union. It kept a fairly low profile and I suspect that quite a number of people in SOE had little knowledge of its existence. It was unlike other country sections in that it had nothing to do with encouraging resistance within the country concerned; its duties consisted in liaising with the Soviet security service. The NKVD as it was then known was the successor of the original OGPU of ill repute and, in more modern times, it became known as the KGB. To explain this rather unsavoury connection it is worth looking back into recent history. Between the two wars British Governments and indeed the British people viewed with extreme distaste the communist regime in the Soviet Union: the forced collectivisation of the early thirties and consequent starvation of a million or more peasants, the purges of military officers and intellectuals, indeed of anyone of whom Stalin disapproved, the forced labour camps and, worst of all, the

Soviet avowed intent of spreading the communist revolution to other countries. In Germany Hitler made use of the threat of communism in his rise to power and in the immediate pre-war era the two totalitarian states glared at each other angrily. Ten days before the outbreak of war the Western Allies were completely taken aback by the Molotov-von Ribbentrop non-aggression pact under the terms of which the Soviet Union undertook to remain neutral in the event of war and in return obtained a slice of Poland.

Hitler, with his rear secured, overran the Low Countries and France and, giving up the immediate idea of invading Britain, turned east and invaded the Soviet Union in June 1941. Stalin, recovering from his surprise and with German tanks driving deep into Russia, began calling on Churchill to start a second front in the West in order to relieve the pressure on the Soviet forces. Churchill was not prepared to jeopardise everything by attempting a wholly unprepared attack, neither were the Americans when they came in to the war a year and more later. But if Britain was not prepared to precipitate 'instant invasion', other means of bringing assistance to what were now known as 'Our Gallant Allies' – and Russians were certainly fighting gallantly in defence of Russian soil – were given priority. Chief among these were, of course, the arms convoys escorted by the Royal Navy to Soviet Artic ports, which suffered horrific casualties in 1942; Convoy PQ-17, for example, set out with thirty-six merchant ships of which only eleven reached their destination. SOE, in a very small way, was called upon to make a contribution. An SOE mission under Brigadier Hill[1] was despatched to Moscow and an NKVD counter-part accepted in London. The mutual aid was, one suspects, chiefly one way.

Douglas Dodds-Parker relates in his book how Stalin appealed personally to Churchill for help in parachuting two German communist agents into Germany as the range was too far from any available Soviet base. This, as Douglas points out, was an unpalatable request but at the time impossible to refuse. (One has to remember that not long after the policy was adopted to arm anyone, communists included, who was prepared to attack the Axis powers, Tito being a prime example.) Gubbins and Dodds-Parker were summoned to 10 Downing Street and Douglas was instructed by the prime minister to handle operation WHISKY personally and to keep the agents' identity secret. After a first attempt, the Whitley, heavily laden with fuel, crashed on take-off and

---

[1] This is George Alexander Hill (1892–1968).

the pilot and one agent were killed. At a second attempt, the longer-range Halifax scarcely had sufficient hours of darkness to penetrate Germany and get back before daylight, but under pressure the squadron undertook the flight. The aircraft failed to return.

I became involved with two further operations of a similar nature which went under the code-name PICKAXE but in this case the destinations were in Western European countries other than Germany. I am glad to say that no further aircraft were lost but the first of these indirectly had an influence on my future life.

The NKVD officers lived in Campden Hill, close to Kensington Church Street, and this is where two of them together with the sole agent had been picked up by the section conducting officer and taken for a meal to the Despatch Station. Here I met the party, escorted them to the airfield and saw them through the departure drill. The section officer, as far as I remember, decided to wait on to see the return of the aircraft and I volunteered to take the two NKVD officers back to London, for which I was provided by the Despatch Station with a second car.

The FANY driver was a tall, ruddy faced twenty-year-old, pleasant looking if not exactly beautiful, her tightly belted-in tunic emphasising her good figure. On her shoulder, I noticed an Ensign's single pip.

The two NKVD men got in to the back of the car, looking for all the world like something out of the Greta Garbo film *Ninotchka*, their overcoats reaching far down their shins, their trilby hats square upon their heads and brims close above their eyes. I climbed in beside the driver and we headed off for London.

It was approaching full moon, there was scarcely a cloud in the sky and the shields on our headlights did little to hinder our progress. We just hoped conditions were as favourable across the Channel; if they were, we should be set for a successful night's operations. Our driver handled the car with confidence and once we hit what was still known as the Great North Road we looked forward to a rapid return to London. All went well until we came to the first little slit of red light to which traffic lights had been reduced. The driver dutifully stopped but so did the engine. She then tried the starter but nothing happened. She tried and tried again but all to no effect.

'What's the matter with this darn car?'

'I don't know. I was given it at the last minute and told to drive it to London as it was due for service.'

'I'll say it was! Do you understand what goes on under the bonnet?'

'Not my best subject. Do you?'

I had to admit I didn't. 'What do you suggest we do?'

'You'll have to give me a push-start.'

I leant back to the passengers in the back. 'I'm very sorry but you will have to help me push,' and I made pushing movements with my arms in case they had not got the gist of it.

'Da, da, okay.' They grinned and waggled their heads from side to side, indicating perhaps that similar predicaments were not unknown in their country.

Being fresh and keen we soon had the Hudson crossing the intersection at some lick and, with the engine restarting, we leapt aboard and were on our way again. I leant back to express my thanks and they shrugged their shoulders and grinned, which I interpreted as ready to oblige if you ever need us.

On the next couple of occasions that we met traffic lights, we sailed over on the green and, just when I was beginning to hope that our troubles were over, we again had to stop at a red light and again the engine stalled. Needless to say, the starter still showed no signs of life.

'Now, before I ask these gentlemen to get out and push again,' I said a bit huffily, for I disliked looking foolish and inefficient in front of foreigners – I still do – 'just remember, if we get held up again, put your clutch out as soon as you can and keep the engine revved up with the accelerator. Either that or just ignore the lights unless there is imminent danger of collision.' A stubborn look had settled on the driver's face and I was not certain that my advice had been accepted. However, I had no option but to call out the pushers, whose grins I noticed were not quite so wide as before.

But my fears turned out to have been justified. Our driver clearly had no intention of following my instructions and the closer we came to London the more frequently we had to get out and push. My offer, or perhaps my order, to allow me to drive was equally disdainfully ignored.

By the time we reached Campden Hill I felt both physically and mentally exhausted. So, I suspected, did our driver but I could not bring myself to feel sorry for her. Our NKVD friends had, of course, to give one more push to be shot of us and I had a final glimpse of their legless feet pounding away under their overcoats and their identical hats still immovable on their heads.

We drove through the streets of Kensington, deserted except for the occasional patrolling ARP warden, and turned eastwards into the Bayswater Road. We spoke not a word but our nerves were on edge, so close to home and yet perhaps still too far. Our luck held as we drove alongside Hyde Park, the silhouettes of leafless trees and the barrage balloons high in the sky plainly visible in the moonlight. I kept my fingers firmly crossed and we managed to keep going past Marble Arch and left into Portman Street but here disaster struck again. The lights leading into Portman Square turned red as we came up to them, but it was not easy to be quite sure of a clear passage.

'Go on, keep going!' I shouted, but FANY training had instinctively caused the driver to brake and her effort to pick up speed again merely resulted in the temperamental engine packing in.

I opened my door and got out and just in case the young lady was in any doubt, I put my head back in and, maybe rather pompously, declared that if she thought I was going to push a Hudson all by myself she was decidedly mistaken. No, I was going to walk the last three or four hundred yards to the office and once there I would ring up Transport and ask them to collect her from the traffic lights.

I thought, as I walked away, that I would now be able to wash my hands of the whole affair but, as events turned out, this was not to be the case. The argument as to how to have kept the engine running was to spread over the next forty years.

At the end of the war when I had entered civilian life, if the company were suitable I would sometimes tell the story of my frustrating wartime drive to London at one of our dinner parties. My wife at the other end of the table would listen patiently until I had finished.

'I would point out,' she would then say, 'that my husband never drove a Hudson in his life and is not qualified to talk. In any case' – pregnant pause – 'no *gentleman* would ever have left a lady stranded at the traffic lights in the blackout!'

CHAPTER 9

Malta, Gibraltar and the King's Oranges

It came like a bolt from the blue. I had thought that, for the time being at least and for better or worse, I was anchored down in Baker Street. I had, after all, only very recently moved in to more permanent-seeming accommodation at the suggestion of Dick Barry, Gubbins' chief operations and planning officer. He, I thought, would have known, but now unexpectedly the situation had changed.

I followed Douglas at his request into his office. He was not the sort of boss who often sent for you. On the contrary, he would prefer to come into your office and drape his six-foot-four's worth of well-proportioned body in a chair beside your desk or on the edge of a table. He would chat to you and sometimes ask your opinion, even though he had probably already made up his own mind about any given problem. He was, in effect, a boss who made you feel good and in on things and consequently got the best out of you. To be asked to step in to the seclusion of his own office was out of the norm and I began to wonder whether I had made a cock-up of some sort.

'How would you like to take a trip to Malta?'

'To Malta? Yes, you bet I would! What goes on there?'

'Well, I'll tell you briefly what the AL angle is and later we'll get someone to give you more detail on the political background. I expect you've seen from the newspapers that in Yugoslavia guerrillas under one General Mihailovi have taken to the mountains. Getting early wind of this, SOE HQ in Cairo put ashore a British Liaison Officer with a W/T operator three months ago and he succeeded in meeting up with the general. Now unfortunately the W/T link has gone dead and Cairo are completely out of touch. They now intend to parachute in another BLO and W/T operator to find out what's happened to the first man and to re-establish contact with Mihailovi if possible. The operation can only be done by a Whitley from Malta and 138 Squadron are to send out a flight to take on this task. You are to be the AL representative to go out with them and your job will be to keep an eye on the parachuting side. You'll have to brief the crew on the dropping point and be the liaison between the crew and the agents. In order to catch the moon period, you'll have to leave here on Boxing Day, weather permitting, and the agents will be flown in or shipped by submarine from Cairo to arrive in Malta on or before that date.'

'Is there an SOE office in Malta I'll be in touch with?'

'No, but there's the DSO, the Defence Security Officer. He's an MI5 bod and he has his own communications with both London and Cairo. We'll be able to send you any additional instructions through him, but the air side is up to the senior pilot and you, so you'll have to get on with it yourselves. Our good friend Squadron Leader Ron Hockey is, I'm glad to say, organising things at the Newmarket end so you'll have to be in touch with him when the time comes.'

'Can I tell the other chaps in the Section about all this?'

'Yes, they'll have to know but in general I wouldn't bruit it around too much. And by the way, don't hang around once you've done the job. Malta is none too healthy a place just now and there'll be plenty of work waiting for you when you get back.' It was still the non-moon period and I had, in any case, been intending to take the opportunity of seeing my parents as I knew I would have been on duty over Christmas. Now I would be even busier around that time.

My parents were as usual delighted to see me and it was not long before I let drop the 'good' news that I would be away for a while on a trip overseas. Their visible reaction made me realise that from their point of view the news was alarming rather than good. This was partly due to the fact that I was unable to give any hint of where I was going or what I would be doing. I had never said a word of what I had been engaged on in Scotland nor now down in London. But with my knowledge of languages and the parachute wings on my sleeve they knew I was up to something unusual. Now they clearly suspected the worst and when you can't give any information it's not easy to be convincingly reassuring. It brought home to me the problems facing agents who really were disappearing into occupied territory.

I went across to No. 64 to learn a little about the situation in Yugoslavia from an officer with experience of the Balkans, now working in the rear link for the Cairo station. It wasn't entirely essential for the limited part I was to play but I felt that, as the only SOE officer going out, it would be wise to be in possession of some background knowledge. Apart from my own interest, I wanted to be able to reply to any questions I might receive from the aircrews as to what their journey was really all about.

'The State of Yugoslavia, you know, is a recent invention,' he told me, 'but as you ask for a potted historical background, here goes. At the end of the First World War the victorious Allies created its forerunner, the Kingdom of the Serbs, Croats and Slovenes but this also included a mixed bag of other Balkan odds and sods of mixed religions. It was designated a constitutional parliamentary monarchy under the hereditary Serbian King Alexander I. But with the Serbs bossing it over the others, the Croats quickly took umbrage. There is, of course, an in-built animosity between these two, intensified by the Croats having been part of the Austro-Hungarian empire and having fought alongside the Austrians in the Great War, whereas the Serbs sided with the Allies and suffered a disastrous defeat.

'Alexander became more and more fed up with all the squabbling and finally dissolved parliament. Later he brought in a new constitution increasing his own powers and at the same time the name of the country was changed to Yugoslavia, that is to say the Southern Slav State. But not very long after – in 1934 to be exact – King Alexander was assassinated. History, you will observe, is inclined to repeat itself in the Balkans. Alexander's son Peter was still a boy so his brother Prince Paul was meantime made Regent. And that's what he remained until earlier this year when Hitler's strategic plans necessitated the domination of Yugoslavia and free passage for his troops. Putting great pressure on Paul he persuaded him to sign the Anti-Comintern Pact which had the effect of aligning Yugoslavia with the Axis Powers. This brought forth an immediate coup by Serb officers who deposed Paul and put Peter in his place. Hitler retaliated by flattening Belgrade with his bombers and sending in troops to take over the country. Peter, as you know, escaped to Cairo and is now here in this country.

'We remained uncertain as to quite what was going on inside Yugoslavia until Colonel (as he was then) Mihailovi started broadcasting weak signals from the mountains where he had taken refuge. These were luckily intercepted and Cairo, remarkably quick on the draw for them, landed Hudson, a British officer, and his W/T operator by submarine on the Yugoslav coast. Hudson soon found there were more groups of resisters than we had foreseen as, before even reaching Mikailovi, he ran across a sizeable bunch of Communist-inspired partisans. He went on to find Mikailovi and, W/T contact established, things began to look up. King Peter, knowing Mikailovi to be an ardent and loyal monarchist, promoted him to general and made him Minister of War to his government in exile. Then Hudson without warning went off the air. We suspect it's the set or the generator that's packed in but one can't, of course, be sure. The only way to find out is to send in another BLO and another W/T man. And that's what we hope the RAF and you will do for us.'

'We'll do our best. Where about do you think the dropping zone is likely to be?'

'I reckon it should be somewhere in the Sarajevo area, as that's where he was when we were last in contact. It's up to Cairo and the chaps themselves, of course, to come up with suggestions.'

'That's fine although, mind you, the pilot flying the sortie will have to put his chop on it.'

'Yes, obviously.'

As I thanked my colleague for putting me in the picture, he murmured, half to himself, a hope that those bloody Balkans wouldn't spend as much time fighting each other as they did fighting the Germans. I thought that a bit cynical at the time but, unlike him, I didn't know that part of the world.

The departure date for Malta was confirmed as Boxing Day and, speaking to Ron Hockey on the scrambler, he told me I should be available as from about midday. We would be leaving from Stradishall, 138 Squadron's newly-occupied base, in daylight, making an intermediate stop at Abingdon, where, fully tanked up, we would continue on our way later that evening.

I decided that the best thing I could do would be to spend the evening of Christmas Day at our despatch station, which would be handy for getting to the airfield next morning. I booked a lift in one of the cars going down, since being already in the moon period it was business as usual. I had one bag with me and nothing much else as I knew I would be provided with a flying suit for the flight out.

As far as I remember there were few joes scheduled to fly, which was perhaps fortunate for them as they would have missed a party of some proportions which developed that night. The FANYS had made everything as Christmassy as possible and they celebrated the occasion by being out of uniform and in such glad rags as they had available.

Through my visits of the past couple of months I had got to know most of them, although new girls were always appearing. The FANYs and SOE had hit it off well together and the fact that they did not come under normal military jurisdiction made things easier all round.

The Funny FANYS, as our detachment were nicknamed to distinguish them from the main line branch, could, and did, take on any type of job demanded of them and there were no restrictions, provided their own commanders approved, where they were posted.

We were forgathered for pre-dinner drinks when a smartly dressed figure came up to me. I realised she was the driver whom I had last seen sitting angrily at the wheel of her car at the traffic lights in Portman Square. I was relieved to find that she was now smiling.

'I expect you hoped you wouldn't meet me again but I just wanted to wish you a Happy Christmas.' I wasn't certain whether there was a touch of sarcasm in her words but her smile made me give her the benefit of the doubt.

'Happy Christmas to you. No, I'm glad to see you again.' Indeed, I was, as I wanted to ask her how long she had had to wait to be rescued; I even wanted to apologise for being rude to her but somehow, I didn't get round to either. On the other hand, she didn't seem to have any remorse at having made me push her car all the way from Newmarket to Baker Street. So, we both ignored the subject and began what turned out to be a pleasant conversation.

Dinner was announced by a couple of girls coming in and shouting over the top of the buzz of conversation. The Station Commandant led the joe he was currently talking to off to table and I sat down with my companion, who said that she was excused helping to serve the dinner, as she had been driving all that day. Partly out of politeness, partly out of interest I brought the topic round to herself. Her name was Winifred Hay. Scottish, she said, as one might guess from the name.

'But you don't sound like a Scot.'

'Oh, I can if I want to! No, you see my father's job moved down to London when I was five or six. At first, I thought the other children at school sounded frightful but inevitably it was not long before I began to talk like they did. But I didn't stop being Scottish and it was always a great moment when we set off by train on our annual holiday up north. The excitement reached fever-pitch when we came level with the Lake District and the train began toiling up to the high point of Shap. Then, when it started charging down the other side to Carlisle, I knew we were almost there – the land where the people "talk proper".'

'So, you can do the cockney accent, too.'

'Yes, the Glaswegian glottal stop is a help with it.'

'Tell me, did you have a civilian job before you joined the FANYs?'

'Well, I'd got a place at London University to study journalism and was due to start in autumn 1939 but of course the war washed all that out. I'd previously taken a secretarial course at St James College, so I thought I could perhaps make use of that, I heard that the Foreign Office were short of secretaries so I applied and got a job with them. My parents were pleased and told me I would certainly be helping the war effort that way. I found, however, that you worked in a secretarial pool and every so often you were sent to take a letter from an official, every time a different person from the last. You handed in your typed letter, went back to your desk and went on filing your nails or gossiping quietly to your neighbour. You got thoroughly bored as the lack of continuity meant that you could take no intelligent interest in what you were doing. Then one day I met up with a friend, Vera Aungers, who told me she was joining the FANYs, so I threw in my job and joined up with her.'

'One minute, isn't Vera that titchy little girl who finds it difficult reaching the pedals at the same time as seeing over the steering wheel.'

'Yes, she's now driving in Baker Street. She did well on the training course, whatever you say.'

'Maybe, but one of my colleagues suggested raising a subscription to buy her a periscope to see over the top.'

I wasn't sure this was found to be very funny but at least I got some sort of a smile.

Dancing to the wind-up gramophone went down well with everyone after dinner and, when I turned in, the party was not yet over.

Ron Hockey, briefing me after my arrival at Stradishall, told me that they were now sending four Whitleys out to Malta. The first two were leaving in a couple of hours' time.

'I'm putting you in with an experienced crew. If you're like me, you'll prefer to travel with the grown-up boys rather than with the newcomers. The other crew are splendid fellows but they've not long arrived from New Zealand and they're all aged around the twenty mark. This will only be their third operational sortie, so they tell me, but I'm sure they'll make it. It should be a good experience for them and you have to learn the job quickly these days.'

Hockey drove me out to my Whitley and introduced me to the pilot who, I noted with satisfaction, wore the rings of a flight lieutenant on his sleeve. I climbed into the fuselage for the short hop to Abingdon and the door was closed behind me. I could not see out but I heard first one and then the other engine being churned round by the starter motor and then bursting into life. I knew that the pilot was going through his routine checks and then we started taxiing, presumably round the perimeter towards the end of the runway. I thought nothing of it when we came to a stop but after a minute or two a member of the crew came back and told me that we had grazed a wing-tip against a parked petrol bowser. There was probably no harm done but the squadron engineer was coming to check up on it.

The engineer arrived in his car and after a quick look decreed that it would be inadvisable to proceed without a closer examination. The fuselage door was opened, I climbed down with my small case of luggage, got into the engineer's car and was driven to the other Whitley which was ready for take-off and joined the New Zealand crew.

I had a chance of talking with the crew during our stop-over at Abingdon. They were, I found, a keen and pleasant bunch and I got the impression that they were confident and looking forward to seeing a little more of our end of the world. But I was glad I had done some homework on the Balkan background as this was understandably a closed book to them and they listened intently to my little exposé.

'But you don't want to sit all the way to Gib. cooped up behind, do you?' asked the young pilot. 'We're briefed to fly far out over the Atlantic to keep clear of the long-range Focke-Wulfs based around Brest. It'll be a very long flight. We don't carry a front gunner as you know, so why don't you take his place. You might even prove useful!'

'That's great, but I must tell you I don't know how to work the turret or use that type of gun.'

'No worry. You'll be on the inter-com and when we're well away from the coast we'll give you some instruction and you can have a trial burst or two.'

Thick clouds obscured the moon when it was time to depart and as I climbed into the front turret I couldn't see a single thing. I settled down gingerly as I had a nasty feeling I might cause havoc by accidently pressing a button or getting my feet entangled in something.

We had a smooth if long take-off with our full tanks and as we set off on the first leg of our course, I listened with interest and occasionally participated in the chatter between the crew members. When we were well out to sea the captain called me up.

'Now what about a bit of target practice? I'll get Jim to take you through the drill.'

Jim first indicated how to swivel the turret to the right – or did one say to starboard? It was still as dark as sin and I had to grope with my hand.

'Found it? Okay, now operate it.'

I am not sure what I was expecting but it suddenly felt as if the turret had launched itself free of the aircraft taking me with it. Jim's voice over the headset with further instructions reassured me that I was still attached. Then under Jim's guidance I was able to fire several bursts with the guns. I was nevertheless grateful the chances of being involved in a gun battle at night were extremely slim.

After what seemed many hours of flight, dawn began to break in a cloudless sky. I could now establish that we were flying somewhat east of south, so we were on the inward loop of our detour out to sea.

'It's going to be a lovely day,' pronounced someone.

'A lovely day for Focke-Wulfs?' enquired another voice.

'No, we're out of their range now.'

'Good. So Gib., here we come!'

In fact, it was still a long way to go and it must have been approaching midday when I caught sight of the well-known silhouette of the Rock in the distance. One could sense the touch of excitement and relief in the conversations now taking place. But when we flew over the airfield the mood abruptly changed.

'Christ,' exclaimed the pilot, 'are we expected to put down on *that*? And with all those ships' masts in our path!'

The airstrip was across the neck of the isthmus joining the Rock to the Spanish mainland. Later in the war the runway was extended further into the sea but at this moment it was only used by smaller aircraft and I was told, after landing, that our Whitley was the largest ever to have landed there. In recognition of this, the whole Air Force contingent had turned out to watch us do so.

We circuited the Rock and came in to land over the harbour but we made too much allowance for the ships' masts and we would have put down too far along the short runway. Sitting in the nose I had a good view of all this. We set off round the Rock again and this time skimmed the masts but we only managed to touch down some distance down the asphalt, as there was 'lift' off the warm surface. We came to a halt two hundred yards from the sea facing the way we had come. Under the circumstances the skipper deserved the congratulations we all gave him.

It was some twenty hours since leaving Stradishall and the crew needed a night's sleep. I was driven off to the Rock Hotel where I was billeted. That evening, at an excellent dinner, I was taken aback by a familiar figure coming up to my table and enquiring whether the meal was to my satisfaction. This was Paul Homburger who was one of the Spanish speakers on my course at Lochailort. We exchanged a few knowing looks before he continued on his rounds. It was not for me to ask what he was doing there.

The next evening, we reassembled for the onward journey. The instructions were that we should make Malta just before first light. During the last few days the Luftwaffe from its base in Sicily had stepped up its attacks on Luqa airfield and on the Grand Harbour and dockyards. The unaccustomed appearance of a bomber of our size coming in to land in daylight would attract great attention.

The Germans had long since taken over from the Italians the task of attempting to neutralise Malta, since aircraft and submarines using the island as a base had been interfering with supplies and reinforcements for Rommel's Afrika Korps. The ding-dong battle in Libya between Rommel's forces and the British Desert Rats had only days past taken a turn for the worse for Rommel. General Auchinleck, now in command of the Commonwealth troops, had launched an offensive in mid-November which had relieved the siege of the British in Tobruk and as recently as 24 December had recaptured Benghazi. From this point on the German High Command decided that Malta must be knocked out once and for all, come what may, and the first six months of 1942 were to become the most traumatic in the island's long history.

First of all, we had to get off the ground safely and we were advised to take-off with escape hatches open. Luckily these precautions were unnecessary as we were airborne before we had time to hit the sea. It's perhaps unfair to say that the large audience that chose to see us off were disappointed not to witness a 'wizard prang', but rather that if there had to be one they did not wish to miss it.

Looking at my watch I decided we must now be very close to Malta and when the first streaks of dawn appeared in front of us I strained my eyes for a sight of our destination. When daylight fully took over and no land was in sight I began to feel a bit apprehensive. I was not the only one.

'Where the heck's that island?' the captain asked his navigator. 'We should have hit it by now.'

'We're on course.'

'Can we have overshot it? What happens if we have?'

'A whole lot of bloody ocean and nothing else.'

'We'd better keep on and see.'

Flying into low sun did not help, but three or four voices shouted almost simultaneously as a low shape became apparent on the horizon. As we came closer this divided itself into the islands of Gozo and Malta.

'Keep a watch out for Messerschmitts! I'll get her down as fast as I can.'

Luck was with us, as the morning patrol was not in evidence, and as soon as we landed – no problem with length of runway here – we taxied off to the comparative safety of a sandbagged dispersal bay. Only very comparative, as events were to demonstrate.

Before the crew went off to get their breakfast I made contacting arrangements with the skipper and we both agreed that as we were already well into the moon period the sooner the operation could be laid on the better. We hoped the remaining Whitleys would arrive the following morning, bringing the advantage of pilots being more experienced in this type of work. As we were talking, a young dark-haired Army officer came up and introduced himself as Oliver Churchill. His name made me look at him twice and I recognised a smaller, possibly less extrovert version of Peter Churchill. It was indeed his younger brother who was temporarily attached to the Defence Security Office and who had been detailed to meet me.

After a wash and tidy up, followed by a very welcome breakfast, Oliver and I called on the DSO. He was an older Army officer called back from retirement and he did not exactly overflow with enthusiasm at the sight of me.

'You had a good flight, did you? Good. I've fixed up some discreet accommodation for you, and Oliver will take you over there in a few minutes. You'll need a sleep and perhaps we can find time to have a talk sometime tomorrow. Meanwhile I'll give you a few points on our cover here and what you should or should not say to other officers you may meet. You can also collect some local currency and an identification document.'

I felt the DSO had not quite grasped the urgency of getting on with planning and executing the operation in the remaining days of the moon period. Apart from it being our job to get the men to Mihailovi as soon as possible, there was also the safety of the aircraft on the ground to be considered.

'But, my dear good chap,' he replied rather patronisingly when I politely pointed this out, 'we haven't any agents to parachute. They're still in Cairo.'

'When are they expected?' I asked when I had recovered my breath.

'How should I know? That's up to your people in Cairo.'

'Is there no way of hurrying them up?'

The DSO just looked at me. I already suspected that he was beginning to find me a bit of a pain in the neck, preventing him from getting on with important work.

'I'll let you know through Oliver when we get any news.'

As Oliver drove me off, I pondered the fact that it would be up to me to break the news to the aircrews and I didn't exactly fancy the job.

We circled round Marsamxett Harbour to the township of Sliema which looked across the water to Valletta, the capital. Along Tower Road, skirting the open sea, we stopped at a two-storey house, which had been intended as a private villa. Oliver explained that this was a mess and living quarters for some officers of the Maltese equivalent of Special Branch. I would be billeted on them for the duration of my stay in Malta. I was shown by a smiling other-rank member of the domestic staff to a bedroom on the upper floor with a promise to wake me up in time for the evening meal. When I did appear, still rather dopey, I was overwhelmed by the friendliness and hospitality of my hosts and this continued unabated for my whole stay, which lasted longer than I had envisaged.

Two more Whitleys arrived, but the one which had had the encounter with the petrol bowser had stayed behind. Even so, it seemed to me that we were liberally catered for just to carry out one operation. The aircrews took the delay imposed by the absence of the joes philosophically but the moonlit nights frittered away. Rather ominously the air attacks, if anything, intensified and, although the Germans could not have known for sure what the Whitleys had come for, they clearly objected to their presence.

When the message finally came through that the agents would not arrive until the next moon period, we realised that we had two weeks or more in which to kick our heels.

I made a point of turning up at the airfield as often as possible in the ensuing 'off' period in order to keep in touch with the crews. There were times when Oliver would have the use of a car and he and I would drive to Luqa together. On one such visit a stick of bombs was dropped along the side of the runway scattering rubble over several hundred yards of surface. There was a splendid, if slightly eccentric squadron leader whose exact title I did not know, but whose functions seemed to include keeping the airfield operational. He kept a loaded Lee-Enfield rifle on his desk and, on the very frequent occasions when enemy aircraft were overhead, he would rush into the open and try to bag one himself. But the aircraftsmen were not quite as enthusiastic as he. Some of them had been called out to clear the runway once too often and had been caught in the open when a second attack materialised.

Oliver and I happened to be standing near his office and observed his unsuccessful attempt to gather a posse together to go over to the runway. Seeing us, he charged up and asked us to set an example: if two 'brown jobs' led the way, others might be shamed into following. Oliver and I looked at each other and realised that we had ourselves been shamed into taking action. Two solitary figures walked off together and for a time we feared that the whole job was to be left to us. But slowly an increasing number of blue uniforms started to follow with shovels and other equipment and members of the Whitley crews, who saw what was happening, immediately set out. Oliver and I were not the only ones to be glad when the job was done.

The police mess helped to pass what was inevitably a frustrating period. I spent most evenings there and my hosts watched with interest and a certain degree of amusement as I tackled favourite local dishes. Squid was often on the menu and, although in those days it was virtually never eaten in England and the thought of it turned me off, I managed to consume it with an appearance of pleasure. But when octopus in its own ink appeared, looking like sliced bicycle inner tubes in dirty black water, I had to admit defeat.

Nights were often disturbed, especially the night that the Germans introduced screaming bombs, which had special attachments which made a great shriek as they fell through the air. No doubt they hoped they would frighten the civilian population into surrender but, if so, they misjudged the Maltese. The first one I heard certainly frightened me. It sounded as it was about to score a direct hit and I disappeared under the old-fashioned iron bedstead, fearing the roof would come in. The blast when it came was not very great and it was not even a near-miss. Familiarity did, in time, breed contempt.

If I wanted to visit Valletta, or to get myself up to Luqa under my own steam, I would walk the five minutes to the ferry terminal. The small ferry took you across a mile of water to the capital but you could also share a dicer (as it was pronounced) with one or two others. This was a high-prowed boat, rowed by a colourful and voluble boatman standing upright. Not only was it painted in traditional Mediterranean-style designs but portraits of King George and Queen Elizabeth were given place of honour. It was not unusual for anti-aircraft guns to open up whilst you were being taken across and you could see the expended shell fragments hitting the water round about. Someone was then bound to remark that what went up, must come down.

I walked through the streets, past shop windows, every one of them displaying portraits of the Royal Family and patriotic slogans. This was echoed too in the windows of many private houses. I had wondered whether the Maltese would be resentful of the rain of bombs which British naval and air bases had brought down on them but I neither saw nor felt any evidence of this. Their economy had never been self-supporting and for the past 140 years British naval bases and dockyards had been the island's life-blood. Now they made it clear that they did not want to swap it for domination by neighbouring Italy and certainly not by Germany. It was fortunate that the caves, and in some cases the centuries-old tunnelling in the limestone rock, provided many with ready-made safe shelter and whole families had moved in to them on a semi-permanent basis. The conferring of the George Cross on the Island and its inhabitants three months later by George VI proved an imaginative gesture.

At times, I would lunch at what in peacetime had been the rather select Maltese Club in the centre of Valletta, now more of a general officers' club. The menu was inevitably a trifle limited but I became very partial to the Gozo goat's cheese which they served. Goat's cheese in my family, mainly under my mother's rather than my father's influence, had been looked upon as something almost unclean, on a par with squid, and which some misguided foreigners unaccountably ate. Now I learnt better. The club was also a good place from which to hitch a lift to the airfield. It later fell victim to German bombs but Gozo cheese fortunately survived to delight modern tourists.

Then, the almost inevitable happened; what we had all feared. One of the three Whitleys was destroyed on the ground by enemy action. The young crew who confronted me were not at all happy and who could blame them? There had already been plenty of RAF colleagues prepared to tell them what the loss of their aircraft could entail: running the gauntlet by sea to Alexandria and, assuming they survived that ordeal, returning by stages round the Cape of Good Hope to England. One hoped, of course, that they could return to their base as passengers on the remaining Whitleys when the operation had been completed, but as we were as yet scarcely half way through the non-moon period, and as the Germans clearly wanted to eliminate these unexplained bombers, this could far from be relied upon. All one could really do was to keep one's fingers crossed. My own particular fear, which I kept to myself, was that the agents might once again fail to materialise.

After receiving this upsetting piece of news, it came time for me to leave and I wandered off in search of some form of transport going into town. January had the reputation of being the chilliest and one of the wettest months of the year and we had been experiencing a rainy spell. The rain had held off that afternoon but there were plenty of surface pools of water around. I skirted a small petrol bowser which was parked thirty yards or so from the entrance to the underground ops room. This was the nerve centre of the whole place and had been carved out of the deep limestone rock. There was not, as far as I knew, an air-raid alert but that did not perhaps mean very much.

A twin-engine fighter-bomber flying at right angles across the runway at around 500 feet was in line to pass right over the top of my head. I thought it might be a Beaufighter although I didn't remember seeing any so far in Malta. I realised my ignorance when, standing looking up, I saw a stick of bombs emerge from its belly, seeming to spread out as they fell and likely, I thought, to straddle where I stood. I turned and there seemed to be two alternatives: to throw myself down into a large muddy puddle in front of me which afforded no real cover, or to try to reach the entrance to the ops centre thirty or more yards distant. I wasn't certain I would make it but I knew I must try. I was just through the doorway and tackling the first few steps, which led straight away down from the entrance, when the explosions came. I was conscious of debris hurled past the doorway but I was busy concentrating on getting down the rocky steps as fast as I could. So fast indeed that when the first hair-pin bend came, I cannoned off the rock face in front of me before going down the second flight. But now the noise and racket was over and there was little point in going further. I slowly climbed the steps again and came out into the open.

The first thing I saw was that the bowser was no longer there. It must have received a direct hit; the crater was negligible but the wreckage was spread over a very large area. It had been hit by the first bomb and the rest of the stick stretched out behind it. I was sure that this sneaky attack had not been directed at the bowser but at the entrance through which I had disappeared and at the vital centre to which it led.

The excitement over, I became aware of the fact that I had banged my knee on the rock face tumbling down the steps. Nothing more than a graze and a bruise. My first 'wound', I thought to myself and I'll be lucky if I get away with nothing worse than this before this war is over. But, in fact, my luck held.

On my way back to Sliema I pondered on the events of the day. Pretty grim, on the whole. If this sort of thing continued, not only might we lose all means of carrying out our mission but, into the bargain, none of us would be likely to get home in a hurry. I only hoped they didn't serve up inky bloody octopus for dinner again tonight!

I presented myself at the DSO's office first thing next morning. When I was shown in, I told him of the loss of our Whitley, although I had the impression he had already heard through his own channels. I asked him if he would kindly send a message to my headquarters and handed it to him written on a piece of paper. Apart from reporting the loss, I stated that we would attempt the operation at the earliest opportunity in the coming moon period, provided we had any agents to parachute and provided we still had a serviceable aircraft.

The DSO read it through and after a pause looked up from his desk.

'You seem to imagine that we have a London bus service between Cairo and Malta. I thought you might have realised it's not quite so easy as that for agents to get here.'

He had a point, of course, but from the little I had picked up in London I had a suspicion there was perhaps more to the delay than merely lack of transport. I was afraid the DSO would take it upon himself to edit my message, which he was perhaps entitled to do as it was to go over his channels, but I knew that Gubbins would by now be on the warpath. He was not, as yet, overall chief of SOE and Cairo did not come under him but he at least had a responsibility to 138 Squadron for their aircraft.

I was back in the DSO's office a couple of days later. I handed him a second message for London, informing them that a second Whitley had been put out of action and that Flight Lieutenant Austin's aircraft was the only one still operational.

The DSO was expecting me and countered with the good news that the agents had just arrived in Malta. I remember the surge of relief which swept over me but exactly which form of 'London bus service' they had used to get there now escapes me. He had them all in safe accommodation and we arranged a meeting when we could discuss details of the operation with Austin and his navigator. Whilst I was sorry for the other two crews, I was glad that it was John Austin's aircraft which had so far survived as he was one of the squadron 'old hands' with a number of very successful operations to his credit.

The BLO was a Major Elliot, a quiet and reliable looking man, as I remember him. He had with him four Yugoslavs, one of whom was his W/T operator. They were all in uniform and were indeed to be parachuted in uniform. One of them was a large man wearing just a khaki sweater over his battledress trousers and over his rather ample stomach. He would, I supposed, lose weight once he had to start climbing mountains. Elliot himself looked in fighting trim.

Maps were produced and we started discussing a dropping point. They had already selected a ground a few miles outside Sarajevo with which one or more of them were familiar. The airmen thought, given reasonable visibility, it would not be too difficult to find and it was provisionally agreed upon. Their equipment had been packed into standard containers and two W/T sets into separate packages. They had brought their own parachutes with them and appeared to be well trained in their use. There was not much more that we could do for the moment other than pray for good weather early in the moon period and wish them all good luck over a drink.

The moon period did not immediately bring good weather over the target area but it slowly improved sufficiently for Austin to decide to have a go. On the chosen day, I was up at the airfield most of the day and, in the afternoon, it was decided to load the containers into the bomb bays. Back at home these were winched up into the bay but the appropriate equipment was not available on Luqa. A few of us, including some of the aircraft-less crews, accompanied the containers out to the Whitley, parked in one of the more distant dispersal areas.

The acting bomb-aimer now took charge. Packed with weapons, ammunition, supplies, personal kit and heaven knows what, the containers were extremely heavy. Eight of us, in the manner of pallbearers, stood beside one of them which we had lugged to a position immediately below the open doors of the bomb-bay. At the word of command from the bomb-aimer who had disappeared half-way inside the bay we struggled to lift the container on to our shoulders.

'A bit further forward, no, back, back. Now lift it a few inches,' came the voice as its owner tried to engage the ring on the container with the bomb release mechanism and we strained to obey the shouted directions.

At that critical moment, there came the roar of an attacking aircraft firing all its guns.

'Drop the bloody thing!' 'Hang on to it!' We were all shouting different instructions and, as a result, when a few seconds later the Messerschmitt had disappeared, we were still standing there with the dead weight on our shoulders. But in the adjoining shelter to ours an ominous plume of smoke was arising.

'Now, let's get it done before the bugger comes back again,' came the voice from above our heads. Strangely enough we did do it – and in double-quick time!

Darkness fell and there were, luckily, no further alarms before I watched the Whitley with its precious cargo aboard disappear into the blackness above Malta.

I had to return that evening to my billet as there was nowhere on Luqa I could wait all night without arousing undesirable curiosity. I had, however, to be back again to meet the returning aircraft and, in case it had been an abortive sortie, I had to have a car to take care of Elliot and his companions. Oliver therefore picked me up well before daybreak and we drove the six or seven miles from Sliema to the airfield.

We met up with other members of 138 Squadron, waiting to welcome their colleagues home. The first excitement was the arrival overhead of the Whitley and the second, equally satisfying, the news that the joes had been successfully parachuted. Austin reported that the weather on the long outward journey had, to say the least of it, been most unpromising but, as they approached the target area, the cloud dispersed and they found a patch of clear weather centred around Sarajevo. The dropping zone had been identified and the men and their containers dropped on target. Starting the return flight, they ran into the same lousy conditions again.

This seemed almost too good to be true after our run of bad luck, and Oliver and I presented ourselves at the DSO Office at the start of play with a message for London already drafted. The reply was not long in arriving back. It contained congratulations to all concerned and instructions to me to return by Austin's Whitley soonest. This order was hardly necessary as there was no argument about us getting the hell out of Malta whilst we still could.

The Air Officer Commanding Malta was Air Commodore Hugh Lloyd, subsequently Air Chief Marshall Sir Hugh Lloyd. I had, of course, never met him and knew nothing of his background. Had I known then that his previous appointment had been Air ADC to the King, his action would perhaps have seemed less quixotic. He had delivered to the Whitley a large and heavy crate of Maltese oranges addressed to H.M King George VI, Buckingham Palace, London, and requested Austin to fly it home with him. A request was a command and the crate was duly stowed forward in the fuselage.

Our flight back to Gibraltar was, as far as I was able to judge, without incident. I was in the fuselage with the King's oranges and with several members of the plane-wrecked crews and had no view of what was happening outside. The landing at Gib. appeared to be less fraught than before, but this time I was deprived of a grandstand view and not privy to the captain's comments over the inter-com. Under the circumstances I think I preferred it.

We split up again in Gib, the airmen going to service accommodation and I back to The Rock Hotel. The day after arrival Austin got in touch and said there would be no take-off that night as there was insufficient wind. With our load, we needed a minimum of ten mph to help us to get off the runway. I was not dismayed at this as it gave me the opportunity to buy a few souvenirs to take home and to have a look around this famous garrison town. I noticed that there did indeed seem to be something approaching a dead-calm as the ensigns on the ships were scarcely stirring.

The next day I got the same message and I spent the time wandering around again and maybe some of the crew came in to The Rock for a drink and a chat. There was still no wind the day following and this went on for three or four more. The one great advantage was that there were unlikely to be any enemy aircraft within range to attack us and our Whitley was in that respect out of danger. So, we just had to bide our time. I was comfortable, well-fed and in no desperate hurry to get back. If the sunshine at that time of year had been slightly more powerful I would have been in even less of a rush. Strangely enough, without my knowing it, the enforced delay was playing to the advantage of both a friend of mine and of F Section as a whole.

Came the night when the wind had got up sufficiently for us to get away. It was arranged that Austin and two or three others would come to The Rock Hotel after dinner, have one drink in the bar and then we would all return up the road to the airfield. We were sitting on bar stools having our drink when someone slapped me on the back. To my astonishment it was Peter Churchill.

'Good God, Peter, what are you doing here?' I exclaimed.

'It's great to see you again Van, but what are you doing here? I've just crossed the frontier in the boot of a car and now I've got to get back to England as fast as I bloody well can. Have you any idea how often 'planes go back from here?'

'Not very often, as far as I know, but it so happens that I'm going back in one in an hour's time.'

147

'Can I get on it too?'

'You'll have to ask the skipper,' and I introduced him to John Austin as one of our important French Section agents.

As I ordered Peter a drink I listened eagerly as he explained his situation to John.

'Well, obviously I can't give you all the details but I've just come back from a short mission to the south of France where I had to establish contacts and then make my way back to report. As a means of getting there in the first place, I was sent out here to Gib. on a troopship and after spending a day or two here I boarded a submarine on New Year's Eve.'

'Good heavens,' I interjected, 'you must have been here when I passed through on my way to Malta.'

'Yes, indeed, but they kept me pretty well out of circulation. I was landed, you see, on the coast and then had quite a hectic time seeing people and carrying out my brief. Then came the problem of getting out of France again and taking the results of my visit back to London. All I can say is that if you don't have to cross the Pyrenees on foot at night at this time of year, dodging to avoid guards on both sides of the frontier, well don't try it! Even when safely away from the frontier area all was not plain sailing and delays occurred. But finally, I was lucky and got a lift on the last lap down here and came over shut in the boot.'

'Pretty uncomfortable, I should imagine.'

'Well, yes, but eight days incarcerated in a submarine was not bad training for it!'

Peter had made his case well. I did not need to be convinced of the need to get him home speedily and John was now on our side.

'There's only one big snag,' he said, turning to me. 'We're already loaded to capacity and if we take on another man, let alone a big chap like your friend, this could tip the balance – literally tip us all into the Mediterranean on take-off.'

'No way of lessening the load?'

'Well, yes, I could think of one. We could dump the King's oranges.'

'Well, let's do it. I'm sure the King would understand.'

'Well, I was personally commissioned by the AOC, you see, to make sure that the crate was delivered to Buckingham Palace. I presume you're prepared to assure me that getting Peter home is more important?'

'Yes. I'll take responsibility.' What I really meant was that I was sure Gubbins would back me up, not something one could say of every boss.

'Fine and in any case those oranges are beginning to get a bit smelly after being cooped up all this time. So now there only remains the small problem of a flying-suit for Peter. It'll be difficult to get one at very short notice at this time of night. It'll be darn cold at the back.'

'Couldn't he share mine? One takes the outer and the other the inner half?' I was not prepared to be foiled by a small matter or what I thought to be one.

'Okay, I expect you'll survive. Put on all the clothes you've got underneath.'

When we got to the airfield there was a major snag. The starboard engine refused to start. Peter Churchill described our journey home in his book *Of Their Own Choice*. He recalled that we were due to leave on Friday the 13th (of February 1942) but as the day had so far brought him good luck he was not perturbed. However, it had just become the 14th by the time both engines were functioning satisfactorily, but as it turned out this did not prevent it being an eventful trip.

All the passengers were huddled as far forward as we could get for take-off and, although we could see nothing, we knew it must once again have been a close-run thing.

Unlike the outward journey we were taking a more direct course, planning to make landfall near the tip of Cornwall. As John had predicted, it was extremely cold but Peter and I did survive although sleep was hardly possible. However, all we cared about was getting back home safely and we knew we were in capable hands.

A member of the crew had not long since been back to chat to us and tell us that dawn was breaking and that we now only had a short distance more to go, when we heard one engine stuttering and then stop completely. We could feel that it was the starboard one, which had given trouble before departure, and that the pilot was battling to keep the 'plane on an even keel and to maintain as much height as he could. We were given urgent instructions to huddle forward again.

I could see nothing squeezed up against the partition between us and the cabin and I was forced to wonder whether fate had not decreed that not just two, but all three of our Whitleys should come to grief. But it limped on and, although it seemed long, it was a matter of minutes before we crossed the cliffs of the Cornish coast and were in sight of an airfield. It was now a question of getting down successfully on our one good engine and John brought us in to a perfect landing. He deserved every word of thanks and praise that his relieved passengers showered on him.

The problem of getting back to London was solved by the unexpected appearance of a Baker Street Hudson with a FANY driver at the wheel. The large figure of Jacques de Guélis jumped out and went to embrace Peter. I knew Jacques as an F Section officer and knew he had been much involved in Peter's briefing. Peter had taken up contact with people that Jacques had recruited when he himself was parachuted earlier in 1941. Jacques had received warning that Peter was on his way and had driven through the night to meet him. He didn't realise I was also aboard but there was no difficulty in thumbing a lift.

I sat in the front chatting to the driver and catching up with some of the Baker Street gossip, while Peter and Jacques talked their heads off, switching from French to English and back again as the mood took them.

After dropping the two of them at Orchard Court, I was driven back to the flat. The Swiss housekeeper welcomed me with a vague smile but was chiefly worried that I had not notified her that I would be back for the evening meal. As she had had the benefit of my ration card for six weeks I was not too sorry for her.

I had time to enjoy the luxury of a hot bath before my fellow flatmates came home and, when they did, our conversation over dinner was restricted to banalities since, as the posters informed one, one never knew whether the enemy was listening. I don't think any of us really distrusted the housekeeper but the present occupants no longer knew her background, so we played safe. However, this did not prevent Dick Barry from telling me that we both had a date with Gubbins the next morning.

Gubbins welcomed me with a smile and a handshake and asked me to give a short account of my trip. When I reached the part about the non-arrival of the agents from Cairo, he interrupted me several times with questions which seemed to indicate his own dissatisfaction with the reasons given for the delay. I came to the return journey and my meeting with Peter Churchill.

'I have one thing I must report to you, sir.'

'And what is that?'

I told the story of the King's oranges and of my taking responsibility for leaving them to rot on Gib. airfield. By the time I had finished both Gubbins and Barry were smiling broadly.

'Well done! It was certainly important to get Churchill back quickly. If I had been in your shoes I would have taken exactly the same decision. Don't worry. If there should be any repercussions, which I doubt, I'll

The reunion with Maquis veterans shortly after the unveiling of the memorial to Xavier near Nantua in France. Van (centre) is pictured with Marius Roche (left), one of those who had flashed the torches to guide in aeroplane from which he parachuted, and Tardi, who had driven the getaway car.

A poignant visitation. Van at the ruins of the farm building where he was hidden on his first night after landing in France. With him are Marius Roche and Tardi who had taken him there.

The site where Van landed when he was parachuted in to work with the Maquis; it now looks quite flat and peaceful but in 1944 was a place of secrecy and potential danger.

The Halcrow family, accompanying Van on a visit, at the Maquis Memorial near Nantua close to the field that Van was parachuted into. From left to right are Gillian, Bridget, Alastair, Richard, Van and Dani Roche, wife of Marius.

Van and Marius Roche at the RAF memorial plaque near Nantua. This is one of the many memorials to those who had played major roles against the Nazis in the area.

The re-born relationship continued into old age. Van and Marius Roche drinking to commemorate the brave departed at a later day reunion.

A monument to some of those who helped the Maquis. In this symbolic monument lie the ashes of those who came to the aid of the Maquis de L'Ain in 1943 and 1944.

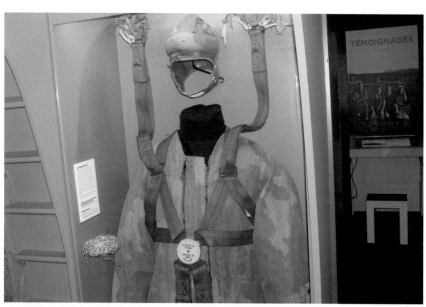

The people of Nantua and the Haute Jura celebrated the heroism of the Maquis as well as those who helped them and The Museum of the Resistance was founded by them. Here Van's jump suit is displayed along with other memorabilia.

Marius Roche strove to get Van's work with the Maquis recognised by the French government. He finally succeeded when Van was invested as a Chevalier of the Legion d'Honneur. Here is Van with son, John, and daughter, Gillian, at the ceremony.

Daughter Gillian and Van beside the West Highland Line steam engine on the route between Fort William and Mallaig where Van had trained prospective agents how to blow up trains and railway lines.

The award ceremony in London in July 2003 during which Van was presented with the Legion d'Honneur by the French Ambassador, Defence Attaché and other members of the French Embassy staff.

Van and his grandchildren at the award ceremony. From left to right are Edward (recently married to Louisa) and then grandchildren Louisa, Alastair, Sophie, Caroline and Bridget.

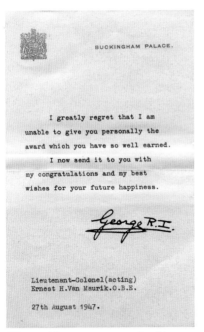

The certificate accompanying his award of the Military OBE.

The Military OBE.

Chevalier of the Legion d'Honneur.

The Fairburn–Sykes Fighting Knife originally given to Van by Fairburn and Sykes at Arisaig and later sewn into his jump suit when he was parachuted into France.

Van in later years. Always the diplomat as well as loving family man, he was, nevertheless, still discrete about his post war work in the diplomatic service.

field them. Now, I expect you'd like to know that we are once again in W/T contact with Mihailovi'

'Oh, good!'

'Not quite so good, as it's the original set, now repaired by some local wizard, that's on the air. Cairo tell us that the team which you parachuted were briefed to use extreme caution as it was not clear whether Mikhailovich's men or the Germans currently occupied Sarajevo. One can only imagine they were misinformed after landing as we now learn that they walked into the town, only to find they were sharing the pavement with German soldiers. They turned tail and nearly succeeded in walking out again but then some observant German queried their uniforms and they were arrested.'

It took a moment or two for this to sink in. 'So, it was all for nothing?'

'As it unexpectedly turned out, yes. But, just remember, we've been given high priority to foster Yugoslav resistance and to keep German troops tied down there, so we couldn't just have sat back indefinitely and done nothing. So your journey was necessary.'

At least, I said to myself as I made my way to start work again in AL Section, we managed, with a bit of luck, to get Peter back again.

Exactly how lucky we had all been I did not discover until many years later when I met John Austin and recalled our trip home from Gib.

'You obviously only know half the story,' he told me. 'When they came to examine the Whitley, they discovered that sand filters had not been fitted to the engines, as should have been for that part of the world. The engine that failed was completely gummed up with sand and so indeed was the other one which was ready to pack in at any moment!'

CHAPTER 10

The White Rabbit

It is a fairly common phenomenon, I believe, when returning back home from a spell abroad, be it a long or a short one, to expect to find changes in familiar things around and to be slightly surprised and perhaps gratified to discover this has not been the case. I remember an extreme example of this after the war when, coming home after six years' posting overseas, I restarted commuting up to London, only to find the same people waiting for the 08.12 train, wearing the same hats, carrying the same umbrellas and with the same newspapers tucked under their arms. Furthermore, they were all standing on their own exact pre-ordained spot on Sevenoaks platform where I had last left them. I must admit I found this depressing rather than comforting, especially as no one appeared to notice my return nor presumably have been aware of my disappearance. Things in wartime, however, tended to move faster and when I re-joined AL Section I was surprised by all the changes I found.

Douglas Dodds-Parker was still the boss but it was rumoured that it would not be long before he moved on to other fields. It seemed that I was now in charge of an enlarged sub-section dealing with the country sections over parachute operations, clearing their dropping grounds with the Air Ministry and preparing the briefs for the squadron. We also continued to brief the agents on dropping procedures and, where necessary, accompanied them to the airfield.

I now had two new officers as yet inexperienced in our work to look after. One was an amiable-seeming chap but rather older than the rest of us. Even so, Rex Turner was probably on the right side of forty. The other, Lionel Drage, was small and dark-haired and although rather retiring, perhaps a bit shy, gave the impression of quick intelligence. He was a member of the Drage family who owned a network of furniture shops. Drage furniture was synonymous with inexpensive, serviceable but not exactly high-class goods, but Lionel turned out to be good value in all respects.

'They say that Douglas is importing FANY labour into this section,' they told me. 'What's more, it seems that you are getting a FANY secretary. Apparently, she's standing in as secretary to the FANY Queen Bee at this moment but is shortly coming over here.'

'Is that so? What's her name?'

'Oh, we haven't heard that.'

I was soon escorting agents and their conducting officers down to their aircraft again. The two squadrons, 138 and 161, had just taken up permanent home at a newly completed airfield at Tempsford just off the Great North Road below St. Neots. A large house hidden standing in its own grounds twenty minutes' drive away had been requisitioned as the new Despatch Station. The stately Audley End House was to become a holding school for Poles. On these expeditions, I always hoped to bump into John Austin and his crew again but there was only a slight chance of this, as either they were getting ready to fly a sortie or they were taking advantage of being off duty. However, I knew they were successfully back on the job from the operational debriefing reports which reached my desk in Baker Street.

On one stormy night, I arrived at Special Training School 51, for this was the official designation of the Despatch Station, with a group of Norwegians hoping to parachute into the snowy mountains of their homeland. Here I met several Canadian girls who had come over to England to join the FANYs and we left for Tempsford in two cars, one of these driven by a Canadian. We saw these tough Norwegians into their aircraft and returned to STS 51. Later that night we received a message telling us that, with the bad weather unexpectedly extending right across to the target, the operation had been aborted and would we please collect the joes.

We set off in the two cars again and I sat in the front with the Canadian FANY to make sure she knew the way. She was a blonde young girl overflowing with enthusiasm at being close to the action rather than several thousand miles away across the Atlantic. We picked up the disappointed passengers and began the return journey. The Canadian, quite confident, led the way with a car full of joes and I followed in the second car with the conducting officer and a couple of the agents. The weather was wet and murky and the road had become narrow and twisty. Perhaps not fully accustomed to black-out driving, the girl in the front car failed to pick out the rear lights of a large slow-moving van, the only other vehicle abroad at that hour of the morning. The resulting collision wrote off the Hudson and the agents suffered horrendous injuries although some of them, when recovered months later, volunteered for a second attempt and landed safely in Norway. The Canadian, when we got her door open, was already dead, impaled on the steering column.

More cheering was a message passed to me via F Section from Peter Churchill suggesting we met for lunch. He had been flown out again to Gibraltar barely two weeks after our return together, but this time in a smaller and more comfortable aircraft. He had escorted four agents by submarine to his own 'private' landing spot in Antibes, paddled them ashore and then returned to the submarine. He was now back and awaiting his next assignment. I said that if he were parachuted next time I would try to see him off.

Our flat, too, was not immune from change. Major Peter Boughey, who specialised in Balkan affairs, moved in. Tall, round and ruddy faced, horn-rimmed spectacled and with brown wavy hair, his frequent laughs were interspersed with the occasional wheezy cough. He had at one time suffered lung trouble. He was good company and events proved him to have been a good acquisition.

Dick Barry, now the oldest inhabitant, still smoked his all-metal pipe. One Sunday when the Swiss housekeeper had the day off, he decided that the pipe needed more than just a routine pull-through and, selecting what he felt was the least used saucepan in the kitchen, embarked on the makers' recommended periodical service. He stripped the pipe down, placed the component parts in the saucepan and put the lot on to boil. A strong odour of nicotine spread through the flat but with the operation completed and all windows thrown open, none of us worried too much. After washing and drying up, Dick declared that the reassembled pipe was functioning better than ever.

We had finished the scratch supper which had been left for us and were catching up with the Sunday newspapers, when the front door opened and the housekeeper stepped in. One could practically see her nostrils twitching as, without a word, she followed the scent into her kitchen. We all held our breath and sure enough she was back again in a few moments brandishing the offending saucepan. Dick proved to be no match for her and the horrible truth was squeezed out of him in no time at all.

It may have been pure coincidence but Mademoiselle handed in her notice quite shortly afterwards.

This really set the cat among the pigeons. None of us wanted to take on the time-consuming job of finding a replacement and checking on her bona fides, but we all agreed we could not just take on anybody without knowing something about her background. Besides this, single women prepared to live in wartime London and who were not already employed on war work did not exactly grow on trees. On the night that the news hit us Peter Boughey was away and we finally decided to defer action until his return, just in case he volunteered to take the job on.

Dick explained the situation to Peter next evening and the safeguards necessary in choosing a replacement. Peter listened intently and then his smile broke out.

'My dear chap, I've got the perfect solution. Ma, that's to say my mother, will be delighted to take on the job and you won't need any security clearance for her.'

There was a momentary stunned silence. Splendid, perhaps, but what if she were a disaster and we couldn't get rid of her?

'But I thought she was looking after your house in Buckinghamshire,' said Dick, taken aback by Peter's somewhat cavalier approach to his mother's services.

'She is, but I think I've got a buyer for it, so she'll have to move out.' This was the first we'd heard of Peter's dealing in houses – but not the last.

'But would she be prepared to do the housekeeping for all of us?'

'Oh, she'll love it.'

Peter spoke the truth. Mrs Boughey was a small, smiling, motherly person and, in addition, an excellent cook. She doted on her son and, by extension, on his friends. We all never had it so good as under her care, but as time went on we began to see how Peter exploited his mother in connection with his business deals. When we charged him good-humouredly with this, he laughed his asthmatic laugh and pointed out that she really loved being involved and it was good for her to be kept busy. But this proved to be only partly true, as emerged later.

Back in the office, the FANY infiltration of Norgeby House had begun. The first arrival in our section was Pauline Laughton, known as the blonde bombshell, who had married a close relative of Charles Laughton, the film actor. The second was my new secretary.

She arrived unexpectedly one morning and was brought along by Dodds-Parker to meet me.

'I don't know whether you've met Winifred.' Fate had, as I had already suspected, brought the Scottish driver of the NKVD trip and myself together again. We both signified, simultaneously, that we did indeed know each other.

'Good, so I'll leave you both to get on with it. Winifred is a qualified shorthand-typist and has been working for Phyllis Bingham for the last few weeks but she's keen to help out in all aspects of the work here.'

'I trust you don't think I had anything to do with my posting to you,' said my new secretary, when Douglas had left, 'because I didn't. I hope you don't mind my coming.'

'On the contrary, we need all the help we can get.'

It was luckily between moon periods and I had time to take Win, as she said she preferred to be known, round the Section, introducing her to the others and explaining the work. When we completed our round I felt she was just what we wanted – quick on the uptake and probably a serious and accurate worker.

I was worried on the other hand about Rex Turner as I felt he was our one weak link. He was a pleasant chap but he did not always display the dedicated enthusiasm most of us felt the job deserved. It was, after all, the airmen and the joes who were risking their lives and it was up to us at least to see no errors occurred in our work. He was not a natural staff officer and errors were not infrequently picked up in his operational briefings by the double-checking officer. His heart seemed to be in the West Country where he had a wife and a small-holding and he squeezed every opportunity he could to dash down there for twenty-four hours, mainly, some colleagues maintained, to see the animals. It seemed ironic when, a couple of years later, he fell for an older woman in the office and abandoned both wife and animals.

Not all the operations we laid on from London were destined for Western Europe or Scandinavia. Apart from the Poles, the occasional sortie went further afield. I was involved in the operational briefing of an agent to be dropped in Estonia, the most distant of the three Baltic States, which were then occupied by Germany. The agent, Ronald Seth by name, had been a professor of English at Tallinn University before the war and had acquired the language. He volunteered to go back to Estonia with the object of recruiting friends of his for acts of sabotage. When I arrived at the safe-flat with my suitcase of tricks, I was confronted with a small, fair-haired man, whose nerves were on edge, or so it seemed to me; he chain-smoked and his fingers were stained with nicotine. Understandable, perhaps, in view of the dangerous job he had undertaken to perform. I demonstrated the equipment he would take, the necessity of disposing of his parachute and we pored over the map and discussed his dropping point. As I came away from my meeting with him, I admired his courage but wondered whether he fully realised what he could be letting himself in for, dropping blind and with little prospect of future back-up operations.

It was not until Seth wrote his memoirs after the war that I learnt what had happened to him.[1] He landed successfully but was taken prisoner before he could put his plans into action. He suffered torture at the hands of his German interrogators but was able to save his life by agreeing to collaborate. It seems he succeeded in being of little use to the Germans although just before the final collapse he was entrusted with a peace offer from Himmler which he took to London. After the war, he become an established writer on various aspects of espionage and was certainly more qualified to do so than some of his fellow exponents.

The qualifications for FANYs to work in AL Section included a knowledge of typing and preferably some experience of office work and this resulted in the posting to us of Muriel Smith. When she came to report for work, Win and I were in discussion in my office. I should explain that as an alternative to the traditional cap the FANYs had been issued recently with a rather wide beret which Baker Street FANYs were wearing at a rakish angle. When I looked up at the newcomer, there was Muriel, a slim, good-looking brunette giving a smart salute. The only thing that spoiled the picture was the fact that she was wearing her beret horizontally across the top of her head like some deflated pancake.

'May I?' asked Win.

She went across to the new recruit and readjusted her beret at an angle of forty-five degrees.

'Oh, I didn't dare,' said a red-faced Muriel.

'You'd better take Muriel around the Section and then we might introduce her to Mr Cole's.'

Mr Cole was an irrepressible Cockney and he ran a snack bar just round the corner in Dorset Street.

'Three coffees, Mr Cole, please,' I ordered.

'Three burnin' 'ot coffees,' Mr Cole shouted back to his wife in the small compartment at the back of the bar.

As we drank our coffees, which indeed were always burnin' 'ot, Win explained.

---

[1] *A Spy Has No Friends*, first published in 1952.

157

'Muriel's going to move in with me in what I call the garret in 91, Gloucester Place, just a minute's walk from here. It's five flights' climb but there are a couple of bedrooms and the usual facilities. It'll be nice to have company.'

So started a friendship which was to last a lifetime.

With more staff arriving, even though the work-load was also increasing, we were able to compile better records of parachute and landing grounds, both those already used and those recommended for future use by the Field. This helped us to act fast when urgent operations were called for. We had not, of course, the benefit of modern computerised records but we were supplied with an ingenious form of card-index which we nicknamed the knitting needle method.

Each card in this system had a row of perforations along its top edge, each of which bore a number, and we composed our own guide to the numbers. In the case of France, we allocated numbers to geographical regions, to grounds reserved for aircraft landing only, to F Section, to R/F Section (Free French) and to various other categories. A girl making out a new card would snip away any hole which did not apply to the data on it. Someone subsequently using the index was provided with a number of long spikes – our knitting needles – and, if wishing to consult, say, F Section grounds in Central France suitable for landing operations, would slip spikes through the appropriate holes and cards on which these holes had not been cut away would be lifted out by the spikes. A bit Heath Robinsonesque but it worked. It also helped us in our responsibility for ensuring that F and R/F Section operations did not clash.

It was at this stage that I received a letter from Roddy Clube, with whom I had been maintaining a desultory correspondence since I left the 4th Wilts. He had, I guessed, attended a signals course at Catterick and had, I knew, become the battalion signals officer. Now he told me he had been involved in an accident whilst on his motor-bike, had seriously damaged his leg and was judged medically unfit for active service. Condemned to some boring desk job, he supposed,

I marched into Group Captain Grierson's office, who had just taken over from Dick Barry. The latter, only on loan to SOE, had had to return to normal Army duties. Grierson, a gallant pilot, had not yet recovered from the shock of finding himself in such unconventional surroundings, and with Dodds-Parker due to take up other duties, needing all the help he could get. I told him about Roddy, about his languages and his good French, which was now becoming more or less a *sine qua non* in AL Section.

'Get him! And tell Personnel that we need him urgently.'

Roddy's arrival a few weeks later solved another problem. With Dick Barry's departure, we had become few on the ground in our flat, just Peter Boughey, his mother and myself. Roddy improved the position by moving in straightaway. The four of us became good friends and life in the flat ran on an even keel. Mrs Boughey loved to have an evening gossip with Roddy and me and to discuss the events of her day. Peter had now bought the definitive house, the one they would live in when the war was over. There was a lot to be done to it and Mrs Boughey would go off after completing the morning chores with her shopping bag and take a suburban train out to supervise the work on it. There were still elderly decorators and building workers prepared to come in but Mrs Boughey needed to supervise them. 'Needed' was perhaps not quite the right word since she loved doing it. She would also take the opportunity whilst down there of searching round the local food shops and would be proud of any lucky purchase off coupons she had made for our table. She would buttonhole Roddy and me, perhaps more receptive than Peter, and give us progress reports on the improvements to the property.

'It's really a perfect little house,' she told us, 'and I just can't wait for this beastly war to be over, so that we can go and live in it.'

If the delightful Mrs Boughey had a fault it was that she was too naive and trusting. But it was hardly for the two of us to tell her that the day would come -and come it did. 'Oh, by the way, Ma,' Peter said somewhat casually over dinner one night, 'I've unexpectedly had an offer for the house, such a good one, really, that we can't afford to turn it down. Oh, don't worry, it so happens I've seen another one. It's larger and I'm sure you'll agree it's nicer. It needs a little bit doing to it, of course, but it's definitely more suitable for us. I'll take you along to see it as soon as I can get a moment off. I know you'll love it.'

Mrs Boughey collared Roddy and me after dinner. For her she was looking quite distressed.

'You know I *do* wish Peter would tell me before he does things. That house really is rather lovely and, although you both may not believe it, I *have* put a great deal of work into it. And now someone else will get the benefit. But still I suppose Peter knows what he's doing. Perhaps the new one really is more suitable for us. I suppose we'll just have to wait and see.'

'I hope Ma isn't too upset,' Peter told us a few minutes later. 'But she'll be all right when she sees this new one. She's only happy, you see, when she's got a house to work on. By the way, I've got a new chap arriving in my office, a young Scot who, remarkably enough, speaks Hungarian. If he seems all right, would you both agree to him taking a bed in here' Fine, good. His name, by the way, is Ormond Uren.'

There were also changes and reinforcements in most of the country sections. Claude Knight was soon to return to his regiment, unwilling to battle further, it was said, with the various warring factions among the Belgian government in exile. His second-in-command, who took over the Belgian Section from him, was Hardy Amies.[2] The girls enjoyed his visits down to our section, not only because they knew he was a young dress-designer of some sort (his world-wide fame was a thing of the future), not only because he was indeed charming but mainly because they liked to get another look at his uniform. Hardy had designed it himself which gave it a particular chic, unlike any other Intelligence Corps outfit. About the only things he had not altered were the buttons because, as he explained, they portrayed a pansy resting on his laurels.

R/F was now transformed with the arrival of a new section head in the person of Lieutenant Colonel Hutchison. 'Hutch', close on fifty, was a man of immense, if occasionally misdirected, enthusiasm. He led the Section for a year or more but with the approach of 'D' Day he handed it over and disappeared into hospital. He was determined to lead one of the uniformed 'Jedburgh' teams to be parachuted to support spontaneous French uprisings on or after 'D' Day. In view of his knowledge of Resistance networks, he felt he must take no risk of being recognised should he fall into enemy hands. He therefore underwent plastic surgery to alter his appearance. How successful this was I cannot personally judge as by that time I was no longer in England, but one colleague related subsequently how he had bumped unexpectedly into the colonel and, without thinking, hailed him as 'Hello, Hutch', much to the latter's irritation. But heavily disguised or no, he earned the DSO for his bravery in action.

Someone with whom we had a closer working relationship was 'Tommy' Yeo-Thomas, particularly so Win, who, after I left AL, took over responsibility for R/F operations and worked on a daily basis with him. We all liked Tommy, he was so human and approachable. He never flapped and his sense of humour never deserted him. He liked his cigar and his drink and felt that life was there to be lived. His superhuman endurance and spirit, which enabled him to survive what was to come,

---

[2] Sir Edwin Hardy Amies became the official dressmaker to Queen Elizabeth.

were not displayed on the surface for all to see but were available to him when the need came. Win handled the operational details when the 'White Rabbit' made his first visit by parachute to France. When successfully exfiltrated again by Lysander he presented Muriel and her with small enamelled brooches bearing the arms of Paris. The rarity value at that time was scarcely less than that of stones brought back later by astronauts from the moon! It was on his second mission to Paris that Tommy was arrested.

I was not to see Tommy again until after the German capitulation in 1945. I had taken the SOE mission known as ME42 to Germany as the war in Germany was coming to its close. One of the several tasks foreseen for us was to search out and repatriate SOE agents of any nationality who had ended up in German captivity. In the event most of our surviving agents were rescued by the advancing British and American armies and Yeo-Thomas, who had gone through hell in Buchenwald and other camps, was one of these. Our HQ was situated close to HQ 21 Army Group south-west of Hanover, and a telegram arrived from Baker Street telling me that Yeo-Thomas was flying out to us and would explain his requirements on arrival. Despite recent revelations of concentration camp atrocities, I was profoundly shocked by Tommy's still almost unrecognisable appearance and by his grim unsmiling mien. He asked me to drive him personally to Paderborn, an hour and a half distant, and to interpret for him when he interviewed a German on behalf of the War Crimes Commission. Tommy told me in the car that this decidedly unsavoury character had saved his life and that he now intended in return to honour his promise to save him from execution. Tommy's intervention had so far spared him imprisonment and he had meanwhile married a former inmate of the Buchenwald brothel, which had been only available to guards and *kapos* (prevailed prisoners).

We found our way to a modest house on the outskirts of the town and were greeted at the door by a small, middle-aged man with beady eyes and a head shaved completely bare, overall of unprepossessing appearance. He sat us down in the living-room at a round table with the obligatory German betassled table-cloth and before long his wife appeared with three cups of ersatz coffee.

The interview commenced and although I translated word for word I had a feeling that Tommy understood somewhat more German than he was prepared to concede, but had no intention of letting a word of the hated language pass his lips. As the questioning proceeded and we started to probe the nightmare scenario of Buchenwald, I began to piece together a story more horrendous than any horror movie. It transpired that Herr Dietzsch, sitting opposite me, had been the kapo of the Guinea Pig Block where he had been responsible for injecting fellow prisoners with doses of typhus so that SS doctors could study the advance of the usually fatal symptoms. About how many had he thus injected? I had to ask him. Difficult to be sure but it certainly ran into a hundred or more, said the German, sipping his acorn coffee. I learnt how half the SOE agents held in the camp had been hung from hooks in the crematorium, convenient for their subsequent cremation, and how Tommy and the remaining twenty were daily awaiting a similar fate. How Tommy had persuaded the Sturmbannführer of the block and Dietzsch himself to attempt to save their own skins, in view of the imminent collapse of Germany, by agreeing to a plan whereby SOE agents swopped identities with prisoners already dying of typhus. Dietzsch gave Tommy and two others (the Germans insisted it would only be feasible to save three lives and Tommy must be one of them) non-lethal injections which brought on high fever similar to typhus and which necessitated their removal to the typhus block. Shortly afterwards three corpses left the block bearing the names of the three British officers in the place of their own.[3]

After Dietzsch had been questioned on atrocities committed by other camp officials, I drove Tommy back to our mess in quite a daze. Next morning, I put him on an aircraft back to the UK and, as it happened, our paths never crossed again.

Returning back to the August moon period of 1942, Peter Churchill was due to be parachuted in to France once again and, knowing which code name he hid his identity under, I was able to keep a watch on it. When his operation came up on the board, as I had promised him, I went down to Tempsford to see him off. He was as cheerful and confident as ever and I sincerely wished him well. I was relieved when a message came over the waves reporting his safe arrival. It had not, as he told me later, been an easy landing. He had dropped blind but, as luck would have it, he had landed on the only rock in the whole field. Decidedly

---

[3] Arthur Dietzsch, though a German Army officer cadet, was arrested for helping his girlfriend's father, a communist, escape imprisonment and was sentenced to fourteen years imprisonment. After being released following the war, he was arrested again by the German authorities in December 1946, and sentenced to fifteen years in prison for accessory to murder due to his activities in Buchenwald.

uncomfortable but no bones were broken. After six months' work in the Field he returned to London to report, travelling in a Lysander piloted by Hugh Verity.

It was now just on a year since I came down to Baker Street from Scotland and I began to think that if I did not make a move I might spend the rest of the war despatching others off to their fate. I knew that my old battalion, like many others, was still in England awaiting the opportunity of going into action and that I was doing a more useful and certainly more rewarding job than if I had stopped with them. I did not fool myself that I was equipped to take on underground work in France as my French, although very serviceable, would nevertheless endanger both me and anyone I worked with. But others around me, without first-class language qualifications, had disappeared to what I suspected was more active work. I was never one of those brave firebrands who had to be in any scrap that was going, but men such as Peter and Tommy made me feel I must do whatever I was fitted for rather than sit tight. I decided to speak to General Gubbins, as he had now become, and his secretary Margaret Jackson arranged for me to see him.

I explained what I felt to the general.

'But you don't dislike the work in AL?'

'Far from it, sir, but I would like to move on to something more demanding.'

'You're doing a useful job there, so I think you'd better keep on at it for the present. Just carry on the good work.'

I'd had my say, so I returned to my work which I did indeed enjoy.

But it was not all work and no play. Roddy, Muriel, Win and I had chummed up together. We all had the same sense of humour and, if we were not on duty of an evening, we would go off to a cinema or the girls might manage some sort of a supper in the garret. The films of Bing Crosby and Bob Hope were very popular and took us into a different world. We were keen to see their latest *The Road to Morocco* and discovered it was being shown at a not-too-distant Odeon. We needed a little exercise and Roddy said walking was good for his leg. We asked Mr Brown, the elderly caretaker of our flats, how to get there.

'Make sure you follow the Arrer Road.'

'The Arrer Road?' queried Roddy.

'That's right, sir, the Arrer Road,' and he told us how to find it.

We all four set off in the black-out, singing quietly to ourselves the theme song, 'We're off on the Road to Morocco', adding a few Bing Crosby touches as we went. After a while we began to wonder whether we were going in the right direction. Stopping, we heard footsteps approaching and soon a man and his dog loomed out of the darkness.

'Excuse me,' said Roddy, 'we're looking for the Arrer Road.'

There was a short silence while the figure seemed to be leaning forward to examine our outlines. Had we but known it, he was probably lamenting the fact that such uneducated riff-raff got into officer uniform these days. When he spoke it was in almost painfully high-class tones.

'If it should be (*pause*) Harrow Road you are looking for, you are now in it.'

He must have wondered at the barely suppressed laughter as he went on his way.

The fact that Rex Turner was still paying flying visits to the West Country, albeit with the group-captain's permission, made us think that we must surely be overdue some leave ourselves. Working it out, we decided we could all four justify being away together for a long weekend during a non-moon period. The question was where to go. As we were entitled to free railway warrants to anywhere in the British Isles, we decided to go as far as we reasonably could. The overnight Inverness train attracted us and someone told us of a little hotel in Kingussie, eight or so miles short of Aviemore. We could get there wasting a minimum of daylight hours.

The Duke of Gordon was a small, unpretentious but comfortable hotel but one which has now been enlarged, modernised. We came to walk – there wasn't much else to do anyway – and walk we did. On the second day, we hiked twelve or more miles up and down dale coming out at Aviemore station. The girls were in civvies and one had a frying-pan attached to her belt and the other a saucepan and we had had an excellent fry-up over a camp-fire on the way. Arriving at Aviemore we found a local train ready to leave for Kingussie and with pots and pans rattling and haversacks flying we charged up the metal footbridge to cross to the down platform. Half way up there was a shout from Roddy and looking round we found him holding one foot in the air with his boot, its sole flapping loose and two rows of sharp nails exposed, looking for all the world like a hungry alligator.

'Caught it in a rung of the steps,' gasped Roddy. Two of us caught an arm each and, with Roddy hopping on one foot, propelled him down on to the other platform and into the nearest carriage.

'If today hasn't cured your leg,' said Muriel when she had stopped laughing, 'nothing will!'

Aviemore, now having become a ski resort, is today unrecognisable but I was delighted to discover on a recent visit that the metal bridge still exists.

Looking ahead, the next summer when I was no longer in the Section but still working in Norgeby House, our holiday had a less auspicious start. We thought for a change the West Country, possibly Devon, might be pleasant. Rex Turner said that he knew just the place for us, just outside Totnes. It was a big place standing in parkland and they still managed to produce very good food. The dining-room tended to get booked up but accommodation should offer no problem. Being Rex, he found he could not remember its name and scratching his greying hair brought no result, but when one of the girls produced an old AA handbook he immediately identified it as the Dartvale Manor.

The train took us to Totnes station and there we found a taxi waiting for a fare.

'Do you know the Dartvale Manor?' we asked.

'Yes, surr.'

We expected the driver to head out of town but we seemed to be getting further into the centre. We began to become suspicious.

'I'm told the hotel stands in its own grounds,' remarked Roddy in his politest voice.

'Ah don't know about that, surr, but it's certainly next door to the antique shop. They do say the lady as runs the guest house does the antiques as well.'

We all felt stunned as we stood outside the house adjoining the antique shop. There was no doubt about it; a small sign announcing the Dartvale Manor hung above the front door. But further surprises awaited us inside.

The proprietress welcomed us into her small hall which had various pieces of brass and china scattered around, which had clearly escaped from the antique shop next door. One could not complain about the warmth of her welcome but we soon found she was considerably more broad-minded than were the four of us.

'Now which couple,' she asked with a knowing smile, 'will have the double bed and which the twin-bedded room?'

In a less permissive age than the present we had remained nothing more than good friends and it did not enter our heads to alter our mode of behaviours now. After some discussion, which rather perplexed the landlady, the girls took the double and Roddy and I the two single beds.

At high tea that evening, which fell far short of the standard of cuisine promised us by Rex, we decided to look for alternative accommodation first thing in the morning. But first we had to share the communal breakfast table with the archetypal railway bore. He was small, grey-haired and officious and his wife silent and mouse-like, weighed down by a lifetime's recital of railway timetables.

'Now how did you come down here? You took the 12.15 from Paddington? Now, mark my words, if you had taken the 12.47, changed at Taunton into the 16.05 you would have been here seventeen minutes earlier. But then again ...' He spent the rest of breakfast enlarging on further variations, throwing in a few personal travel itineraries for good measure.

'Mind you,' he ended as we rose from the table, 'I'm less good on the Great Western. I'm a Southern man myself.'

We explored the town and not finding accommodation we fancied, decided to take a walk and find Dartington Manor, which we now realised must have been Rex's choice. The weather was fine, the exercise invigorating and our spirits fully revived when we came to the impressive building, standing indeed in its own grounds. When, however, we discovered the price difference between it and our guest house we hesitated.

'I suppose we could put up with the Dartvale Manor,' said Muriel. 'After all, we'll only be sleeping there.'

'Why don't we give it another day or so and spend the money we save on coming out here for a good dinner, taxis both ways' I suggested.

We never did move out and we coped with the 'Southern Man' by leading him on to such an extent that his wife finally revolted and made him shut up.

Wing Commander John Corby had now been appointed head of AL Section under Group Captain Grierson. It was a sensible move to get an active airman, known to the squadrons at Tempsford, on to the job, but like everyone else he had to feel his way at first. He had hardly settled behind his desk when he had a fast one thrown at him. An idea had been floated that a highly portable air directional beacon should be produced for issue to certain reception committees in occupied territory, on to which the parachuting aircraft could home. This, it was hoped, would cut down the number of abortive sorties when reception committees could not be located. John was given the task from on high of selling the idea to Robert Watson-Watt, the prestigious pioneer of radar.

John was of course well equipped to talk from the airman's point of view but as yet knew little of the problems on the ground. He asked me to accompany him down to the radar research establishment at Malvern. Watson-Watt put us to the test and I found myself having to answer a great many of his searching questions. We left without getting any firm assurance that what we wanted was either feasible or that the great man was prepared to devote research to it. I personally heard no more of it for some time but a year later REBECCA/EUREKA became fully operational, REBECCA being the unit installed in the aircraft and EUREKA a portable D/F set for use by reception committees.

At the end of 1942 my démarche to Gubbins bore fruit. I was appointed to a post on his personal staff and as it furthermore carried the rank of major I was doubly pleased. It was not exactly what I had aimed for but I hoped, rightly as it turned out, that it might later lead to something more active. Meanwhile an experience in staff duties and a broadening of my knowledge of SOE could only be to the good. I soon moved to an office on another floor but I remained an 'honorary member', as it were, of AL Section. If they had to work late and my desk had closed down, I would sometimes give them a hand until such a time as my friends there were free to come for a meal.

After I left, new members joined the Section who were to remain life-long friends. Nadine Ekserdjian was a FANY of great ability, bi-lingual in French and possessing a sparkling sense of humour. Right at the end of the war Win and I, newly married, attended a colleague's wedding with Nadine. For those days, the reception was smart and formal and a flunky was announcing the guests' names at the door.

Asked our name I rather proudly gave: 'Mr and Mrs van Maurik.'

'Mr and Mrs van ...?' queried the flunky. It took him several attempts before the poor man got it right. He then turned to Nadine.

'Your name, madam?'

'Ek-serd-jian', spelled out Nadine syllable by syllable, but this was, even so, too much for him. After patient tuition from Nadine he managed a poor version of the name and drew himself up to make the announcement. He hesitated and then turned back.

'Excuse me, madam, but is it Mrs or Miss?'

Nadine gave him a scornful look and snapped back: 'You don't think I'd marry a man with a name like that, do you?'

Nancy Frazer-Campbell was another FANY who became a close friend of Winifred's. Now Mrs Nancy Roberts, she still likes to tell the story of her arrival in the Section. She came straight off her training course to Norgeby House and reported to Win. After an introductory chat, Win said she would take her in to meet the Wing Commander. Young Nancy, still in her teens, was prepared to be overawed but was taken aback to find Win taking her into the boss's office with a cigarette between her fingers and the words, 'John, this is Nancy'. Yes, the 'Baker Street Irregulars' could be very informal but they did get on with the job.

From the Women's Auxiliary Air Force, we had an infusion of two good officers. Jean Wollaston was brought in to organise a professional operations room as opposed to the rather makeshift arrangements which had seen us through the early days. Now provision had to be made for handling the great wave of air operations leading up to 'D' Day and thereafter. It was fortunate that Jean found no difficulty in fitting in to the unusual, if not unique, Baker Street atmosphere and indeed thrived on it. Once the ops room was set up Jean needed assistance in manning it and Flight Lieutenant Bill Simpson joined her.

When war broke out in September 1939 Bill was the pilot of a Battle bomber. His squadron formed part of what was known as the Advanced Air Striking Force which was immediately despatched to France. There was little action for them for the next six months of 'Phoney' war and then in May 1940 the might of the German army was unleased against neutral Holland and Belgium and the tanks skirted round the French Maginot Line and began to roll back the Anglo-French armies. Now there was more than enough action and Bill's aircraft, making a low-level attack on an enemy column, was hit by anti-aircraft fire, caught fire and crashed. He himself was trapped in his cockpit until rescued by his two crewmen. His burns were truly horrific and in his book *One of our Pilots is Safe* published at about the time he joined us, he describes how he looked down through the flames at his hands where the skin hung down like white icicles and the fingers were curled and pointed like the claw of a great wild bird. His face and other parts of his body were also horribly burnt. Bill, against expectation, survived and was evacuated to England. After many months in the hands of the plastic surgeons at East Grinstead he arrived in Norgeby House to take up his first job since leaving hospital.

When I first walked in to the ops room and found Bill sitting behind his desk, I found the shock almost unbearable and could scarcely bring myself to look at him. His face was still a livid mask with the eyes seeming the only normal part. His fingers no longer existed but he sat upright, smartly and proudly attired in his RAF uniform. It was above all the shame and disgrace I felt at not being able to disguise my involuntary aversion to his appearance. But this passed and Bill became a popular and respected colleague. Such was his determination that he managed most jobs without assistance. He wrote with a pen the handle of which had been whittled down to a thin blade. This he held between two vestigial finger stumps on his right hand. To get home he took an underground train from Baker Street Station for which he needed two or three coins to put in the ticket machine. Before leaving the office, he would skilfully settle his RAF cap on his head and then, sitting at his desk, slide the coins to the edge and manoeuvre them into his grasp. Volunteers would willingly have accompanied him to the station, but he would have none of it.

Faith Townend was the second WAAF officer to join the ranks of AL Section. At a later date, she was posted to SOE headquarters in Ceylon where she was responsible for liaison between Force 136, as it was known, and the RAF. It was here that she met Freddie Spencer Chapman in 1945, who had just been evacuated from the Malayan jungle after spending three-and-a-half arduous years there behind the Japanese lines, so graphically described in *The Jungle is Neutral*, one of the classic books to emerge from the war. A budding romance developed between Faith and Freddie. In August, the Japanese surrendered after the dropping of two atomic bombs but the situation in Malaya remained unclear with fears being expressed that the guerrillas might take the law into their own hands. Freddie volunteered to parachute back into Malaya to help sort matters out and Faith had to make the arrangements for the daylight operation. There was only one snag: Freddie had never parachuted before and was not prepared to waste time attending a course. With only verbal instruction what to do he climbed into an RAF Liberator and jumped through the hole to his waiting reception committee. As luck would have it he was caught on a back-swing of the parachute and was thrown heavily on his back. Faith was only partly reassured by receiving the returning pilot's report which read: 'Body appeared to land on his head but got up and waved.'

Thus, another of SOE's romances ended happily!

CHAPTER 11

Code-Name Paterson: Planning the Mission to France

It must have been close on the end of 1942, perhaps early 1943, that I took up my new appointment. I worked in the first place under Lieutenant Colonel Arthur Nicholls, a tall, elegant, good-looking, heavily moustached Coldstream Guards officer, who had nine months previously been posted to SOE direct from the Army Staff College to be senior staff officer to Gubbins. He had always struck me as a serious, rather unsmiling but undoubtedly efficient officer and I wondered not a little what he would make of me, with no formal staff training of any kind and little conception of what would be expected of me.

I soon discovered that I could not have had a nicer or more considerate boss. He set out to teach me my job but in such a way that he never made me feel embarrassed at my inexperience. I would have to draft papers or projects for his signature and in the early days he probably spent more time redrafting them into shape than if he had dictated them himself in the first place. But under his guidance I learnt, and after a while I was, I hoped, being of assistance to him, particularly, of course, on the air operations and training side of which I had more background than he had.

One of the early papers to be submitted through me to Nicholls, and thence to Gubbins, was entitled 'Bad Odours as a Weapon of Offence'. Station IX near Welwyn Garden City, one of SOE's two main research establishments, had developed a liquid with a truly disgusting smell and the paper set out possible uses for it; for example, spraying it on German greatcoats hung up in restaurants or bumped into in the street. Not only would the owner become a pariah but the coat would need to be destroyed and replaced. Arthur Nicholls suggested I visited Station IX both to report on the odour and generally to be brought up to date on the other various projects. The smell, tested out on a swab held at arm's length, was fearsome – they refused to disclose the ingredients used in its preparation – but if it was eventually used in the field, I never heard tell of it.

One paper which came through my hands and which did evolve into a very successful operation was the blueprint for the Jedburgh teams, who were to be parachuted into France on or after D-Day to coordinate the activities of spontaneous groups of resisters with the Allied invasion plans. These consisted of Anglo-American-French teams, usually of three men of whom one was a W/T operator. Having affixed my comments, I sent the paper on its way to Colin Gubbins with the further statement: 'I would like to be the first volunteer to take part in this scheme.' It eventually arrived back on my desk with the general's agreement to my request. I did not in the event become a Jedburgh as Gubbins put me forward for a mission to France and Switzerland at a date prior to D-Day.

I did not serve under Arthur Nicholls for more than four or five months as he was posted away, to the Middle East one gathered. I was sorry to see him go but, thanks to him, I had acquired sufficient knowledge and self-reliance to face his successor with confidence.

I only heard the full Arthur Nicholls story much later in the war. After a year's exemplary service under Gubbins he volunteered for active service in the Balkans and was posted out to Cairo. At the beginning of winter 1943 he was parachuted into Albania where he was second-in-command of an SOE Mission attempting to liaise with the partisans. In an encounter with the Germans in January 1944, the head of mission was wounded and captured and Nicholls, taking command, extricated the remainder and led them into the hills. They survived but Nicholls, suffering from extreme frostbite, died of gangrene. For exceptional bravery and selfless devotion to duty he was one of only three or four members of SOE to be awarded the George Cross.

One of the few others to be given that award was, of course, Odette Sansom. I did not meet her during the course of the war but I always seemed to be bumping into her husband-to-be, Peter Churchill. It was around lunchtime on a day in April 1943 when Peter's voice came through on the telephone. Agents going to the field were not permitted to know where our headquarters were located – although one imagined that the Gestapo had discovered this by now – and so Vera Atkins or some other member of F Section would make the connection from the safe flat in Orchard Court.

'Van, my dear chap, I've just heard I'm "on" tonight, returning to you know where. I do hope you can come and see me off as usual. You know you bring me luck!'

If I had still been working in AL Section it would probably have been easy, but there must have been some commitment or other which prevented me asking Arthur Nicholls to let me go down to the airfield. I was genuinely sorry to have to make my excuses but there was nothing to be done.

I was very much upset, and could not avoid an irrational feeling of guilt, when shortly afterwards the sad news came through of the arrest of Peter and of his courier Odette within hours of his arrival back in France. The book *Odette*, as well as the film of that name, told a vast post-war audience the story of this brave couple and how Odette's inspiration in claiming to be Peter's wife and Peter to be related to Winston Churchill (which he was not) saved their lives, but still could not save them from torture and the horrors of German concentration camps. Peter did indeed marry Odette after the war and I have always regretted that service overseas on my part made it difficult to meet up with him again.

For a while, domestic life in our flat remained little changed. Peter Boughey, Roddy Clube and I had now been joined by Peter's protégé, Ormond Uren. Ormond was a young captain in the Highland Light Infantry and, although we tried to make him feel at home, and Mrs Boughey did her best to 'mother' him, he remained a misfit. He seemed to have some sort of a chip on his shoulder and preferred to keep his distance. We decided he was a loner and indeed he kept his own company and seldom spent the evening in the flat.

Mrs Boughey became quite worried about Ormond and confided to Roddy that Ormond seemed to have rather funny friends and girls with, frankly, rather common accents, phoned up asking for him. This seemed to confirm suspicions about Ormond's sex life which the rest of us had been harbouring and Roddy explained, as tactfully as only he could, that boys would be boys!

Came the day when Peter let it be known that both he and Ormond had been posted out to SOE Middle East and Roddy and I assumed that the Hungarian Section was now coming under the aegis of Cairo, hence the move. His mother, he considered, should now move into his most recently acquired house until such a time as he returned, supervising the inevitable improvements it required. This suited Roddy and me as we felt we could do our basic catering ourselves and either go out for our evening meal or encourage Win and Muriel to cook it for us.

Indeed, we got on very well together looking after ourselves and, although we rattled like two peas in an otherwise empty pod in such a large flat, we preferred not to take anyone else in, unless someone particularly compatible turned up in the office. Roddy became quite proficient in strumming on the grand piano in our spacious sitting room and we both resumed the practice started in the old 4th Wilts. days, of brushing up on our languages by turning on the BBC foreign news broadcasts in French and German. We even listened to the news in Dutch which, already more or less knowing the contents, we became quite adept at following.

Mrs Brown, the porter's wife, came in every so often to tidy around. She was not, unfortunately for her, an attractive looking person, having an outsize carbuncle on the side of her nose which, against one's will, insisted on riveting one's attention. She also appeared periodically at our front door with some little dish or other she had cooked and which she handed over with the words seemingly borrowed from the Tommy Handley radio show: 'I made this for you, sir.' It was difficult not to reply in the same idiom: 'Oh, *thank you*, Mrs Mop ... but *what is* it?' She was kind, however, and we appreciated her attention.

We now had to do our own little bits of shopping, that is to say, as much as our two ration cards and the kindness of Mrs Jones, who ran the little dairy down the road in Ivor Place, allowed. Her catch-phrase was, 'We can't let the major and the captain down', as she discreetly added perhaps an egg or an extra minute cube of cheese to our weekly allowance. She may well have done the same, when and if she could, for some other favoured customers but, if so, we were happy to be counted among them. It was not our fault that Win and Mur (as Muriel had now become) claimed to be outraged at this blatant pandering to the male sex.

Roddy and I used to listen to the BBC news – this time in English – as we made our breakfast. At long last there seemed to be more good news than bad. The Germans and Italians had finally been driven out of North Africa, Sicily successfully invaded and Mussolini ousted by King Victor Emmanuel and replaced by Marshal Badoglio. (My ex-boss Douglas Dodds-Parker took a leading role in organising an SOE clandestine W/T link with Badoglio which enabled the latter to negotiate a separate Italian armistice with the Allies under the noses of the Germans).

But no piece of news had such an electrifying effect on Roddy and me as a short final item broadcast one morning. Captain Ormond Uren of the Highland Light Infantry, the BBC announced, had been tried and sentenced to seven years' imprisonment for passing highly classified information to the Communist Party of Great Britain. We looked at each other aghast and then recollected that 'naïve' Mrs Boughey with her tales of Ormond's 'funny friends' had perhaps got slightly nearer the mark than had the rest of us.

The story emerged that Ormond, leaving the flat with Peter, had been arrested by Special Branch just as they were about to set out on the first stage of their journey overseas. This avoided all but a very few in Baker Street from learning immediately of the arrest. Ormond had been passing on to the CPGB everything he knew of the doings of SOE (which had probably been of a fairly limited nature) and this in turn had been passed on to our Soviet wartime allies, who, unlike the mass of the British public, had no illusions about post-war cooperation with the West.

Peter, who, I suspect, had been given no advance warning of Uren's disloyalty, continued on his way to the Middle East. After much delay, he persuaded the SOE mission in Bari to parachute him and three companions into Hungary in spring 1944, with the object of making clandestine contact with the Hungarian government. Dropped blind, but in uniform, his small party was soon rounded up and Peter, after imprisonment by both the Hungarians and the Germans, was eventually able to make his way back to Britain by way of the Soviet Union. With the end of the war he resumed his business career and Mrs Boughey enthused to me, over lunch at her West End ladies club, of her happy life settled at last by Peter in a house outside London.

Arthur Nichols' place on Gubbins' staff had been taken by Lieutenant Colonel Ram; short, dark and bespectacled, he lacked Arthur's presence and easy charm although he was efficient and easy to work with. Alongside me sat a fellow wartime soldier, Major John Mann; he had a good-natured round face and a jolly laugh and we got on well together. Ram, and to some extent John Mann, were inclined to bleat their names when answering the telephone; I was not conscious of bleating mine but even so Van was close enough to Ram and Mann. When one takes into account the fact that John and I had a secretary whose name was Ann, one can see that the opportunities for confusion were considerable.

The Office of Strategic Studies (OSS), behind which title the American counterpart of SOE hid itself, had now been in existence for a year and selected OSS officers began to be attached to sections in Baker Street so that they could learn how we did things and be prepared for the running of a number of joint operations as D-Day approached. Two such officers whom it was considered should have an overall insight into SOE operations were put into my charge.

The first to arrive was Major George Brewer. George was an older man than many of us but a nicer one would have been difficult to find. He clearly came from a sophisticated milieu but I do not know what he officially gave as his peacetime profession, if any. He was a man of parts and had written the not particularly successful novel on which the highly successful film of *Dark Victory*, starring Bette Davies had been based. I enjoyed introducing him round to the various sections and in general looking after him. Later he was posted to the OSS Station in Stockholm.

Our paths did not cross again after the war but he was the indirect cause of one of the meaner social tricks once being played on me. Serving in the British Embassy in Moscow in the late forties, I found myself talking to a young American at one of the embassy cocktail parties. How the subject came up I no longer remember but it was established that I had known George Brewer.

'Didn't you feel that basically he was an unpleasant rogue. In fact, an absolute so-and-so?' enquired the rather smooth young diplomat.

Battling to make oneself heard – the KGB microphones must have been having a hard time of it – it would perhaps have been easier to have given some non-committal agreement. But my respect for George was genuine and I told the young man I totally disagreed with him.

'You've passed,' said he, and turning to the girl at his side, 'Meet George's daughter, my wife!'

Johnny Bross was more my age and a pleasant companion but, unlike George, he still had to make his way in the world and was ambitious to do so. He deservedly succeeded since when I next heard of him many years later he was one of the top men in the CIA.

One of the departments I took him over to see was the Training Department. We received an enthusiastic welcome from the new Director of Training, who was none other than my old boss Jimmy Young. He still wore his kilt which enlivened the drabness of wartime Baker Street but his tunic was now adorned with the red tabs of a full colonel. As Jimmy does not reappear in this account, I must give his story its happy ending. Jimmy, a divorcée or widower, I never quite knew which, fell for the charms of the FANY Queen Bee, Phyllis Bingham, and after the war they bought a hotel in the Highlands of Scotland. Winifred and I would have liked to visit our former respective bosses in their mountain eyrie but overseas postings on our part led us to lose touch with a number of old friends, including these. We heard excellent reports at second-hand of ex-colleagues who had made the journey north. It seemed that Jimmy ran his bar on somewhat similar lines to the little mess we had at Garramor; the guests went away charmed by the hospitality they had received but the hotel did not make the profit one might otherwise have expected. But Jimmy and Phyllis enjoyed life nevertheless.

The girls in AL Section also played their part in hosting learner-officers temporarily attached to them. This added a bit of spice to the daily toil, although the phoney accents they were apt to come out with tended to grate on Roddy and me in the long run. One incident did, however, scandalise Win and Mur. A young lieutenant, recently out from the States, came in one morning with a bandaged hand. He explained that after the air-raid warning had sounded he had hurt his hand when running down the basement stairs of his billet to the shelter. He was perhaps not to know that hardened warriors took little notice of the siren until they actually heard bombs dropping. It was the sequel therefore which astonished the girls. A short while later, the bandage long since discarded, he appeared with the Purple Heart sewn on his uniform – awarded for injury sustained in a zone of war. There was of course some similarity between his experience and mine in Malta, the main difference being that in his case there were no bombs dropping and in mine, and rightly so, no medals going free.

Muriel and Win had, of course, long since become accustomed to air-raid warnings, both those which turned out to be false alarms and those which brought bombs in their wake. The narrow, tall terrace house in Gloucester Place happened to be owned by a middle-aged German couple who lived on the ground floor and rented out the rest, with the girls living at the very top of the building. The Germans, who were inclined to be timorous, must have been judged to be no security risk as otherwise they would have been interned somewhere in the country. One night just after the girls had gone to be bed, a heavy raid developed and, looking out, they saw that several small incendiaries had ignited on a flat area of roof outside the window. A regulation stirrup pump stood on the tiny top floor landing but someone had removed the bucket which went with it. The two of them raced down the flights of stairs in their nightdresses and encountering the owners in the entrance hall demanded buckets. Finding the German couple paralysed into inaction, Muriel seized an enormous balloon-shaped flower vase which had always stood on the table in the hall, always full of water but seldom sporting flowers. Clutching it in her arms she started up the stairs accompanied by Win. Half-way up the first flight the unthinkable happened. The giant vase slipped from Muriel's grasp, shattered on the step and a cascade of water and broken glass descended on to the Germans who stood at the bottom of the stairs wringing their hands. Seeing no prospect of help from that quarter, the girls ran upstairs again and to their relief found the incendiaries burning out without having done any damage. Panic over, they used some of their precious ration of coffee powder to make themselves a cup and, as they drank, tears of laughter ran down their cheeks, partly as a reaction but mainly at the thought of the couple downstairs mopping up the deluge.

About this time the AL Section refuge-in-need – Mr Cole's coffee bar – closed down. He had, it seemed, made so much money serving his burnin' 'ot coffees that he was able to start a more upstage restaurant near the junction of Marylebone Road and Baker Street. The original small snack bar had luckily not been patronised by all sections but, as SOE lacked the space for a canteen of its own, staff had to find their own refreshment at lunchtime. The Finance and Administration branches, highly respected unlike those in many other organisations, favoured a pub to the back of No. 64. Its real name no longer comes to mind, since it was universally known as 'The Swinger' after its particularly well-endowed barmaid. Others went elsewhere, but not many people sought a sit-down lunch and a number ate sandwiches over their work.

One evening Roddy, Muriel, Win and I decided to try out Cole's new enterprise. Its decor, perhaps owing to wartime restrictions, was simple but its menu sounded pretentious. Mr Cole, having forsaken his previous shirt sleeves and white apron, advanced upon us in black jacket and striped trousers and, giving us a subdued nod of recognition, proffered the menu. We all chose omelette *aux fines herbes* which, despite its highfalutin title – which he pronounced O finis erbis – we knew could only be made of powdered egg.

Whilst we sat waiting for our meal I glanced round at the other customers and my eye alighted on a horribly familiar face, that of my old prep school music master Denis Wright. He sat alone at a corner table, gazing in deep contemplation at the ceiling. I knew there was a BBC establishment nearby and I imagined that he was devising some new orchestration for a piece in his popular brass band programmes. I drew my companions' attention to him and gave them a brief synopsis of my past experiences with him.

'Why don't you go over and speak to him nicely?' suggested Win, always ready to give a person the benefit of the doubt. 'He may, for all we know, have had you on his conscience all these years.'

Before I could reply, Mr Wright lowered his gaze and then slewed round to look directly at our table, or, to be more exact, directly at me. Great Heavens Alive! Did anyone in this day and age really still wear pince-nez? They glinted just as terrifyingly as they always had and I began to experience the once familiar sensation of my knees turning to jelly. Could he really have identified me as his erstwhile *bête noire*? But no, he had now recommenced examining the ceiling.

'Not bloody likely,' I replied to Win rather brusquely. 'I would be quite happy to remain on his conscience indefinitely.'

Roddy ordered four coffees and we waited to see whether Mr Cole would yell the order back to the kitchen in traditional fashion, but we were disappointed when he meekly made out a chit and despatched it behind the scenes without a word.

We never went there again. The good down-to-earth atmosphere had gone and in any case, we knew places where we could get the same powdered egg for half the price and I, frankly, funked another encounter with the 'Beast of St. Andrews'.

There was nothing out of the ordinary in my being summoned into Gubbins' office nor in the fact that the lanky figure of Maurice Buckmaster was stretched out in a chair. Probably some minor problem over next moon period's F Section operations. But when the General started to talk I realised that something more interesting was afoot.

'Sit down, Van. Now I know that you want to do something of a more active nature and I remember that you volunteered to be a Jedburgh. How would you like an operational mission without waiting for D-Day?'

'I certainly would, sir.' I felt a surge of excitement. This was indeed what I wanted but I could not help wondering what I had let myself in for. My conscience would not let me sit the war out in Baker Street but nevertheless I had dug myself out a pretty comfortable hole there among good friends

'Let me put you in the picture. As you know we have a station in the embassy in Berne. The only home-based officer out there is Jock McCaffery, the head of station; he went out there two and more years ago when one could still reach Switzerland through Unoccupied France.

He is an Italian speaker and since the Italian capitulation the workload has increased enormously. Added to this, the station is becoming more and more involved as a channel of communication with neighbouring F Section circuits in France. Yesterday we received a telegram reporting that McCaffery was suffering from nervous exhaustion and had gone into a sanatorium. We hope of course that he'll be able to get back to work in a week or two, but obviously we can't afford to take any chances.

'Now both Buckmaster and I think you would be a good person to send out there. You don't of course speak Italian but McCaffery has an efficient locally-recruited assistant who, if the worst comes to the worst, would be able to take over that commitment. As you are well up on the air operational side and already have a reasonable knowledge of F Section work, you would be well equipped to become F Section representative in Switzerland and Deputy Head of the station.

'The nub of the question is how to get you there. Switzerland is an island in a sea of German-occupied territory. They only haven't invaded Switzerland too because it hasn't served their purpose. No British official has been able to get into the country for the past year or so but the Swiss have allowed the embassy to recruit some British service escapees to help with the work. To ask the Swiss to connive in your parachuting direct into Switzerland would probably be counter-productive, let alone unacceptable to our own Foreign Office. So, we're forced to consider parachuting you to an F Section set-up and getting them to assist you to cross into Switzerland clandestinely. How do you feel about that?'

'I'm game, sir.'

'Fine. Well, what we'll do is find a replacement for you here as quickly as possible and then attach you to Maurice, who'll work out the operational details and be responsible for your despatch.'

The first plan put forward was that I should be parachuted to Tony Brooks, one of F Section's star performers. Tony had been parachuted blind into France in July 1942 when he had scarcely reached the age of twenty. He proceeded to build a network, centred on railway workers, stretching from the Mediterranean through Lyons up to close to the Swiss frontier. After fourteen months' highly successful work he had come back as a passenger on a Hudson pickup piloted by Wing Commander Bob Hodges for refresher courses and new briefing in London.

I met Tony on several occasions and we hit it off well together, starting a friendship, which is still unbroken. His main line of communication to London was through Switzerland and he briefed me on the character of his courier and good friend Réné Bertholet. This proved to be of considerable assistance when I subsequently took up the contact.

Tony was parachuted back into France in December 1943 but, to my regret, found it necessary to send back a message suggesting I went by another route, since he was not satisfied with the security of his parachute ground near the Swiss frontier.

Richard Heslop, code-named MARKSMAN but known in the Field as Xavier, was now consulted and he signalled that he could accept me. He was an F Section officer of considerable experience and had originally been landed by boat in Southern France but through no fault of his own had been arrested by the Vichy police with two other SOE agents whilst on his way to take up contacts in Angers. Released by a friendly prison governor when the Germans entered Unoccupied France, he continued his interrupted journey and subsequently was lifted home by a Lysander flown by Hugh Verity. In October 1943, he returned to France as leader of an Inter-Allied Mission to the emergent guerrilla groups, or Maquis as they were known, in the Jura, Haute-Savoie and more particularly the Département de 1'Ain.

For reasons best known to F Section, I was described in the first message as a high-ranking officer and this was subsequently abbreviated to HRO. The W/T operator at the other end was the American OSS member of the Mission, Denis Owen Johnson, known as Paul. He was a great personage whom, however, I was not destined to know until many years later as it was then policy to attempt to keep him separate from the direct firing line. This did not long prove to be possible.

The detailed planning of the operation soon got under way but, once safely arrived in France, the method of my infiltration into Switzerland obviously had to be left in the hands of Xavier and his French colleagues. To get to the frontier I would have to move away from the mountainous Maquis country and therefore had to be equipped to fit into the local picture. To this end I was given a forged French identity card and a cover story to go with it. It was hoped that my French would be good enough to pass a perfunctory police check or a questioning from a German with inadequate French. But the probability of my being unable to sustain this story under closer interrogation had to be catered for and it was decided I should have, in addition, the fall-back cover of a shot-down RAF airman. This would coincide with the story I would, in any case, have to tell once I reached Switzerland.

The concoction of my French cover story was a routine matter for the F Section expert in conjunction with the false document section. My fall-back story of a shot-down airman however was very much a one-off job. Our Security Section in 64 Baker Street stressed the importance to the Air Ministry of providing us with an identity and a service number which would stand up to investigation in the event of my falling into enemy hands. They came up with the name of J.W. Paterson and a number to match. They also agreed to make available the captain and rear gunner of a Halifax bomber who had been shot down in Belgium, made their way on escape lines to the Spanish frontier and very recently arrived home via Gibraltar.

I asked to interview these two RAF officers myself. It had already been decided I should pose as one of those Army officers who, three years into the war, had been permitted to volunteer to switch over to the RAF and train as aircrews. This enabled me to keep to my early Army history but omitting, of course, any mention of joining SOE. Now, with the two airmen enjoying a dinner cooked by Winifred and Muriel in Roddy's and my flat, I started the process of picking their brains. The meal served, the two cooks got out their shorthand notebooks and we took down details of the ill-fated Halifax sortie over Belgium and the crew's escape down through France. From the point where they began to go west towards the Pyrenees I had to invent my own route south-east to the Swiss frontier. The fact that no shot-down airman would be prepared to give away incriminating details about patriots who had helped him on his way would, I hoped, allow me to blur over some of the details where required.

When the time came for our guests to leave we had made good progress and they had enjoyed relating their experiences to an appreciative audience. But there was more I wanted to ask the rear gunner and I had little difficulty in persuading him to come for a repeat performance the following night. My late transfer to the RAF could account for limited flying experience but I wanted to be word perfect on the training courses he had attended and the type of armament installed in the Halifax. As it turned out I was glad that I had taken this precaution.

As a back-up to my story I was provided with identity tags with name and number on them. Instead of wearing these round my neck they were sewn into the waistline of my trousers, allegedly by an obliging French woman, only to be produced if needs be. I was to wear my own skiing trousers and boots which I had pre-war brought back from Switzerland, but the remaining articles of my get-up were of a type which might have been given to me by an escape organisation. Obeying instructions to get used to wearing these newly acquired items, I changed into them when visiting my parents one Sunday in Tunbridge Wells. My mother, one of whose dictums had always been, 'I like to see my two boys well turned out', took one look at me and asked pointedly whether I really had to wear such shocking clothes when out of uniform. Security prevented me from assuring her that indeed I did.

I visited Leo Marks, in charge of agents' codes, to be instructed in my own personal code, the key for which one carried in one's memory and which in my case was for use in an emergency only. Luckily, I never had to use it. Leo, in his early twenties, was a young man of quite outstanding ability; with his extra-long and no doubt expensive cigarettes – everyone else was happy to guard jealously their monthly issue of Players or Senior Service – he was an impressive person, verging perhaps on the dramatic. To keep up with him mentally one had to run whilst he strolled. When he learnt my destination he at once realised that this might be an opportunity of getting fresh mainline cypher books out to the Berne station.

The one-time pads used by Berne consisted of pages of groups of five figures which, as the name suggested, were only supposed to be used once and then destroyed. But when Berne found itself physically cut off from headquarters, it ceased destroying the pads and was now being forced to use them a second time over. This, theoretically at least, rendered them less secure and if the point was reached when they had to be used yet again, it might have led to a field day for the enemy cryptoanalysts. The task of photographing a new set of one-time pads and reducing each page to a microdot was now undertaken. A microdot came out about the size of a typewritten full stop but its operational use was normally very limited since the recipient had to have the use of a microscope to read its contents. The finished article in my case was a foot or more of narrow photographic film and this was sewn into a leather belt which I could use to hold my trousers up. It was an excellent job and I had no qualms in accepting it.

I now had a telephone call from one of Jimmy Young's subordinates in the Training Section. They had looked up their records and found that I had done no parachuting for nearly two-and-a-half-years and I had never done a night jump. They would be happy to fix up a couple of jumps for me – a day refresher and either a night jump from an aircraft but, if this was not possible, then a night jump from a balloon. I did not need to think before I replied. I hoped I would jump on the night but I had no intention of breaking my neck before then.

What I did require was physical exercise to toughen me up again and I took to going for runs in Regents Park – the term 'jogging' had not so far been adopted. Winter having arrived, it was normally dark before I was free to go out and on one occasion I was running along a narrow passage, which ran from the Outer Circle Road towards our flat, when I collided with a lamppost in the black-out. I arrived home with a bloodied face which alarmed Roddy and the girls who were waiting for me with supper but luckily the damage was only superficial. It did, though, rather discourage me from taking the exercise which I did not realise I was in such need of until I started climbing mountains in France.

By the middle of December 1943, I was all set to leave, and my operation, code-named CHEF, was scheduled for the next moon period beginning around the end of the year. My F Section briefing was complete and Buckmaster had lent me his own Christian name of Maurice for my field name; I could hardly go around calling myself HRO. My dropping ground was to be in the Ain at Izernore, a few kilometres north-west of Nantua. The Swiss frontier at Geneva was some seventy kilometres to the east.

Winifred and I spent Christmas together and shared it between our two sets of parents. I had visited the Hays several times previously in their tiny wartime flat in Welwyn Garden City. John Hay was Chief Labour Officer of Imperial Chemical Industries and his department had been evacuated there after the beginning of war. He was a silent, pipe-smoking Scot, straight and meticulous in all his dealings but kind-hearted when he got to know you. Fanny, his wife, like John, a Glaswegian born and bred, was much more outgoing and keen to socialise and John, a loyal husband if ever there was one, was prepared to play his part. ICI had taken over many of the flats in the complex and, although there was only one small spare room per flat, by common consent spare rooms were made available when any colleague had more than one overnight guest. Hence, I was farmed out if I stopped the night.

Fanny prided herself, and rightly so, on her entertaining and in this she was aided by her husband. John's department managed every Christmas to get hold of a turkey – a rare beast those days – and it was raffled among the members of his staff, and John, who possessed the lucky touch, walked away, not for the first time, with the prize that

Christmas. Christmas dinner, to which I was invited, was a memorable meal but was nearly marred by an unintentional but serious gaffe on my part. Coffee was served and John produced a long-hoarded bottle of liqueur. He also passed me a large cigar in a metal tube. I really felt I could not tackle it at that moment, so thanking my host most profusely I said I would reserve it to smoke after a really good meal. The effect of my remark on my hostess was devastating and it took abject apologies and explanations from me, much cajoling from her daughter and soothing remarks from her husband before she began to see the funny side of it. For many years thereafter she did not allow me to forget this example of how not to curry favour with one's future mother-in-law.

We spent time in Tunbridge Wells in between Christmas and New Year. Neither of our parents had any inkling that I was about to disappear. It would probably have been in order to tell my mother and father but we felt it would relieve them of worry if Winifred visited them and put them in the picture once I was safely in Switzerland.

I had never really discussed my relationship with Win with my mother; it was not something either of us easily did. I could tell that my mother now accepted that I was serious about her and was glad. She told me later that after Win and I had paid a courtesy call on my grandmother sometime previously, Gingy, lacking my mother's intellect but full of worldly wisdom, had declared that Ernest would end up marrying that girl and he couldn't do better than that. How right she was!

CHAPTER 12

Parachuting to the Maquis

O nce again, I found myself in a bomber – this time a modern four-engine Halifax – but unlike other occasions I was not really worried about having to parachute. Jumping this time was a means to an end, not the end itself and it was the latter which held my attention. I knew I had a reception committee awaiting me and I assumed Xavier would be on the ground to meet me. At the back of my mind I knew also of operations where the Gestapo stepped in and took over the reception arrangements but, no, in this case this possibility could be discounted. I was excited, yes very, but not, I think, unduly scared.

I had walked into the office that morning at midday quite prepared to be told once again that operation CHEF had not gone up on the board. But Win was waiting for me at the door of the Conference Room (as the operations centre was now known) to tell me that I was 'on' that night. I reported in to F Section, then took Win for a quick pub lunch and early afternoon drove down to the Despatch Station with the F Section officer seeing me off. After a meal, we went on to Tempsford.

We went through the routine drill that was so familiar to me, although it seemed strangely unreal that it should now be happening to me. My conducting officer examined the pockets of my French-style civilian clothes as well as my personal effects, which I carried in a canvas sling bag, to make certain there was no give-away object such as English money or a London bus ticket. He handed over my identity papers and some small change in French currency and then watched me tighten the belt with its precious cargo around my trousers.

Charles Tice, formerly parachute instructor at Ringway and now our liaison officer at the airfield, arrived and helped me into my camouflaged jumpsuit. I stuffed the spine pad down into the seat of the trousers and put the rubber crash-helmet on my head. I found a handy pocket for my Colt .32 before pulling on the silk gloves handed to me which went inside leather gauntlets. It would be cold in the fuselage on the four-hour outward journey as well as when I actually jumped.

Then my parachute was fixed over the top of everything and I waddled like a duck to the car which was to take me to the aircraft. There I was put in charge of the RAF despatcher who was responsible for looking after me during the flight and preparing my jump.

It was a fine night and the weather forecast was good. The fuselage was not designed for comfort but a sleeping bag big enough to take my bulky figure was set out on the floor. Heating pads, activated by adding water to their contents, had been inserted into special compartments in the bag to help to keep out the cold.

I am not sure whether I actually achieved any sleep but I was aroused from my day-dreams by the aircraft suddenly taking violent evasive action. The despatcher, plugged into the aircraft intercom, shouted in my ear that we were encountering flak over the French coast. In a short time, we were clear of it and we resumed our even progress.

Shortly before our estimated time of arrival, the despatcher gave me a shake and handed me sandwiches and hot coffee well laced with rum. But he made no movement to take the cover off the hole or to get ready for parachuting. Finally, he shouted above the roar of the engines that there was thick mist over the dropping point making identification impossible and that the skipper sent his apologies but had decided to return to base.

Home again, I was delivered back to the Despatch Station by one of the ubiquitous FANY drivers, where I enjoyed the traditional compensation for an abortive sortie: the rare delight of an egg and bacon breakfast. As a headquarters officer, the commandant gave me the option of staying on at his establishment or going back to Baker Street in a car returning to London. Knowing from experience that aborted operations seldom seemed to be rescheduled for sometimes several days later, I opted for the latter, only to find on arrival at Norgeby House that I was 'on' again that very night.

Wing Commander John Corby, who was now in charge of AL Section and hence Win's boss, was gallant enough to detail her to escort me to the airfield. After a sandwich lunch in a pub, and an early dinner at the Despatch Station, we were driven by a new-intake young FANY to Tempsford where I climbed into my parachuting gear for a second night running. The young driver was given instructions where the aircraft was parked and we set off in search of it. Win and I, who were not new to the game, were soon issuing agitated advice to the scared young woman but she clearly felt it was not up to her to take orders from her passengers. We crossed the path of a taxiing aircraft and were in danger of coming face to face with another before, thankfully, discovering our own. By this time, although worried at the thought of Win's return journey round the airfield, I was nevertheless more than a little relieved to have survived this first stage of my journey. I embraced Win, then climbed into the aircraft and the door was soon closed behind me. What I did not learn until a year later was that the little gaggle of persons seeing us off, realising the relationship between us, insisted that Win scale the ladder and make sure the door was firmly secured. This they said would bring us luck. In the long run, it did.

We met no flak over the French coast and the weather remained good right to the target. Some minutes before our arrival the despatcher pulled out a length of webbing from my parachute and attached it to the static line, which in turn was firmly anchored to the interior of the fuselage. Following regulations, he demonstrated to me that he had correctly carried this out. When you jumped, the static line followed you out and automatically opened your parachute when you fell its full length.

The despatcher had now received the order to uncover the hole and, as I swung my legs over the edge, I could see the ground down below, covered in snow and bathed in brilliant moonlight. Now the ground seemed far below and then suddenly the side of a mountain surged up towards the aircraft, almost appearing to touch it as we flew over the top; then once again the mountain fell away. I watched no more, as the red light had come on and the despatcher stood close at my side, his arm raised. I was just conscious that the pilot had throttled back the engines but their roar and the noise of the slipstream below my feet scarcely seemed to have diminished. The lamp turned green, the despatcher shouted and dropped his arm and I jerked forward into the middle of the hole, trying to adopt the rigid position of attention. When my vision cleared, I was gently swinging on the end of my parachute, suspended between hills and valley with the cold mountain air pressing against my face.

The usual feeling of euphoria, a reaction to the tension before the jump, overcame me and I had time to admire the scene. I appeared to be floating down to a wide flat valley, bounded on either side by wooded hills. I saw people, black against the snow, motionless and

187

gazing upwards. When it finally became clear where on the large expanse of landing area I was about to descend, the black figures began running but I had already experienced a soft landing in the snow and picked myself up before they reached me. They pulled up two or three metres from me and for a moment we gazed at each other. With the full moon reflecting off the snow I could both see and sense that these lads, dressed in a motley assortment of clothing, were straining at the leash. I felt it up to me to make some move and the best I could do was to greet them with, 'Bonsoir, Messieurs.' This broke the spell and a score of maquisards darted forward, not so much with the object of welcoming me, I realised, as with the urgent aim of getting their hands on my parachute. They then set to, ripping up the camouflaged silk and converting it into fashionable mountain neckwear. Meanwhile others were chasing after the nine or ten packages which had been parachuted after me, containing the special radio and other stores and equipment.

A tough-looking individual, his *canadienne* jacket enhancing his naturally thick-set figure, pushed his way through the group around me with an air of authority and I knew this must be Heslop known as Xavier. He was closely followed by a somewhat smaller man – Romans-Petit, the Frenchman who had originally helped to create and coordinate the Maquis camps in the whole area. There was a certain amount of back-slapping and introductory chatter between the three of us before Xavier declared that we must clear the landing zone without delay.

I had been relieved of my jumpsuit and other incriminating equipment by the same lads who accounted for my parachute. Compared with those agents who landed blind and had to dispose of their impedimenta under their own steam, this was money for jam. I hung on to my revolver for the time being, since everyone else carried a weapon of some sort.

We walked to the road which ran down the centre of the valley where an old Citroën was awaiting us. Xavier, Romans and I squeezed into the back and the lanky figure of Marius Roche, who had flashed the recognition letter up from the ground, travelled beside the driver as bodyguard. Xavier, it seemed, when seeing the aircraft making its run-in at right-angles to the lights, had been extremely indignant but Marius and his twin brother Julien, also a torch-bearer, had pacified him by pointing out that the pilot had upheld the traditions of the Royal Air Force by dropping his load plumb on target.

There were no German troops in the immediate vicinity at that moment I was assured but, as our small convoy of cars drove around the edge of Nantua, there were nevertheless detachments of maquisards guarding crossroads. Well before the night was out we, and everybody else, were back in the comparative safety of the mountains. After forty minutes climbing up small mountain roads, which scarcely concerned me as I was being bombarded by Xavier with questions and busy passing back news and instructions from Buckmaster, we arrived at a disused farmhouse, clearly a Maquis hide-out. The night was well advanced and it was not long before we were dossing down on a straw-covered floor to catch up on a little sleep. The straw was on the wet side of damp, and as I began dropping off I can remember thinking how ironic it would be if I now caught pneumonia from it. Thus had two years of headquarters work in London undermined the toughness acquired in Scotland.

I must have slept soundly, as by the time I emerged into the open, the day's chores were well under way. The farmhouse, which had once housed the farmer's family, his hay and even some of his cattle, stood on the brow of a hill, well screened by trees at the rear and sides, with a snow-covered meadow sloping away in front. Men were carrying our fatigues or stripping and cleaning weapons, others just smoking and chatting. I was somewhat naturally an object of interest, especially as I was the first man to be parachuted to the Maquis in this corner of France and, as it turned out, the only one, others being landed by Hudson or Lysander. When I chatted to them I realised that most of them were even younger than they had appeared the night before. Hardly surprising when one remembered how they came to be there.

A year earlier the Germans, working through the puppet Petain government, had introduced the *relève*. Desperate for labour in their factories and on the land, this proposed an exchange of French prisoners of war in return for able-bodied young volunteers prepared to work in Germany. When no volunteers came forward, they invented the *Service du Travail Obligatoire* which put an obligation on certain age groups of young Frenchmen to go to work in Germany. To escape the round-ups which followed, the men left home and in many cases, took to the mountains. Thus, to a great extent the Germans had themselves to blame for the formation of Maquis groups which were to become a thorn in their side. In mid-1943 Captaine Henri Petit, alias Romans, took over the task of bringing some sort of organisation into the various camps in the area and, once shelter and food had been assured, of developing them into a viable guerrilla force. For this a plentiful supply of arms and explosives was required and in October of that year the Inter-Allied mission under Heslop arrived to provide them with logistics support by bringing them into direct W/T contact with London.

'I'm afraid it's going to be ten days or more before your crossing into Switzerland can be laid on,' Xavier explained to me as we talked over a hot drink. 'Romans is arranging it through one of the Maquis groups in the Haute-Savoie, so you'll have to wait here until the go-ahead comes through from them. By the way I've located Paul, our American W/T man, in a quiet spot in the Haute-Savoie and I communicate with him by courier, but unless there is great urgency he won't be able to send a message to London about your arrival for a couple of days or so. Is this okay?'

'Yes, no urgency,' I replied, but at the same time I spared a thought for close friends in Baker Street awaiting news. They must however have received a positive report from the pilot.

'But to fill in the time profitably,' Xavier went on, 'I think Romans is going to ask you whether you'd be prepared to accompany him on an inspection of the camps in this district, so you can judge the situation here for yourself. You'd then be able to report back on it when you reach your destination. You'll have seen that we do have a selection of small arms here – our Stens and a couple of Brens were distributed to us from earlier drops to the so-called Secret Army network – but your op last night was the very first we've had ourselves. It was a new experience for the lads and that is why they are displaying their silk mufflers so proudly today! In the eight or nine weeks I've been here, ops have been held up by bad weather but also, I guess, by priority being awarded elsewhere. The chaps were obviously disappointed last night that no major drop of arms took place but they don't yet realise that, among other essential stores, we received a Eureka which should help pilots to find us in bad visibility and we also got an S-phone, so I'll be able in future to radio-telephone the 'plane. But we've got to get it over to London that we urgently need more weapons and explosives, both to harry the enemy and to be able to defend ourselves. The Germans won't remain in the valleys indefinitely. They don't like coming up here now in small numbers but sooner rather than later they'll attempt a large-scale raid.'

I did not comment immediately on Romans' proposal to go visiting. I had in mind my last interview with Gubbins, during which he stressed that my job was to get into Switzerland without delay and without drawing attention to myself and, as he put it, to avoid the temptation to get involved in blowing anything up on the way. Nevertheless, I did not fancy chickening-out on what appeared to be an interesting request and by the time Romans came up to join us I had my answer ready.

He was stocky with blond hair brushed back from a broad forehead, his Roman nose and prominent chin drawing one's gaze. Old enough to have fought – but certainly as a very young man – in the First World War, in 1940 as a reserve air force officer he refused to give up the struggle when the French capitulated. Early on, he become involved in underground resistance which led to the local Free French giving him his present Maquis command. He was not at first sight an impressive figure in his old windcheater and baggy trousers (needing to move around his large parish he could not afford to indulge in quasi-paramilitary garb) but he had a way with men – 'mes petits' he called his young maquisards – and they responded and accepted his authority.

Romans received my agreement to an inspection of the troops with some enthusiasm and suggested we start straight away with the local set-up. The farm where we slept, known as 'Le Fort', was deep in the splendid mountainous countryside immediately to the south of Nantua. It was currently Romans' HQ and his immediate entourage, apart from Xavier, included Chabot (Henri Girousse) a regular army officer who had been given command of the southern sector in which we were situated, and Marius and Julien Roche. Chabot and Marius had inherited my parachuting gloves, one taking the inner pair, the other the outer. Neither pair of gloves survived the war, Marius's going up in flames in La Ferme de la Montagne and Chabot's finally disappearing in the confusion of active operations. Happily, both men themselves lived to see the Germans quit their country but Julien sadly did not.

We walked a few hundred yards up the road, not much more than a track under winter conditions, to Camp Michel. This occupied a much larger farm complex and the strength, I was told, amounted to around ninety men. It was they who provided the protection for the drop at Izernore and I had indeed been impressed by their behaviour and by the fact that even our car had been stopped last night and checked before being allowed through to the farm.

'Yes, they're a good bunch but it was not an easy process to train them,' said Romans, after we had chatted to some of the men and I had complimented them on their turn-out the previous night. 'They'd had no previous military experience and at the beginning we had few if any men capable of acting as instructors. Now that we're in business we are attracting some more experienced men. We're fortunate to have Chabot with us, an officer of outstanding ability, but even he's had

191

to learn to adapt himself to guerrilla warfare. Camp Michel is one of our best armed but even so, you'll know yourself, taking on an enemy equipped with machine-guns and mortars with only short-range Stens is a bit of a lost cause. Mind you, we try to avoid confrontation by employing hit and run tactics but situations can arise when you need heavier weapons to hold back the Boche and to cover your retreat. For instance, if they came up here in force and attacked our camps. Then again, when the Allied invasion comes, we'll need better armament to make our contribution and this can't be sent to us overnight. And we must have explosives in ample quantities. At present, we have to ration ourselves and we couldn't carry out a sustained and widespread attack against enemy communications which will certainly be expected of us when the time comes. My good friend Xavier – and I could not ask for a better colleague – has attempted to drive home these points to London but space in our radio communications is limited. To sum up, we need more arms and explosives and more emphasis on heavier weapons. If you can support our plea when you get to Switzerland we'll be more than grateful.'

This continued to be the main theme as we went from camp to camp, some small, some major, in the next few days. Xavier would accompany us if he had no pressing work of his own – instructing, reconnoitring, inspecting possible dropping zones. On one day, indeed, I went off with him alone, not to see a camp but to visit the Leopold family in the village of Poncin. They were stalwart resisters and Xavier could always find shelter with them if needed. We drove down from the mountains to the valley of the river Ain. On our way, we stopped off at a farm where Xavier went to check that the road to Pontin was clear. He explained that the farmer's wife was part of a chain which gave warning of any German movement out of their garrison areas. Mme Leopold had cooked us a lunch which was a delight after the spartan fare of the Maquis camps. Her pretty daughter Janine, helping to serve the meal, lent a touch of glamour to the proceedings.

On the way back, Xavier talked of the tightrope which in his first few weeks he had had to walk. London somewhat naturally looked upon him, as head of the Anglo-French-American mission, to be in command on the spot. The local underground Free French organisation in Lyons, whose appointee Romans was, regarded the latter as the boss and were scared of Romans becoming 'London's man'. But Romans was both a patriot and a realist. He kept his allegiance to Lyons but he collaborated fully with Xavier as this was where the future source of material aid lay, without which the Maquis might not survive. By a piece of good fortune Romans and Xavier saw eye-to-eye on virtually all issues, and a potent friendship based on mutual respect had already taken root. Romans remained in command, Xavier his indispensable adviser.

Apart from Pierre Marcault's group tucked away in the area of Hauteville, and where I was introduced to the excellent local eau-de-vie, I clearly remember one camp I visited but can no longer pinpoint. Romans and I were driven to a spot at the bottom of a hillside and we then proceeded to climb up what was presumably a path hidden beneath deep snow. At times, it was so steep that for every two paces upwards we slid back one. Romans, fifteen or more years my senior, took this in his stride but it was hard going for me although I tried not to show it. My own skiing boots and trousers were fine but my heavy 'escaper's' overcoat was not suited to mountaineering and I was sweating profusely by the time we emerged from the trees some several hundred feet higher up. It was then but a short distance along relatively flat ground to a wooden chalet.

Drawn up in front of it were its fifteen or so inhabitants and fluttering above their heads, next to the Croix de Lorraine, flew a second flag, not an entirely accurate home-made copy but certainly fully recognisable as the Union Jack. At a word of command, they sang their own version of 'God Save the King', followed by a more confident rendering of the Marseillaise. I was more than a little moved as I stood to attention, forgetting the runnels of perspiration trickling down inside my clothing. Nor did it occur to me that at that moment an area, luckily only a small one, of Berne Station's new code pads was being washed away within my sodden belt.

By the end of our tours of inspection I had memorised the locations and strengths of the various camps and composed in my mind's eye the lengthy telegram I would despatch from Berne. As I was not in a position to learn London's reactions to my report until long after, I have to rely on testimony of those at the receiving end.

In his book *Les Obstinés*, published shortly after the end of hostilities, Romans-Petit writes as follows:

'I explained the situation (lack of arms) to a senior British officer who parachuted on one of the grounds in the Ain. He listened with unflagging attention to all my complaints. In the course of his short stay amongst us he discovered a veritable army, he watched manoeuvres and took part in discussions which followed practical exercises.

'We emphasised that even if we were well supplied with Stens, we nevertheless only had six light machine guns in the whole of the department and no heavy ones at all. Our reserves in explosives were meagre.

'He assured me he would report immediately to HQ in London. I had confidence in him as he didn't waste words … and he proved to us that he had a good memory since I do not believe that I am mistaken in attributing to his intervention the numerous drops that followed both in the Ain and Haute-Savoie.

'One thing is certain: the composition of the arms deliveries was completely modified from the beginning of February. We at last received an important number of Bren guns.'

Heslop, in his book *Xavier*,[1] tells that after Christmas 1943 he informed London that the number of men in camps had greatly increased but more arms had not been forthcoming. 'I demanded more stores, more guns, explosives, drugs and clothing. Strangely enough, I got approval for every operation I demanded and, though delighted, I could not understand why. Then I remembered the VIP captain (Romans had 'promoted' me to colonel but I was in fact a major) who had passed through the Ain a little earlier … He told me he would contact London the instant he reached Geneva and add his insistence to my request. Now I believe he kept his word.'

But the German major offensive against the Maquis de l'Ain took place before most of the new arms had time to arrive and be put to use. At dawn on 5 February 1944, German troops took control of the roads surrounding the mountainous country south of the Nantua-Bellegarde-Geneva axis and, deploying 5,000 men equipped with machine-guns and mortars, backed up at times by aircraft based at Ambérieu, set out to eradicate all resistance within these boundaries. A column drove up to Brénod with the intention of eliminating Camp Michel, Le Fort and Le Molard, a nearby farm to which HQ had moved a couple of days previously. Camp Michel just had sufficient warning to organise a delaying action which held off the Germans, labouring on foot in deep snow, that day. At night, they evacuated the camp and next morning the enemy, reinforced by artillery, bombarded the farmhouses, not aware that they were now unoccupied. All that remains fifty years later of the farm I stayed in is one short stretch of wall. Other camps further south suffered similar fates but in general the tactic of disappearing into the forest, where the Germans were not prepared to follow, paid off. But in mid-winter with new snow falling to a depth of nearly two feet

---

[1] *Xavier: A British Secret Agent With The French Resistance.*

this entailed severe difficulties and hardships, but the Maquis survived and regrouped, hardened by their baptism of fire. Some thirty young men lost their lives in battle, the Germans taking no prisoners, and rather more villagers were massacred as reprisals on the orders of the Gestapo. Few arms were lost but food supplies previously 'liberated' from the Germans and French Militia, plus motor transport, had to be abandoned.

It was the HQ staff who perhaps had the hardest time. It so happened that Romans was visiting Haute-Savoie, for which he was also responsible, and had great difficulty in getting back. Chabot was deputising for him; and Paul, the W/T operator, had returned from Haute-Savoie a week or two before and was at HQ. Gestapo informers had done their work and the new location was already known, although this was not realised at first. The small group kept their heads down the first day but the following they had to fight their way out to the safety of the forest and then started on a lengthy slog to La Ferme de la Montagne north-east of Ambérieu. Meanwhile Paul had reported the evening before that the BBC message announcing an arms drop for that very night had been broadcast. Chabot and Xavier decided that business must continue as usual, and Xavier and two escorts made the twelve-mile march to the ground in question. The weather was too foul for the aircraft to find their lights but Xavier managed to make contact on his recently arrived S-phone, but the 'plane had to drop its load blind. As luck would have it, the containers were found several days later by patriots who handed them over to the Maquis.

Xavier now had the misfortune to fall in the deep snow and split his leg open. Bleeding profusely, he was unable to continue and had to shelter with sympathisers until medical aid could be obtained. Meanwhile the HQ group of some twenty arrived at the Ferme de la Montagne and, exhausted, started settling in. Chabot and another went out to reconnoitre defence positions and were shattered to find a German detachment some two hundred-strong advancing up the steep and narrow track and effectively cutting them off from the others. Almost at once the small farmhouse was under attack, and when mortars came into action and the house was afire, the position became untenable. Paul, proving himself as good a fighting soldier as a W/T operator, took control and led out a sortie. A meadow, with no cover save a few folds in the ground, led four hundred yards to the edge of the forest which then climbed steeply away. Ten men ran for it from behind the immediate shelter of an outhouse and were not at once spotted but then the Germans got a machine-gun in position and the gunner began to get the range. Paul set the example zig-zagging, throwing himself down in the snow, getting up and running another spurt. Paul, Marius Roche, some eight in all, reached safety but Julien Roche was one who did not. Ludo (Pierre Chassé) had been hit twice but his comrades dragged him along on yet another marathon march, at the end of which a doctor was found to attend to him. Another ten did not leave the farm alive.

If all this had taken place three weeks earlier, my passage to Switzerland would, to say the least, have been problematical. As it happened, I left the Maquis de l'Ain in the lull before the storm. It would not have been quite correct to say that I was sorry to leave; my job was to get into Switzerland and I was keen to get on with it. But I was grateful for the friendship and assistance I had received. What I had seen had been quite a revelation and I had genuinely been impressed by the spirit and the potential of the Maquis. That Baker Street seemed to have acted on my recommendations was probably due to the fact that I was, as it were, one of them and had no reason not to be objective.

Romans had announced two or three days previously that he needed to pay a quick visit to Geneva and was taking the opportunity to accompany me. I did not enquire, nor did I discover, the nature of his business, except that it was a one-off expedition on his part, but I welcomed his company.

Octave Tardy, who had driven us away from my landing ground, again provided the transport. We left on 14 January *'en voiture gazo'*. This was a car adapted to run on gas generated in a wood-burner, and not only did this save precious petrol but, as a civilian vehicle, probably attracted less attention to itself. We headed for St. Julien-en-Genevois a few miles our side of the frontier from Geneva, where we were to meet a car from an Haute-Savoie Maquis. We only had one slight excitement; going round a bend in the road we saw two hundred yards ahead a French police check-point. Tardy pulled up, executed a quick three-point turn in someone's driveway and we were retreating the way we had come. This seemed to go unnoticed and we soon turned off to make a fairly extensive detour back to our original road.

'If we can avoid having our false papers examined, so much the better,' said Romans, and I entirely agreed with him.

We made our rendezvous and said goodbye to Tardy, whom I next met forty-five years later when he was still 'messing about in cars' and running his own garage in Brénod.

The small Maquis, where we were to stay overnight, was housed in what was more a primitive chalet than a farmhouse. It was lodged rather precariously on a thickly-wooded slope, somewhere in the mountains immediately above the French frontier town of Annemasse. Romans was soon in deep discussion with two of the leaders and I took a short walk around. Compared with what I had seen in the Ain I was unimpressed. The cheerfulness and the sense of purpose were less evident, indeed I did not particularly like the feel of the place. The evening meal was not a very joyful occasion and then we were subjected to an 'entertainment' which I and, I suspect, Romans could have done without. A thirty-year-old Frenchman was brought in and made to sit on a kitchen chair in the middle of the room. An aggressive looking maquisard stood behind his back with the muzzle of an extremely large automatic – not one I could identify – held to the nape of his neck. If it had been fired one could have imagined it would have just about have blown his head off. He was then accused of treachery and collaboration and every effort made to force a confession out of him, although he was not beaten to any serious extent. One knew of course that traitors had to pay for their wrong deeds but it was pretty obvious that they had laid on a set-piece for Romans' and my benefit, but with what object in view was not clear to me. Maybe they wanted to demonstrate their own toughness; certainly, they terrified their victim out of his wits but this did not necessarily make him guilty. Eventually they hauled him outside again and, although I for one kept an ear open for the sound of a shot, none was to be heard.

Romans and I left early in the morning before it was fully light. I was not sorry to go as neither the place nor the people inspired me with much confidence. But to be fair, the arrangements made for our onward passage certainly worked. We were dropped close to the Poste de Douanes in one of the main streets of the little town of Annemasse. We were expected and were hustled down a flight of stairs which led to a small basement room, used as a store for old archives. The official looking after us was understandably a bit jumpy, now having a Maquis leader and a supposed British escaping aviator in his cellar. He looked both of us over and was not very happy with what he saw, particularly my appearance. Couldn't I do something about it? I didn't explain that my naturally heavy beard had not enjoyed shaving with a blunt razor at a half-frozen pump in the backyard before dawn, that my clothes had been slept in for the last twelve days and, worst of all, SOE had not provided me with the French equivalent of Brylcreem so that my shock of fair hair insisted on standing on end in mute protest. Unremarkable in a Maquis context but perhaps less so in a frontier town. He fetched me a cup of hot water and I did what little I could to remedy matters.

We spent three hours behind locked doors, fortified by a bottle of wine and a chunk of bread. Romans quite enjoyed himself as he delved into the archives, finding them fascinating, emitting occasional exclamations of astonishment or chuckles of amusement, but they meant little or nothing to me and I soon gave them up.

At last we heard our mentor pitter-pattering down the stairs and unlocking the door.

'Now collect your things and follow my instructions. Go up the stairs – I will remain here – and leave the building. No rushing, no haste. Against the wall directly opposite you, you will see two bicycles. Also, a uniformed *douanier* ready to ride off. Show no signs of recognition. When he rides off, take a bicycle each and first you,' signalling to Romans, 'follow him but keeping thirty metres behind him. Then your friend follows you, also thirty metres distance behind. If any incident occurs there is no connection between any of you. You will arrive at the bridge crossing the river which forms the frontier. Follow the instructions you will be given there.'

It was a strange and somewhat unnerving sensation riding close past German soldiery walking or standing and chatting on the pavement. In Britain, we had at least been spared occupation and it was an unaccustomed and rather unnerving sensation having to rub shoulders with the enemy. After the remarks made about my appearance I felt even more conspicuous than I might have done and I was glad when one after another we turned down a side street.

We arrived at what must have been in peacetime one of the main crossing points over the River Forun. Now barbed-wire barriers straddled the roadway leading across, and even the parapets either side were topped with wire for a short distance of their length. There were no buildings at this point except for a little hut thirty yards back from the river housing two *douaniers* but what their duties were, unless the barriers were sometimes removed, was difficult to guess. Whilst our original *douanier* cycled back the way we had come, his colleagues started shouting instructions at us but were not prepared to leave their hut. Put the cycles against the trees, that was simple, but climb round the edge of the bridge was perplexing.

'Get a shift on before the boche come back,' they urged but were unwilling to demonstrate.

It was I who finally understood their flow of admonitions. On the outside of the parapet, about three feet down, there ran a ledge of about a brick and a half's width right across to the other side, 150 yards away. There was a way, perhaps surreptitiously engineered, of getting past the wire and stepping on to the ledge. The first little bit was more difficult, holding on to the wire and shuffling one's feet sideways, but then the wire ceased and one could hold the top of the parapet itself. It was now that I realised that the river was thirty feet below running in a gorge with steep banks topped on both sides with wire. I also became conscious of the Swiss *douaniers* enjoying the spectacle and cheering the two of us on, but neither of us had any intention of falling off our perch.

To the Swiss customs officials we must have been just two more escapers but they gave us a warm welcome, shaking our hands and clapping us on our backs. They took us into their hut as they explained that they did not want us seen by the German patrol which was soon due to pass along the French bank. It was now discovered, to our hosts' amusement but not to his, that Romans had split the seat of his trousers from top to bottom on the barbed-wire. But aid was close at hand, since the wife of one of the *douaniers* was visiting the post and, with exemplary Swiss efficiency, she produced needle and thread from her handbag and set about repairing the damage.

Romans was still sitting in his underpants when a hefty young man appeared at the door in civilian clothes.

'I belong to Swiss Field Security,' he announced in excellent English. 'Which of you claims to be a British escaper?'

'That's me. I would like to report to the British Consulate.'

'Yes, indeed, but first I must have details or your identity.'

Formalities over, I said goodbye to Romans and was driven by the young man the eight kilometres into Geneva, straight to the Consulate, which was housed separately from the Consulate-General. We were both shown into the office of a Mr Farrell who, rather to my surprise, turned out to be well acquainted with my Swiss official. I did not yet realise that Vic Farrell knew everyone worth knowing in Geneva and that his fame as supposed head of the 'Secret Service' had spread across the frontier into France, enabling those with intelligence to impart to know whom to contact.

'The usual drill, if you agree,' the Swiss told Farrell. 'You'll be responsible, won't you, for him until the morning and a sergeant will then escort him from the hotel to Berne.'

When we were left alone, Vic came round from behind his desk and shook me warmly by the hand, in contrast to his previous polite but non-committal greeting.

'Well done! We've been expecting you for the last day or two, although we did know you'd been somewhat delayed. Not too many problems on the way?'

'So, you're in touch with Jock McCaffery?' I knew that one should only confide in those in the know.

'Yes, very much so. We – er – collaborate a certain amount together. I'll let him know you've arrived and you'll meet him tomorrow afternoon. The Swiss army will question you when you arrive in Berne in mid-morning to make certain you're above board and then hand you over to the legation. Now let's have a chat but I won't detain you longer than I would normally do with any other escaper.'

He listened with interest to my short account of my doings and I was impressed by his considerable background knowledge of events and personalities. As we talked I warmed to this older but very enthusiastic man and I recognised him as a true professional at his work. I began to get the feeling that he, for his part, approved of me, which was fortunate since, in days to come, he had to rely on my discretion and tradecraft not to put him in a very embarrassing position with his employers.

'Right then. Off to your hotel where there'll be a room booked under the name of Paterson. Have a good dinner and above all a good sleep. They'll let you know what time you're being picked up tomorrow. We'll surely meet again.'

It was still daylight when I went into the bathroom for a proper shave and then luxuriated in a wonderful hot bath. I thought back on the friends I had made over the last ten days, experiencing a touch of guilt at leaving them to their uncertain fate. How, I wondered, would Romans get back to France again? I might never know. But chiefly I looked forward rather than back with a mix of excitement and curiosity.

When I stepped back into my bedroom I was stopped in my tracks. Then I went to the window and looked out in amazement. The street and flood lighting of Geneva blazed forth, the first I had seen for close on four and a half years.

I had well and truly arrived in neutral Switzerland!

CHAPTER 13

Clandestine to Switzerland

I had a companion to travel to Berne with me, a crew member of an American Flying Fortress which had been shot down over an unspecified area of France. He had been put in the same hotel as me and we had had the opportunity to talk. He was not the least interested how I had happened to arrive in Switzerland, which suited me, but he was intensely anxious to know what was likely to happen to him now that some Frenchmen, with whom he had be unable to communicate, had smuggled him over the frontier. It began to emerge that not having been in Europe very long and not having been the navigator or pilot, he had no idea where his aircraft had been shot down, not the slightest knowledge of any towns or areas of France he had traversed in the company of French patriots and, to top it all, only the vaguest impression of where and what Switzerland was.

Our escorting gendarme took the two of us to a set of modest offices somewhere in Central Berne and handed us over to the senior NCO clerk. After a while a small, dapper, well-groomed captain came out of his office and called in the American. He was in there close on an hour which, judging by the NCO's facial expressions and anxious looks at his watch – the lunch hour was approaching – was an abnormally long session. At times, I could hear raised voices through the door and when the two finally came out, I noticed that it seemed to be the captain who looked ruffled rather than the American.

'Now, I hope you are not going to tell me that you also know nothing, but *absolutely* nothing, of where you have been or what you have done over the last three weeks,' the captain told me in a slightly strangled voice, as he led me back into his office. '*Du lieber Gott!*' he continued half to himself, 'it takes an act of faith to believe anyone can be genuinely so ignorant and so stupid, yes, stupid!'

I offered up a vote of thanks to my American colleague as I felt that unwittingly he had paved the way for me. Only I must not come out with my well-rehearsed story too blithely, in case the very contrast raised any doubts. I soon found that the captain, perhaps keen to catch up on his schedule, was egging me on and happy with my fluency. The crucial point, on which all bona fide airmen were briefed, was to claim, at some stage in one's story, that one had been captured by the enemy and then escaped. One was then categorised under the Geneva Convention as an escapee with the right to be put back over the frontier at any time one requested and not as an internee who could only leave the country at the termination of hostilities. It was rumoured that some Swiss interrogators actually gave RAF airmen a nudge if they forgot to make this claim. I was not prepared to take a risk on this and so, as a seeming afterthought, I related how I had been picked up in Belgium by a German patrol and then had seized an opportunity of jumping out of the back of their truck.

'Quite, exactly, yes,' said the captain, smiling as he noted down this important fact. After this, the interrogation proceeded at even greater speed and my reluctance to give any exact details of people who had helped me on my way down to Switzerland was accepted without demur.

'That is all I have to ask you,' concluded the captain, 'and thank you for making my task easy. Have you any Swiss money?'

'None at all.'

'Well, I will give you transport across to the British Legation where you must report to the Air Attaché's office. He will look after your needs and then send you to join the other RAF officers billeted in Arosa. By the way, do you ski?'

'Only very inexpertly.'

'You'll be taught to ski properly there. They say the snow is good at the moment. I envy you!'

I had been briefed in London that Air Commodore Freddy West, who had lost a leg in the Flying Corps during the First World War but in compensation gained a VC, would know all about me. He would see that I met McCaffery but the rank and file of the legation were solely to be given my cover story. I was a bit disconcerted when I was told on arrival that the Air Commodore, artificial leg and all, had just gone off on a long weekend's skiing and, more so, when it became obvious that his assistant, Wing Commander Jones, had not been put in the picture.

Jones sat me down, ready to compose a telegram for despatch to the Air Ministry about my escape. I tried to play for a little time as I debated whether I fed him with my bogus story or committed the cardinal sin of blowing my own cover within a couple of minutes of arrival. Jones wanted to get on with things – perhaps he also had a skiing appointment – so I took the easy way out and gave him the phoney details.

Jones, whom I later learnt was himself an escapee, handed his draft telegram to his clerk and then explained that once formalities had been completed and I had been kitted out with some essential clothing, I would be sent up to Arosa. Clearly some other action on my part was essential.

'By the way, when I passed through the consulate in Geneva I was entrusted with a personal message to be given to a Mr McCaffery.'

'Oh, yes, that's the Assistant Press Attaché. If you give it to me I'll see he gets it.'

'I'm afraid they were most insistent that I handed it over to him in person.'

The wing commander looked for a moment as if he were going to pull his rank on this precocious pilot officer but then changed his mind and picked up the telephone.

'I've got a newly-arrived escapee here who says he was given a message for you … Oh, right.'

'He's coming down.'

We sat in silence for a short while until a man of not more than medium height with a round face, somewhat heightened complexion and curly brown hair burst into the room. His Irish eyes were twinkling and he had a great grin on his face. I was smiling in relief as we shook hands rather formally.

'I have been expecting this message and, if you have no objection, I think I had better take our friend here up to my office for a minute or two.'

We went up to a suite of offices on the first floor, cluttered with filing cabinets and card-indices and overlooking the busy Thunstrasse. Jock McCaffery bubbled over with questions and congratulations on my safe arrival. The three other current members of the staff crowded round and more chatter ensued. It took some time until I could remind Jock of the misleading telegram which Jones was proposing to send to London.

'Yes, I think we have no option but to indoctrinate Jones into our little ploy. Look, I think it would be more tactful if I go down and have a word with him while you stop here and chat.'

'He was completely taken in,' said Jock on return. 'But he's a solid chap and I have no doubt he'll be discreet. However, he was a bit embarrassed as I was just too late to prevent him sending his telegram to the Air Ministry.

'He shouldn't worry.' I was quite confident. 'The Air Ministry have a big red star against the name of Paterson and they'll probably notify Baker Street of my safe arrival before even we do.'

'That's fine then. He says there's a spare room in his digs round the corner and then Monday morning he'll send you out to buy some clothes and then give you tickets and instructions to get to Arosa. I'm afraid you'll have to do a few weeks up there as Freddy, and indeed, the ambassador insist we go through the usual drill and draw no attention to you. It should be no hardship to you and you'll find some fifty RAF aircrew up there under Swiss Army supervision. The plan is that, as soon as thought fit, you'll be called down ostensibly to reinforce the section attached to the legation which administers and pays escapees and internees. There are, of course, many more Army than RAF in Switzerland, mostly POWs who made their way here after the Italian capitulation, before the Germans could round them up again. So, you might as well have a rest and enjoy yourself while you can.'

'That's okay with me, but before I go off I would like to draft a rather lengthy telegram to London giving them the low-down on Xavier's Maquis and detailing the arms and equipment they urgently need. Talking of telegrams, that reminds me.' I stripped off my belt and handed it over.

'How do we read the pages?' asked Jock after I had described its hidden contents.

'I'm afraid you'll have to beg or borrow a microscope,' I explained to a somewhat disbelieving head of station. 'The signals people are genuinely worried about your having to double up on your one-time pads and they want you to switch to these new ones as soon as you can.'

'Gosh, transcribing your microdots is going to be a job and a half but if they say so we'll have to find a way of doing it.'

My telegram drafted and despatched, I had dinner in the head secretary's flat – unaccustomed luxuries ending up with defrosted raspberries and loads of real (!) cream. Ann Moore, other than Jock the only home-based member of staff, told me how alarmed they had all been when Jock went off to the nursing-home but, luckily, he seemed to have bounced back. But with the work-load likely to go on increasing in 1944 it was reassuring to have help at hand. There would be more than enough to do once I got established in Berne.

The next morning, I reported again to Wing Commander Jones, who, nice chap though he was, could not resist getting a little of his own back by informing me that the Air Ministry, in response to his telegram announcing my arrival, stated that they had no record of a Paterson of my description, that my alleged RAF number contained an incorrect number of digits and that I must therefore be considered an imposter.

I sat for a while dumbfounded, considering what would have been my fate if I had been made a POW by the Germans and the Red Cross had delivered this judgement to my captors. The 'red star' against the name of Paterson must either have failed to do its stuff or, perhaps more likely, the Air Ministry had never taken the question of my cover very seriously and no warning marker had ever been inserted in their records. Then I pulled myself together, accepted the fact that the worst had not occurred and stopped worrying.

I set off, this time unaccompanied, to Zurich where I changed trains for Chur. I had some time to spare in Chur, feeling it was a strange circumstance in which to visit for the very first time the town from which the Swiss branch of my family hailed. There was, I knew, still some relatives in or around the town; I had never met them and this was clearly not the moment to do so. I continued my journey on the little mountain railway up to Arosa, where I reported to the Rothorn Hotel.

When being briefed in London, my fall-back cover of a shot-down airman envisaged the prospect of having to sustain my story to the Swiss and, at the very worst, to the Germans, but having to fool a large contingent of RAF aircrew in Switzerland during an extended period of cohabitation had not been foreseen. McCaffery and I had had a short discussion before I left Berne on the subject and we both agreed that to let the senior RAF officer in Arosa – an unknown factor as far as we were concerned – into the know might end up being counter-productive. No, counselled Jock, you hoodwinked the Assistant Air Attaché, just do the same to the others.

The Rothorn, at the top end of the town, was a medium-sized hotel, no longer very smart and which, lacking the peacetime influx of foreign tourists, had been requisitioned to accommodate the RAF escapers. Until recently, whilst welcoming an intermittent trickle of new evaders, it had also seen a fairly regular outflow of officers, whose exit from Switzerland and passage to the Spanish frontier via underground escape lines had been organised by the Air Attaché and British Intelligence. For one reason or another, this had now come to a halt – a temporary one the inmates hoped.

There were two Swiss Army reserve officers in charge of the place but the senior British officer was responsible to them for day to day discipline and also for distributing the meagre pocket money allowance sent up from the Air Attaché's office. It was to this officer that I reported since the Swiss, after conclusion of the day's skiing, went back to their families.

I was invited to join the wing commander at a table where he was having a glass of beer. He asked me a few general questions but when he discovered I had been a tail-gunner on a Halifax he called over a young man to join us, who, as I feared, turned out to be a genuine gunner. All very politely and innocent-seeming, the newcomer went over my past history and when I told him the number and location of the air gunnery school I claimed to have attended, he declared that was where he had been sent as well.

'Which gunnery instructor were you under?'

'Oh, Handlebar Smith. Did you come across him?'

'Good Heavens, yes. Splendid chap. And those moustaches, quite extraordinary!' As my interrogator transformed into a nostalgic narrator, I sat and thanked my lucky stars for that evening in the flat beside Regents Park, when I debriefed my 'look-alike' young airman. From the benevolent smile on the wing commander's face it was clear I had passed my test.

The next morning the Swiss major in change, who I had learnt was a top ski instructor in civilian life, took a few details from me but chiefly seemed concerned to know of my skiing ability. When I admitted that I was little more than a beginner, he lost interest and passed me on to the captain.

The major, who like the rest of us never appeared in uniform, but who nevertheless managed to convey his rank, took a selected group of the better skiers and set himself the task of turning them into gold medallists. The captain took the remainder. The latter, I soon discovered, was not only older in age but in technique and outlook as well. He was an altogether charming man, as un-militaristic as they made them. He may have lacked the push and drive of his superior but he had one accomplishment that no one could remove from him, the reputation, so they said, of being the finest exponent of Telemark skiing in the country.

Skiing instruction took place every weekday morning and of an afternoon one could ski under one's own steam or do what one liked. The only restriction on one's movement was the fact that it was not permitted to leave Arosa. I was soon fitted up with skis – I had my own boots – and, after one morning on the nursery slopes finding my feet again, I joined the captain's class. He was the kindliest of instructors and one of the most elegant of skiers. If the snow was right, his class would beg him to give a demonstration of the already outdated but stylish Telemark. Then to the warm applause of his pupils, he would gently zigzag down the snowy slope with the ease of a ballerina. It was on an occasion such as this that I would suddenly shake myself and wonder how the heck I had landed up in the middle of a war in a place like this!

As time went on, and there was still no word from Berne, I became a reasonably proficient skier and I would join companions on the piste in the afternoon. But as the season developed and my colleagues became more and more foolhardy, the number of broken limbs began to reach epidemic proportions. I particularly remember two Polish pilots who, when not risking their own necks, spent their time urging others: 'Just point 'em down, boy. Point 'em down'. I knew it was up to me to try to remain in one piece but friends hobbling around the Rothorn on crutches did rather alarm me.

I found myself at meal-times sitting next to an officer of the South African Airforce. A shade older than most, he did not fit in too comfortably with the young RAF crowd but I liked him both for himself and for the fact that he was less likely to present a danger to my cover. Jerry Orr and I became good friends and it was he who first led me off to sample the limited wartime après-ski of Arosa.

'I must tell you I've only got enough to pay for one, maximum two drinks,' I pointed out to him.

'That's all any of us have, so you just have to find a girl who'll pay for you. With not too many Swiss up here, the RAF are quite popular. You shouldn't have much difficulty.'

We stood at the bar of the cafe and paid over precious currency for a drink apiece. Almost immediately Jerry was pulled on to the dance floor by a female acquaintance and I knew his evening drinking was secured. I looked around and pinpointed a well-built but rather attractive young lady sitting at a table with two older couples. Worth a try I thought and went over and asked the girl to dance. I cannot recollect whether I addressed her in French or German but I quickly realised that she was a highly intelligent and educated person and we seemed to enjoy each other's company.

The music stopped and I escorted Anneliese back to her table where she introduced me to her parents. They at once invited me to join them and, as I sat down, I caught sight of Jerry giving me a surreptitious thumbs-up.

The first thing I was made aware of, with a certain amount of relief on my part, was that all members of the party were fully aware of the financial restrictions placed upon me. Anneliese's father, I then discovered, was an industrialist from Rorschach on the Swiss side of Lake Constance, her mother was French and hence desperately pro-Allied and she herself had come up for the mountain air because of a chest complaint – not infectious, I was assured. The other man in the group was one of the top bosses of the World Bank.

For the next ten or twelve days, the same group met up in the cafe virtually every evening until it was time for the parents to return home leaving Anneliese to continue her cure. Her father told me that they would be happy if I cared to continue meeting their daughter and of course, don't be embarrassed, she would be able to pay any expenses. I gratefully agreed, especially as I had taken care to let Anneliese know that I had a girl in England whom I proposed to marry once I got back and this had not disturbed the pleasure we had in each other's company.

One morning the wing-commander came up to me at breakfast and said he wanted a word with me. He had no office so I drank the remains of my coffee and went across to his table.

'I've had a message up from the attaché's office,' he told me, 'saying that they'd be glad of you back in Berne for some office job or other. Now before you comment, I must tell you that this has happened before and the chap concerned turned the offer down, partly because he was afraid it might prejudice his chances of being chosen to go out via Spain and partly because, if he had to kick his heels about in Switzerland, he preferred to do it up here. Now if you should feel the same way I'm prepared to tell them so.'

To say that I was actually tempted by the wing commander's offer would be an exaggeration but I did enjoy a fleeting vision of the consternation I would cause both in Berne and Baker Street if I allowed him to go ahead!

'Well, they did comment on my knowledge of languages when I passed through the legation,' I began rather hesitantly, 'and I suppose they feel I can be of some help. I would in fact like to improve my French and German as this might be useful to me later on. No, I think I would like to go.' I could see that this did not go down too well, not the attitude of a keen young airman.

'Very well then, I tell them you're coming.'

McCaffery was waiting to see me when I reported in to the legation.

'I'm terribly sorry, Pat, but the local powers-that-be decided that it would be more natural for you to do a week or two at the consulate-general in Geneva before being transferred to Berne. I can't see the logic of it but there is nothing we can do about it. You'll find they are expecting you there and they'll fix you up with accommodation and anything else you need. Obviously if they have some useful work you can do on their behalf, just do it until we can get you back here again.'

But work was just what the consulate-general did not have for me. An empty office and empty In and Out trays, yes, but no work. None of the staff asked me what I was doing there – it was not fashionable to do so in wartime – and if they had I would not have known what to reply since escapers were administered from Berne not Geneva. Instead I read the *Journal de Genève* and any other newspapers I could get hold of from cover to cover and practised Leo Marks' sophisticated newly-invented personal code to make sure I still remembered it. But luckily, I am one of those who never entirely get bored in a strange city and, as frequently as I dared, I deserted my desk and walked the streets of Geneva. This orientation was subsequently of some assistance to me.

I chiefly remember my three or four weeks in Geneva for the kindness of the head of SIS in Switzerland. He of course knew about me from McCaffery and, being less worried about the delicacy of my cover than some others, he took me under his wing, found me accommodation in his residential hotel and both he and his wife could not have been more charming.

Finally, I came to rest back in Berne, I moved into Wing Commander Jones's digs once more and shared the breakfast table with him for the next five months. In the office, with McCaffery working at full strength and fortunately showing no signs of his previous breakdown, I took over French Section work from Peter Jellinek who now concentrated on German affairs. Peter, resident in Switzerland, had worked for the Bally Shoe Company before joining the SOE station and, after the war, he ran the British end of Bally. Probably because he was locally recruited and Switzerland was so cut off, little seemed to be known about him in London and I had not even been briefed about him by Buckmaster or anyone else. But, despite no first-hand knowledge of the London end, he had clearly been operating most efficiently and I felt a twinge of guilt at taking his job over.

The main innovation in the office was the temporary attachment from the escapee administration of four officers, ranging from a brigadier down to a squadron leader.

'Ah,' said Brigadier Younghusband as I was introduced to them, 'you're the chap responsible for us becoming cross-eyed!' They had on a desk a microscope and, as they explained, they worked in teams of two. One man peered through the microscope reading out the numbers from one of the microdots from my belt while the other copied them down on paper. When the first team could no longer see straight, the second took over. They told me that a patch of the film had been spoilt by moisture and I remembered my sweaty climb up a mountainside with the Maquis. However, there were plenty of pages undamaged and their transcription would keep them busy for weeks.

During our hand-over Peter took me to meet Harry Rée who had sought refuge in Switzerland for urgent medical treatment and who was about to re-cross into France bound for the Spanish frontier, Gibraltar and ultimately England. It was he who organised the 'blackmail sabotage' of the Peugeot factory near Montbéliard which was being forced to manufacture tank turrets for the Germans. In return for a guarantee of no further RAF raids with their inevitable loss of life, he persuaded the management to assist in putting their own factory out of action. Subsequently he had been carried across the frontier on a stretcher after a hand-to-hand struggle worthy of a Hollywood thriller with a member of the German Feldpolizei. Despite six shots fired at him at close range, one bullet grazing his heart, he still managed to floor his opponent and escape across fields to friends. He showed me his pullover with the bullet holes in it; he had indeed had a miraculous escape.

Apart from assisting any SOE agents who landed up in our territory, my main work consisted of dealing with couriers coming in from F Section agents who used Switzerland as a channel for communications to London. This was either because the agents were without a W/T link of their own or because they had more to send home than their own vulnerable link could safely take. We in the station were of course entirely dependent on radio ourselves and one had to summarise and prune pretty stringently to avoid overloading our channel. In this connection one of the agents who regularly sent in voluminous reports was George Millar, who operated very successfully in the area of Besançon. I would read his great chunk of literature enthralled, that is until I began to work out how to condense it into a shorter telegram. When I later read his

Maquis,[1] one of the earliest and one of the very best of the Resistance books, I knew I had perused considerable portions of it before.

Every so often I had a call to meet René Bertholet bearing mail and news from Tony Brooks. René was more than just a courier; he had from the very beginning helped Tony to set up his *reseau*. In the process, he had acquired an almost passionate admiration for this, the youngest of all F Section agents. The fact that Tony and I were friends gave me a head-start with him. René was a remarkable individual. He was a leading activist in the small and tightly-knit left-wing *Internationaler Sozialistischer Kampfbund (ISK)* or Socialist Vanguard Movement which was formed in Germany in the 1920s as a sort of ginger group. They had done their best to stir up resistance to the Nazi take-over of the country and a few stalwarts remained loyal and unidentified throughout the war. SOE was in touch with their exiled leader, Willi Eichler, in London and managed to make some tentative contact with these 'sleepers' in Germany during the latter stages of the conflict.

René was a Swiss national and was able, in his capacity of a Red Cross official, to cross backwards and forwards between Switzerland and France. Luckily for us he had no qualms about using this facility for doing down the Germans; the ISK preached 'ethical realism', which he interpreted as allowing him to break the law in a good cause. I had been briefed by Tony when we met in London that René was, like all other members of his clan, a vegetarian, based on the fact that they were not only against the exploitation of man by man but also of animals by man. He was furthermore supposed to shun alcohol and tobacco, since these might distract an adherent from his socialist endeavours. Somewhere down the line René must have strayed because he had learnt to smoke like a chimney.

My meetings with René were always a pleasure as he had a quick wit and we were able to indulge in mutual admiration of Tony. It was good to get first-hand news of this paragon and operational data was passed both ways – proposals for or acceptances of new parachute landing grounds, details of derailments and other operations and much else. Meetings always took place in Geneva which meant that I had to take the train there, breaking the travel ban imposed on me as an escapee. I had been tipped off to use a side exit at Geneva station, which contributed to the fact that I never got caught in a Swiss snap check.

---

[1] *Maquis: An Englishman in the French Resistance* (William Heinemann Ltd., 1945).

Another rendezvous I sometimes kept, deputising for McCaffery, was with Allen Dulles, head of OSS in Switzerland and the brother of John Foster Dulles who later became President Eisenhower's Secretary of State. He was lively and approachable, and it did not surprise me when, after the war, he became head of the CIA, the successor to OSS. We would have coffee together and exchange the contents of our briefcases. I remember he used the pseudonym of 'Sioux' in his dealings with us.

The British Legation with the minister's Residence alongside (in those days ambassadors and embassies were reserved for the large missions but, with the coming of post-war fair shares for all, the head of even the smallest mission was not denied ambassadorial rank) stood towards the top of the Thunstrasse, one of the main routes leading southwards out of the city. A few hundred yards further up the hill on the Thunplatz stood the more modern, but uglier, German Legation. But if you walked downhill instead of up you reached the bridge over the swiftly flowing River Aar and ended up in the largely unspoilt old town.

The Four Musketeers comprising our microscope teams had, like me, to find their own midday meal and when we felt flush and in need of hot food we would walk down to the old town. All the small streets around the Marktgasse were flanked at street level by the arcades of solid but attractive old buildings. We found, tucked away within an arcade, a good and reasonably priced *bürgerlich* restaurant which we liked to visit. But we soon established that a group from the German Legation, equally deprived of good eating near their place of work, had a reserved *Stammtisch*[2] near the front of the restaurant. This had the effect of spoiling by their presence the pleasant view from the window of one of Berne's traditional fountains. But we saw no reason why we should have to forego the excellent menu which obligingly fell within the scope of our official allowances, although we made it clear to the staff that we would accept no table close to our enemies.

When we first visited our restaurant, the Germans were relatively cocky, even noisy at times. Then came D-Day and both nationalities were on edge waiting to see which way the battle went. When the Normandy bridgehead appeared to be contained the Germans cheered up but after that their spirits visibly went up and down according to the news, chiefly down. It was when the Americans landed in the south of France that our opposite numbers became permanently silent

---

[2] Regular table.

and dejected. Then one day they came no more and we were left in possession of the field of battle! The canny Swiss did not actually give us drinks on the house to celebrate but the warmth of their welcome from then on went up several degrees. Maybe they feared to lose our custom as well.

D-Day brought its excitement and tensions but its effect on our work took a little time to develop. There had been no call for London to take up time and cypher space keeping Berne informed of general instructions being sent to Resistance reseaux and to the ever more numerous Maquis, but I had a fair idea up to the time I left London of what was being planned. From reports coming through from the field, and from one or two participants taking temporary refuge in Switzerland, we built up a good picture. The Anglo/French/American Jedburgh teams, for which I had been the first volunteer, had gone into action and were proving in most cases very effective. Widespread rail sabotage was hindering German reinforcements moving towards Normandy and 'my' Maquis was going great guns. Arms were continuing to descend on them culminating in a daylight drop by thirty-six flying fortresses. This drop was not without its serio-comic side. US Airforce Flying Fortresses tended to hunt in packs and individual pilots had instructions, in the event of becoming detached from their pack, to attempt to latch on to another. Thus arose the case of the '37th Flying Fortress'. The crews of the Fortresses on their way to the Prairie d'Echallon with supplies for the Maquis de l'Ain were dismayed to find that a 'lost' aircraft had joined up with them. Strict radio silence forbade anything but visual communication and attempts to wave it away merely provoked fraternal waving back. The newcomers must eventually have been astonished to find that their target was a large clearing in the mountain forest and that the other aircraft were parachuting literally hundreds of containers down on it. Luckily, they decided in time to hold back their bombs!

Not all Maquis' fared so well. The Vercors, a high and extensive plateau difficult of access, south-west of Grenoble, contained some 3,000 guerrillas and shortly after D-Day the Germans determined to eradicate this danger in their rear. SOE already had plans to parachute in a mission to arrange further supply drops and also, in line with normal guerrilla practice, to caution against open confrontation with the enemy. This team code-named *Eucalyptus*, consisting of two SOE friends of mine, Desmond Longe and John Houseman, and two W/T operators, went in in uniform at the end of June. Unfortunately, the Maquis command was already bent on standing its ground and denying access to the plateau at all costs. It was only when the Germans sent in a glider armada carrying heavily armed SS troops, who refused to be dislodged, that the order was given to disperse. The main German force now swarmed in and Desmond and John in the resulting mayhem became separated both from their W/T operators, who had also acted as their interpreters since they spoke no French, and from anyone in a position of command.

Apart from what had appeared in the press, the first I knew about all this was when word came through that Longe and Houseman, having made their way through a countryside alive with Germans on full alert, had arrived in Switzerland. They were passed on to me and were very relieved to be told that, with a little patience, they could be sent on their way back to England. Meanwhile I debriefed them and sent the good news of their safety to London. I did not see Desmond again until years later when, having just retired from the job of running Norwich Union, he slapped me on the back in Special Forces Club and insisted on thanking me for getting him out of Switzerland – forty-five years after the event.

Jock McCaffery, a fluent Italian-speaking Irish ex-journalist, was fully busy keeping in touch with Italian resistance groups which were fighting against the German occupation of their country subsequent to Italy's capitulation to the Allies. But, like everyone, he needed the occasional break and I recall a Sunday when he drove his secretary Ann Moore and me into the countryside. He much wanted to see one particular village and being impatient by nature he drove ahead, taking not much notice of Ann who was map-reading in the front seat beside him. Before too long none of us knew where we were and as Jock spoke not one word of German – we all in wartime preferred in any case to speak French rather than German even in German-speaking Berne – he was forced to ask Ann to question a Swiss peasant on the roadside.

She used her good German to do so, since she knew the man would only speak Swiss German.

'Gradoos,' was the reply, being his version of the German *gerade aus*, straight on.

Further down the road Jock pulled up again and Ann, putting her head out of the window, received exactly the same reply. Now Jock was the nicest of bosses but, even so, he did not like to seem too reliant on his secretary, and by now he thought he had got the hang of things. Seeing another man pushing a bicycle on this rather deserted road he pulled up a third time, wound down his own window and shouted '*Gradoos*'.

The peasant looked momentarily bewildered but then grinned at the mad foreigner and waved us straight on. As luck would have it we came to the wanted village a mile down the road.

I was lucky enough to have one weekend away from Berne during my time there. I had kept up a correspondence with Anneliese ever since leaving Arosa. I had no social life outside the office and this human link gave me considerable pleasure. One day she passed on an invitation to visit her parents' home in Rorschach and there was no difficulty in getting special permission from the Swiss to go. I was made extremely welcome and two nights in a comfortable private home was a great treat, as was the cheese fondue prepared by her mother. When the time eventually came for me to leave Switzerland I wrote to them thanking for all their kindness and hospitality, hoping that we would remain friends when the war was finally over; and what I did not add – when difficulties over my dual identity also no longer existed. I could not have known then that fifteen months later when I was demobilised and had joined the Foreign Office, I would be advised to drop any 'Paterson' contacts in Switzerland since they might be a cause of embarrassment if I were to be posted there at a later date. I never was posted there, yet I was prevented from re-contacting these kind friends.

But the war was by no means over. With the Americans pushing up from the south, the area north of the Swiss frontier, the Franche-Comté and the Haute-Saône, formed a natural route of retreat towards the German frontier. We had good lines to resistance groups there thanks to one Jacques Weil. Jacques, considerably older than most of us, had been a businessman in Paris and with Jean Worms jointly ran *Juggler*, an offshoot of the large F Section *Prosper* organisation. The Gestapo penetrated the whole set-up in summer 1943 and Jacques, luckily for him arriving late at a rendezvous, saw Worms being led out of the restaurant in handcuffs. Having Swiss nationality Jacques took refuge in Switzerland. Being a persuasive chap, he developed friendly contact with local Swiss officials at the frontier and was thereby able to keep contact with resisters over the border. He would travel in to Berne where I would meet him and transact our business in a café. I became quite friendly with him and was upset when I got back to London to be told that he had been arrested by the Swiss. He had probably pushed his luck that much too far, but he was released very soon, by which time there was little more in any case for him to do. We did correspond for a while after he re-established himself in Paris, there being no 'Paterson' hitch-up as far as he was concerned.

But not all lines into France were dealt with by Berne station themselves. Indeed, far from it. What I only realised when I started to take over the job, and what Baker Street never really appreciated, was the role Victor Farrell played on our behalf. Vic, whose office was on the ground floor of the Geneva Consulate, ran the SIS Geneva station single-handed as far as I was aware, whilst the SIS Swiss headquarters was on an upper floor. Vic was a brilliant field officer who knew his area backwards, the sort of man senior officers find invaluable but at the same time slightly disapprove of because of their lack of conformity and maybe their untidy staff work. He had, metaphorically speaking, tacked a notice on his door saying: 'Secret Service. Those with contributions to make, please enter.' It was not surprising that at the same time he also attracted contacts which were more applicable to SOE than to SIS. SIS, understandably perhaps, until this stage in the war at least, had found SOE a difficult bedfellow since the latter's 'bangs' stirred up the Germans and could thereby disrupt SIS activities. Vic feared that for this reason he might be instructed not to assist SOE but his attitude was uncomplicated: we're all in the same war and anything that will make life difficult for the Germans should be encouraged. He therefore adopted what seemed to him the right course under the circumstances: he acted as a go-between for the SOE Berne station without informing his superiors.

Taking over the French side at a relatively late stage, I found that many of our connections with Resistance in France were handled by Vic and, without our own man in Geneva, it would indeed have posed a problem if it had not been so. It was when I had occasion to speak privately with Vic and had to sneak into his office without the knowledge of his upper floor that I might have felt guilty vis-à-vis his boss, had I not felt, like Vic, that the war took precedence over everything else.

It goes without saying that over the past months the Lysanders and Hudsons of 161 Squadron had continued their brilliant work of landing clandestinely in Occupied France and ferrying backwards and forwards agents and French VIPs, who included the future President Mitterand. In early July 1944, the US special duties squadron, who nicknamed themselves the Carpetbaggers, added a further dimension by making their first landing in enemy territory on the same ground at Izernore where I had parachuted six months earlier on. To prove the added carrying capacity of the Dakotas with which they were equipped, and as a 'gift' for the Maquis de l'Ain who organised the reception, they squeezed a Jeep into the fuselage! From then on, they continued operating clandestinely until the area was liberated and thereafter for a while they ran transport flights, chiefly for the benefit of the Allied clandestine services.

It was September, and all but Jacques Weil's northern-most contacts had seen the Germans pushed back, when one midday McCaffery asked me to go to his office. There I found the SIS Swiss head who gave me a typically warm greeting. Jock was his usual smiling self but I noticed that he gave me a bit of a twinkle as he pointed me to a chair.

'Our friend has just been telling me,' Jock began, 'that his head office has instructed him to report home for consultation. He's come straight up here this morning as it seems that your old Maquis is running an impromptu 'plane service back to London and he's been told that we'll fix up all details for him to travel on it, when and where to report inside France etc. You'd know how to do all that, wouldn't you, Pat?'

'Yes, with pleasure. It'll take a day or two to arrange, I would guess, but there shouldn't be any difficulty.'

'That's very kind of you, Pat. I'll wait to hear from you.'

As soon as his opposite number had left. Jock came into my office.

'He's not taking a train until around four this afternoon. So, if you go straight off you'll beat him to it.'

On my way to Geneva I trusted that this might be the last time circumstances would oblige us to mislead such a very nice man. I had my meeting with Vic Parrell who undertook to make the arrangements and we agreed the method of sending me the eventual details, so that I could then pass them back to his boss. I then took the next train back to Berne.

Several days later I got my own marching orders. There was little more to retain me in Switzerland and, officially an escapee, I was entitled to leave the country when I wished. I asked Farrell to book me on Xavier's 'airline' and after saying farewell in Berne, I took the train down to Geneva for the last time. With some time to wait there, Vic Farrell drove me out for a look at the bridge at Annemasse where, with barbed-wire gone for good, traffic was again moving normally.

I also had time to shake René Bertholet by the hand and to express the hope that we should bump into each other again sometime. This wish came true the following year when, as commanding officer of the SOE mopping-up mission to Occupied Germany, I was able to give René the logistic back-up – chiefly petrol, food and not forgetting his cigarettes – to track down his ISK colleagues in what was now the Soviet Zone. In return, he brought back first-hand news of what was afoot behind the Iron Curtain. Whilst our mission was not officially an intelligence gathering one, René's contributions were eagerly snapped up by the Army. Post-war, René emigrated to Brazil where he set up a socialist commune in one of the poorest areas of northern Brazil. When I was posted to the embassy in Rio much later on, I just missed meeting him again. By pure chance I discovered that there was an apartment under his name one block from the embassy. A telephone call was answered by his sister who said that her brother had died the week previously.

I was driven through liberated territory to what could still be described as Romans' and Xavier's headquarters. We three consumed, I remember, a considerable amount of alcohol that evening and next morning we drove to the waiting Dakota. According to Xavier's account in his book, the Carpetbaggers had already moved base from Izernore to Ambérieu airfield, not so long vacated by the Luftwaffe. I am hazy on that point but I remember well that F Section agents from near and far, their job now completed, gathered for the flight back to Britain. Not many did I know personally but I did identify one or two including George Millar, whom I was able to thank for the excellent reports he had sent through me.

Saying goodbye to Xavier and Romans I little thought that I would see neither of them again. That this was so was my fault, not theirs.

The aircraft took off from the grass runway and we still seemed to be picking our way through the surrounding hills when the cabin door opened and the pilot, smoking a large cigar, walked down the aisle.

'Christ,' exclaimed someone, 'who's flying this bloody plane?'

'Don't worry,' intercepted the pilot, 'we'll get you home.'

And they sure did!

CHAPTER 14

Foreign Office, Farewell and Reunion in the Jura

It was June 1984 when I received a letter from Vera Atkins. It was not a long note, and it told me that the veterans of the Maquis de l'Ain would shortly be celebrating the fortieth anniversary of the liberation of their area. Vera and Hugh Verity were driving to Nantua to take part in the commemorations and, as there was a spare seat in the car, they all agreed that I must go with them.

I sat long over my breakfast table before finally getting up and writing a reply to Vera, thanking her for her kindness and thoughtfulness. However, I really could not bring myself to go anywhere for the time being and in any case, I had never remade contact with that area and there would be few who would remember me or me them.

I had spent much of the time since Winifred died of cancer, only three or four weeks previously, looking back on our thirty-nine years together, although the pain was still too acute to get any real comfort from doing so.

We had been married on 3 April 1945, with Muriel as bridesmaid and Roddy as best man. We had taken over from a colleague a top floor flat at 28 Westbourne Terrace just north of Hyde Park, which was reached by climbing ninety-three stairs. It was small and cosy when you reached it and by putting our heads out of the porthole windows in our bedroom we could just see the street below. But within two weeks of returning from our honeymoon in Cornwall I left for Germany with the SOE mission and Muriel moved in to keep Win company.

By December SOE was on its last legs and, with the few remaining members of Baker Street packing their bags, my unit was dissolved.

219

Some officers stayed on in Germany but, offered an appointment with the Foreign Office, I came home for Christmas and demobilisation. Winifred and I had a few months to enjoy our first home but before the end of 1946 we were posted to Cairo and then on to Ismailia on the Suez Canal where we liaised with the British Army now concentrated in the Canal Zone.

Neither of us enjoyed Egypt and when I was offered the chance to go to Cambridge University on a year's Russian course, I jumped at it. Win, who was now pregnant, was slightly worried whether we would not end up taking a small baby to Stalin's Moscow. I reassured her by telling her that no government department would ever take such a logical step.

I was wrong. With the Berlin Airlift at its height and young John in a carry-cot, we sailed off on a Soviet ship to Leningrad. The fact that it was impossible to meet Russians socially meant that the diplomatic colony in Moscow turned inwards and entertained each other. With Win learning albeit a somewhat unusual Russian from her Ukrainian nanny and her cook, we were enabled not only to enjoy the ballet but the Russian theatre as well. This interesting and not uncomfortable existence came to an end towards the end of our second year when Win, advised against flying and with Soviet ports icebound, had the sadness of losing her second, and prematurely born, child in a Moscow hospital.

We both had pleasant memories of our posting in 1952 to Germany. Gillian was born two days before I left for Cologne – the Bonn embassy was then being built but Germany was still under Military Government – and Win arrived two weeks later radiant with her tiny daughter. We enjoyed life but, with Gillian a year old and just when we felt we could now explore further afield than the immediate surrounds of Cologne, we were posted to West Berlin, surrounded once again by the Iron Curtain. But Berlin turned out to be a far cry from Moscow; Win became involved with the running of a small first school for children of diplomats and we were quite sorry two-and-a-half years later to be posted home again.

We now had our house in Sevenoaks and a home posting, although great for seeing the family, entailed clearing up after our last lot of tenants and redecorating the house from top to bottom in anticipation of future tenants in two years' time. Win played the lead role in wallpapering and both she and I removed years of old paintwork and applied new. Work well worthwhile as the rent we received paid the mortgage.

Logic seemed to have been abandoned when, with hard-won Soviet and European expertise, I was posted about as far away from it as one could get – to Argentina. For me it was head down into 'Teach Yourself Spanish', but Win knew that with her flair and having to run a house she would pick the language up as she went along. After a sticky start – the only time I ever saw Win in tears of frustration and home-sickness – we became thoroughly acclimatised and at the end of four-and-a-half years took home two Spanish speaking children and left behind many very good friends.

The sheer friendliness and hospitality of its people made Denmark a place apart for Win and me. It was a happy time, especially as our two children, now at boarding school, came across every holiday and loved the place. Win drove them around Copenhagen in her Triumph convertible and, thanks to the generosity of the Danish Steamship Company towards members of the British Embassy, was also able to take her car across home for ten days every half-term. Only one thing wrong – our stay lasted too short a time.

For our last posting overseas, we were invited to express a preference. Win herself suggested we ask to go back to Latin America and use our Spanish. We were indeed sent back there, but to Brazil, the only non-Spanish speaking country, and we had to face the not-too-easy task of converting Spanish into Portuguese. But we felt at home at once out there and the view across the yacht harbour to the Sugar Loaf from our duplex apartment with its small roof garden was a constant joy. The children came out twice a year and Gillian, leaving school, spent six months with us; not wasted as it was there she met Richard, her future husband.

Our time up, we returned to Sevenoaks. With the letting of our house at an end, and the mortgage redeemed, we could afford to have the builders in and have long-planned improvements put in hand. Winifred declared: 'I never want to go to another cocktail party in my life. I just want to enjoy England, my house and be within reach of my children.' I continued to work in London and after a few years Win got herself a part-time job in the same building and we commuted up together. Grandchildren began to appear.

Win was five years younger than I and apparently in fine health when cancer struck. After nine months in and out of hospital I sat beside the bedside of my brave and loving companion while life ebbed away. Knowing for some time that this would be the final outcome made it no less a shattering blow. I realised that life must eventually go on but when Vera's letter arrived I did not yet feel ready to face up to it.

'Van dear,' Vera's soft drawl is instantly recognisable to her friends and the many one-time SOE agents and dependents she still 'mothers'. 'I want you to listen to me. You ARE coming, you MUST come with us.'

'Oh, Vera...'

'I know how you feel but, Van dear, I'm not making a request, I'm ...', her quiet chuckly laugh, 'I'm giving an order!'

I stood by the telephone listening to Vera's kind but persuasive coaxing and finally, as she usually does, she got her way.

I began to relax on the journey through France in such good company and I found myself looking forward to revisiting the dramatic mountain countryside of the Ain. It was the countryside which was uppermost in my mind, since forty years is a long time and the two people, Xavier and Romans Petit, who stood out crystal-clear in my memory were both now dead.

We followed the Saône down to Macon and then turned off on to the route national signed for Bourg-en-Bresse and Geneva. After Bourg, the road climbed steeply into the hills, followed the high ridge and dropped down to cross the wooded gorge burrowed out by the River Ain.

'Now this is more like Maquis country.' opined Vera. 'Do you recognise any of this?'

Frankly I didn't, but it still brought back vivid memories, even though the snow had gone and the meadow clearings in the forest now had wild flowers aplenty.

We drove into Nantua, a thing we wouldn't have dared do forty years before, and I learnt for the first time what an attractive little town it is, nuzzled up at the end of its own small lake and flanked on either side by towering craggy mountain escarpments. We asked the way for Echallon, drove three or four miles further on towards Geneva and then climbed up a twisting road into the mountains again.

We put up at the little village hotel close to the Prairie d'Echallon where the ceremony was to take place the next day. It was obviously a favourite meeting place for Maquis veterans and quite a few were gathered in the bar that evening. As I stood with an aperitif in my hand talking to one of the Frenchmen, he asked me politely what my wartime connection, if any, might be.

'I was parachuted nearby at Izernore and ...'

He gave a gasp of astonishment. 'It is not true! Mon Dieu! you must be Paterson!'

I was equally startled. That someone should immediately know who I was, was remarkable enough but that he should remember the name I scarcely used at all in the Maquis was almost beyond belief. Standing there dazed, my companion flung his arms round me and embraced me. By the time our party was called in to the dining-room several others, claiming acquaintance, had similarly greeted me. One moustachioed gentleman had been a member of my reception committee and he remembered, as if yesterday, how I floated down quite close to him with my tommy-gun under my arm, ready to repel any boche who might be around. I did not wish to spoil his story, knowing from my own experience how memory loves to embroider.

At dinner, I related all this to Vera. 'You must remember,' she told me, 'that for all of them the Maquis was the high point of their war and, what is more important, it quite literally took place on their own doorsteps. We were oh-so fortunate to escape invasion and a similar situation in England. Here reprisals by the Germans could strike at whole families, at the very worst whole villages. Is it surprising they find it difficult to forget? Some of their main characters, Xavier for one, have gained the status of folk-heroes, and deservedly so. They remember you, Van, because, although only briefly amongst them, you did nevertheless help to procure them the arms they wanted. Also, don't forget you were the only one actually parachuted in this area and that must have been a memorable and encouraging sight for them.'

The ceremony on the vast prairie was in front of the imposing Monument to Allied Aid which now contained, at his own request, Xavier's ashes. The participation of a French military band and the Gordon Highlanders pipe band flown across from Germany and orations by several dignitaries, including Maurice Buckmaster, all added up to a very emotional occasion. A lament on the pipes in any case always breaks down my resistance but never more so than on that morning.

Even so, it was, against my expectation, the personal contacts that meant most to me. The ceremonies over and the festivities begun, someone came up to me and informed me that a friend of mine was waiting beside his Jeep and would not leave its side until Paterson sought him out. The tall, shock-haired, beaming figure turned out to be Marius Roche who had guided my aircraft in when I jumped. This, as we used to say in the days of non-stop movie programmes, seemed to be where I came in.

A further ten more years have elapsed and among a number of good friends in and around Nantua, Marius has become my closest and dearest. What gives me greatest pleasure is that my children and grandchildren keep up the contacts and my eldest granddaughter already puts my own spoken French to shame.

But on this first visit, and on every subsequent one, I found myself thinking how much Winifred would have loved it all and how, I felt sure, they would have loved her.

Postscript

Van died in January 2012, some twenty years after he had completed his memoirs. They were an eventful and useful number of years, during which a number of events took place that both tied up loose ends, strengthened certain relationships and, most importantly, brought about a form of healing in one specific area.

Following his original trip down to the Jura with Vera Atkins and others, Van was keen to show Nantua and its surrounds to the rest of the family and so it became a holiday venue for a number of years. I can well recall the first trip in 1988. It was a long drive through France but on arrival we stayed in a charming holiday maisonette in Le Poisat, looking down on Nantua from the Haute Jura. The following day, however, things really started to happen.

Van told us that we would be meeting Marius Roche, the member of the *Maquis* who had shone the torch to guide the aircraft in when Van had jumped and we were all thrilled when this larger-than-life character came to our maisonette to greet us. He was a big man wearing a broad-rim hat who quickly embraced Van and then welcomed me, my wife Sheila and our three daughters with equal gusto.

But Marius was intent on giving us more than a hearty welcome. After a strong cup of coffee, we set off to explore parts of the locality that had a historical significance to both Van's stay with the *Maquis* as well as to the overall battle against the Germans. First of all Marius took us to see the barn where Van had been taken to spend his first night in Occupied France. It was an old, now dilapidated building, set deeply into the countryside and surrounded by woodland. Van had obviously never expected to see the barn again and he patrolled it both inside and out with great curiosity murmuring, as he skirted around the cow manure, 'I can hardly believe that I actually spent a night here.'

The next stop was more emotional, especially for Marius. We were taken to a farm high up in the hills, La Ferme de la Montagne. The farm consisted of a main farmhouse, another building close to it and adjacent to it, and then a long field behind it leading to dense woodland. Marius stopped us outside the farmhouse and explained its significance both for the *Maquis* as well as to himself.

The Ferme de la Montagne had been a base camp for members of the local resistance, somewhere to stay when the Germans were patrolling the area and somewhere to both plan and practice combative resistance techniques. Marius was staying there with his twin brother and several other members of the resistance when early one evening the farmhouse was hit by gunfire. The Germans had moved into the building beside the farmhouse and were using it as a base from which to mount an attack. There was no point in trying to outgun them so Marius and his friends made a quick exit from the side of the house furthest from the other building and sprinted across the field towards the refuge of the woodland.

Unfortunately, the Germans had anticipated this move and had stationed a machine-gunner at one side of the field who sprayed them with bullets as they ran across the open ground. Marius made it but his twin brother was hit and fell in the middle of the field. Marius started to run back to help his brother but was prevented from doing so by the other members of the resistance who knew that he would be killed if he entered the field again. The surviving members of the local *Maquis* made it to safety but Marius never saw his brother again. He explained to us, with tears in his eyes, that he never knew whether his brother had been killed outright or whether he had been captured and tortured for information.

We were all moved by this story, made more dramatic by the fact that we were standing in the very spot where it had taken place. Van put his arm around Marius's shoulders. 'I hope this did not happen because of me,' he said.

'No, no. It was going to happen anyway. You had already left with Ramons.' Van and the rest of us breathed a sigh of relief.

But the tour of the Jura, with its historical significance for van was by no means over.

The following day we visited Le Musee de la Resistance – the Museum of the Resistance. This museum, housed in what had been the town prison in Nantua, consisted of a fascinating set of archives, illustrations and models that gave a vivid account of the local fight against Nazi oppression and the deportation of hundreds of locals to Germany to work as forced labour. The museum had been set up by a local osteopath, Pierre Mercier, who was very eager to show us around and later was to become, with his wife Co, a good friend of the family and a very generous host in future visits.

Pierre was too young to have been in the war. His great interest in the resistance stemmed from the fact that his father, Doctor Mercier, had been the local leader of the resistance and had been captured and was being taken to Boug-en-Bresse, no doubt to be tortured for information, when for reasons unknown the car stopped in the hills, Doctor Mercier was pulled out, and then shot dead. Pierre never knew his father; he had only just been born when this atrocity took place. But he took us to the place where it happened, where there was a monument to the doctor. Another monument was, of course, the museum itself and within it was something rather special.

Van's arrival by parachute was regarded as a landmark by the locals as he was the only Allied person to parachute into the area, and inside the museum was a model of Van landing by parachute. Van had previously been asked to provide a taped commentary to he heard when one looked at the model and although he knew it was there, it was certainly a moving experience for him to actually see it.

The cordial and affectionate relationship with the veterans of the *Maquis* was to continue for many years to come. Marius Roche, on hearing that Van had not received any official recognition from the French government at the end of the war, set out to put things right. This omission stemmed from the fact that General de Gaulle had ordered a stop to the award of medals, stating that too many had been given out. At the time those giving the awards were working alphabetically through those eligible and had got as far as the letter M. Ernest van Maurik was consequently omitted along with many others who deserved recognition. Marius Roche fought hard against French bureaucracy and managed to get things put right. In 2003 Van was awarded the *Legion d'Honneur*. He was initially asked to go to France to receive it but, after so many years, and now being in his late eighties, felt that it should come to him. The award was finally given to him at his club in London by senior officials of the French Embassy, including the Ambassador, the Military and the Naval Attachés. There, also, were all his family and many of his close friends, to applaud the fact that his actions had finally been recognised and to celebrate along with him.

But over and above the justice of final recognition about this time, came a sort of healing in another area. Ever since the initial conversation in 1967 I had been conscious that Van had felt bad about the events connected with Operation *Anthropoid*, the assassination of Heydrich. I did not believe that he felt any guilt at the assassination of this monstrous person but somehow, and illogically, he did feel some guilt at the events that followed. This was when, as retribution, the Nazis wiped out the village of Lidice murdering 199 men, deporting 195 women and ninety-five children, most of whom were never to return. In all, with other retributions, some 1,400 people were killed as reprisals.

Van's guilt, although ill-placed as he did not know what the soldiers he trained were setting out to do, was, I believe, an ongoing pain, not helped by a film made at the end of the war. This was *The Silent Village*, which took the stance of imagining it had happened in the UK, taking the village of Cwmgiedd in South Wales as the UK counterpart, being a mining village of roughly the same size. The film, despite its vintage, is quite harrowing.

But healing can come in all shapes and forms. Just before Van was awarded the *Legion d'Honneur* my wife and I developed strong contacts in Wales and by a huge coincidence, our base was just outside Cwmgiedd. Van came down to visit us on several occasions. On the first visit, he saw what a happy little village it was, and he met several jolly and friendly Welshmen who, as locals when very young, had been in the film and 'murdered'. When these men were now more than happy to chat with him and exchange friendly greetings it was as if a weight had been lifted from his shoulders. All was well. Time – and place – are indeed great healers.

Van continued to be active for several more years, a splendid father to my sister Gillian and myself, a loving and generous grandfather and finally a doting great-grandfather. Ernest van Maurik was much loved and much admired by all.

Appendix

Ernest ('Van') van Maurik (Paterson)

The following is a report written by Van at the request of the Resistance Museum at Nantua, where the dummy parachutist is christened 'Patty':

Before the Second World War I was a member of the Territorial Army (part-time volunteer force) and in November 1939 I was commissioned into the Wiltshire Regiment. During 1940 I spent considerable time on the beaches around Dover and Folkestone awaiting possible German invasion. In February 1941, I joined S.O.E. and spent 7 months on the west coast of Scotland as a training officer. Several different nationalities came through our school but the majority were potential agents for Buckmaster. It was during this period that I first did my parachute training. Later I was transferred to S.O.E. headquarters in Baker Street, London, and was posted to the Air Operations Section. This Section organised the parachute dropping operations into Europe as well as the Lysander pick-ups.

In late 1942, I was promoted to major and became one of General Gubbins' staff officers. The project for Jedburghs to parachute into France on or about D-Day came through my hands. Although my French was not good enough to join a réseau in normal circumstances, I realised that this could be a suitable job for me and I was happy when General Gubbins (later to become the Chief of S.O.E.) accepted my request to be the first volunteer for Jedburgh. However, an opportunity presented itself six months before D-Day when Colonel Maurice Buckmaster needed someone to take charge of the affairs of his Section in Switzerland. There was no direct way of getting to Switzerland so it was decided that I should be parachuted to the Maquis de l'Ain and from there to cross the frontier and get myself interned as an "escapee".

On 4/5 January 1944, I was flown in a Halifax bomber of 138 Squadron RAF to the Izernore ground but over the target there was thick cloud and it was not possible to drop. We returned to base. The next night. 5/6 January the operation was again scheduled and this time the conditions were perfect – bright moonlight – and as I floated down I could see the dark figures of the reception committee against the white snow. I was welcomed by Xavier and Romans-Pétit. We drove to a farm in the woods, which was to be our base for the next 10 days. Paul, who had handled all the messages about the operation, was, for security reasons, staying elsewhere and I did not, in fact, meet him until the 40th Anniversary celebration at Échallon in June 1984.

Xavier explained to me that arrangements for my passage into Switzerland would not be completed for another 10 days. It was planned that Romans-Pétit should accompany and guide me there. Romans-Pétit then asked me whether I would like to use the time available in visiting the various Maquis detachments. It had been emphasised to me in London that my overriding task was to get to Switzerland safely, but, on the other hand, this seemed to be a means of giving an independent report to London on the resources of the Maquis. I agreed and thereafter, usually in the company of Romans-Pétit (for whom I developed a strong liking and respect) but also sometimes with Xavier, I was taken to the individual detachments. One visit, in particular, impressed itself on my memory. Romans-Pétit and I climbed up the side of a steep mountain in the snow and it was then that I realised the many months of desk work in S.O.E. H.Q. had not improved my physical fitness!

At last we reached a clearing in the woods and there, in front of a mountain chalet, were a dozen maquisards, formed up beside a home-made British "Union Jack" flag. As I came up to them they stood to attention and sang their version of "God Save the King". I was immensely touched by this and I have, indeed, never forgotten this emotional moment. It goes without saying that my whole visit to the Maquis de l'Ain was an unforgettable experience, where great friendship was extended to me. I was so happy to meet again some of those who welcomed me at Izernore, in more tranquil circumstances at Échallon in 1984. The more I saw of the Maquis the more I became convinced that those arms which had already been received were in the hands of men determined to use them but that many more were needed.

On or about 15 January Romans-Pétit and I set off by car with two others for the Haute-Savoie. Passing through Annecy I saw my first Germans for several years. By opening the car window, one could have touched them as we drove by. A new sensation for someone who had enjoyed the relative seclusion of London. We may have had air bombing but we had been spared the Germans at close quarters. We spent the night in a chalet in the woods above Annemasse with members of the local Resistance and next morning my companion and I went to the Customs Office in the centre of town. Here we remained for several hours hidden in the cellars among the archives. Eventually we were led up to the street where two bicycles awaited us. We were instructed to follow a douanier also on a bicycle, but each keeping 30 metres distance from the other. We came to a small customs post where the bridge crossed over into Switzerland. The bridge itself was completely blocked by barbed wire. Our arrival had been so timed so that the German patrol was at its most distant point from the bridge. We were instructed how to cross by shuffling along a ledge on the outside wall of the bridge, overhanging the river. In this way, we crossed into Switzerland. The only casualty was to Romans-Pétit's trousers which he had ripped open on the barbed wire. Repairs were made by a douanier's wife on the Swiss side. Here Romans-Pétit and I parted; he had his own task to perform. His last words to me were to ask once again that I should try to ensure that more arms, particularly heavier weapons, should be parachuted to his area.

I was received in Geneva by Vic Farrell, the British Consul, well-known for his assistance to French Resistance. In Berne, whilst being registered by the Swiss authorities as an "escapee", I was able to send a long radio message via the British Embassy to S.O.E. headquarters, giving details of my inspection of the Maquis de l'Ain. It was not until some time later that I learnt that arms supplies had indeed been increased.

Once established, I remained in constant contact with S.O.E. London and for the next 9 months acted as the link in Switzerland for French réseau. When the Germans were finally driven out of Eastern France I was ordered to re-enter France and to contact Romans-Pétit and Xavier. I spent one night renewing my friendship with both of them (and accepting some very generous hospitality!) before returning to London in a U.S. Dakota aircraft, full of other S.O.E. agents, from the Izernore ground.

My final S.O.E. appointment was as Lieutenant-Colonel in command of the S.O.E. Mission which followed the British Army into Germany. This had, among others, the task of searching for S.O.E. agents and contacts who had been imprisoned in Germany.

Note: The S.O.E. code-name of my parachute operation was 'Chef'. My pseudonym was 'Maurice' – Buckmaster 'lent' me his own first name.

Index